# The Classroom as Privileged Space

# Race and Education in the Twenty-First Century

Series Editors: Kenneth J. Fasching-Varner, Roland Mitchell, and Lori Latrice Martin, Louisiana State University

This series asks authors and editors to consider the role of race and education, addressing questions such as "how do communities and educators alike take on issues of race in meaningful and authentic ways?" and "how can education work to disrupt, resolve, and otherwise transform current racial realities?" The series pays close attention to the intersections of difference, recognizing that isolated conversations about race eclipse the dynamic nature of identity development that play out for race as it intersects with gender, sexuality, socioeconomic class, and ability. It welcomes perspectives from across the entire spectrum of education from Pre-K through advanced graduate studies, and it invites work from a variety of disciplines, including counseling, psychology, higher education, curriculum theory, curriculum and instruction, and special education.

**Titles in the Series**

*Big Box Schools: Race, Education, and the Danger of the Wal-Martization of Public Schools in America,* by Lori Latrice Martin

*The Journey Unraveled: African American Students' Career and College Readiness,* edited by Jennifer R. Curry and M. Ann Shillingford

*Race and Pedagogy: Creating Collaborative Spaces for Teacher Transformations,* by Susan R. Adams and Jamie Buffington-Adams

*Asian/Americans, Education, and Crime: The Model Minority as Victim and Perpetrator,* edited by Daisy Ball and Nicholas Daniel Hartlep

*Centering Women of Color in Academic Counterspaces: A Critical Race Analysis of Teaching, Learning, and Classroom Dynamics,* by Annemarie Vaccaro and Melissa Camba-Kelsay

*African Immigrants' Experiences in American Schools: Complicating the Race Discourse,* by Shirley-Mthethwa Sommers and Immaculee Harushimana

*Race, Gender and Curriculum Theorizing: Working in Womanish Ways,* edited by Denise Taliaferro Baszile, Kirsten T. Edwards, and Nichole A. Guillory

*The Lived Experiences of African American Women Mentors: What it Means to Guide as Community Pedagogues,* by Wyletta Gamble-Lomax

*Race, Population Studies, and America's Public Schools: A Critical Demography Perspective,* edited by Hayward Derrick Horton, Lori Latrice Martin, and Kenneth Vasching-Varner

*Curriculum and Students in Classrooms: Everyday Urban Education in an Era of Standardization,* by Walter S. Gershon

*The Classroom as Privileged Space: Psychoanalytic Paradigms for Social Justice in Pedagogy,* by Tapo Chimbganda

# The Classroom as Privileged Space

## *Psychoanalytic Paradigms for Social Justice in Pedagogy*

Tapo Chimbganda

LEXINGTON BOOKS
Lanham • Boulder • New York • London

Published by Lexington Books
An imprint of The Rowman & Littlefield Publishing Group, Inc.
4501 Forbes Boulevard, Suite 200, Lanham, Maryland 20706
www.rowman.com

Unit A, Whitacre Mews, 26-34 Stannary Street, London SE11 4AB



British Library Cataloguing in Publication Information Available

**Library of Congress Cataloging-in-Publication Data**

Names: Chimbganda, Tapo, author.
Title: The classroom as privileged space : psychoanalytic paradigms for social justice in pedagogy / Tapo Chimbganda.
Description: Lanham : Lexington Books, [2017] | Series: Race and education in the twenty-first century | Includes bibliographical references and index.
Identifiers: LCCN 2017027028 (print) | LCCN 2017024796 (ebook) | ISBN 9781498511964 (Electronic) | ISBN 9781498511957 (cloth : alk. paper)
Subjects: LCSH: Critical pedagogy. | Psychoanalysis and education. | Racism in education. | Educational equalization.
Classification: LCC LC196 (print) | LCC LC196 .C44 2017 (ebook) | DDC 370.11/5--dc23
LC record available at https://lccn.loc.gov/2017027028

Printed in the United States of America

To my first teachers: John Jonas, Jenipher, Gerard, Gilda, Godden, and Godfrey Chimbganda.
My family.

# Table of Contents

# Introduction

On April 18, 1979, my mother went into labor dancing on the streets of Salisbury, celebrating the declaration of Zimbabwean independence, an independence later officially declared on April 18, 1980. I have always been confused about my birth story but my mother tells it with a smile that makes it seem like it was the greatest day of her life. I keep asking if I am actually a year younger than they tell me. However, as an adult, I have learned of Zimbabwean history that the details of the story depend on who is telling it. In any case, I share a birthday with Zimbabwe, which means every year my birthday was celebrated extravagantly much to the chagrin of my siblings. I was what was referred to as a "born free" in Zimbabwe, a term reserved for those who never lived under the oppressive rule of the British Monarchy, and later Ian Smith in Rhodesia. Born frees were raised with privileges that older generations had fought for, and we were never allowed to take it for granted.

At school, we learned Zimbabwe's history from Black teachers, not born free but certainly privileged to have been educated in Africa's most literate country at the time. We learned everything in English and learned our native languages as modules we could opt out of as we advanced in the post-colonial education system. I can neither read nor write my native language fluently. We were privileged to experience a transcultural childhood in which we went to school with racially diverse children in the same classes and enjoying the same benefits of a free Zimbabwe. Whether black, white, Indian or colored,[1] as children of Zimbabwe we learned to be proud and to be free. Integration in schooling happened based on economic status with black children whose parents were professionally educated moving into suburbs in the early 1980s.

Unfortunately, even in independent Zimbabwe stratified oppression existed for some, notably against Malawian immigrants and Ndebele people. We called the Malawian immigrants "maBrantyre," which I understood to be a derogatory term to indicate their lack of education and immigrant subjectivities. Ironically, my family had migrated from Malawi over a century ago due to tribal wars. My father did not like to admit the ancestry, probably because he knew very little about it. I do recall learning about mass migrations after the initial Bantu migrations that saw the rise of tribalism in Southern Africa. The Malawian immigrants worked mostly as house cleaners and gardeners, which we were always happy to employ. As a people, they were humble, happy, and always accommodating. Free Zimbabwe took advantage of their economic lack, which to children might have appeared kind and generous even as they lived in our "boy's khaya," served us hand and foot, and existed in our worlds only in servile positions.

Those Malawians, like my family, who had migrated generations earlier, assimilated into the privileged Shona classes. Even with obvious Malawian names like Chimbganda, our loss of all Malawian characteristic stereotypes made us Shona, not "maBrantyre." As children, my siblings and I loved our Malawian help. They played with us, sang to us, and told us stories in their funny accents. In our ignorance, we did not see that we were oppressing them. In my childish mind, I attributed and justified their occupations to their funny accents. They could not speak properly, I thought to myself, and this is probably why they worked as house cleaners and gardeners; otherwise, if they could speak English, like us, they would have different lives.

The Ndebele people, a tribe that had migrated to Zimbabwe long before the white settlers came, had a different story, one I began to understand about ten years ago, after I had several conversations with a fellow Zimbabwean in Toronto. There were tribal conflicts, centuries old, between the Ndebele and Shona. In the early 1980s, hundreds of people died on both sides in the conflict known as the "Gukurahundi." Despite being free from colonialism, we Zimbabweans continued with our internal strife, right from where we had left off before the white people came and disrupted us. I recall Joshua Mqabuko Nkomo, a man revered in Zimbabwean history as instrumental in stopping the tribal conflict. He agreed to let go of historical tensions for the good of independent Zimbabwe. Sometime, after this selfless act, and at a time of peace and prosperity in Zimbabwe, Nkomo died in 1999. He left a void I sensed but could not comprehend, but fully realize now. He had been the voice of reason in Zimbabwean governance. I remember the sadness I felt; mostly, because he was a soft spoken rotund man with snow white hair. In my childish mind, Nkomo was not a hero because he stopped the genocide I knew nothing about. He was a well-known figure I had grown up seeing on TV, speaking in his soft voice things that seemed to make everyone happy. I had associated him with my Zimbabwe, knowing nothing of the tensions in my city or the oppression the Ndebele experienced. My knowledge of the nation was a sheltered ignorance in suburban Zimbabwe.

I went to school with Ndebele children. We played together, and nothing seemed out of place. I had several Ndebele teachers, however, who picked on Shona children quite mercilessly. One particular teacher took great joy in the practice of corporal punishment for Shona children. She called me "ginger hair," a nickname used to bully and torment me on the playground. This woman also taught my younger brother whom she beat regularly, harassed, and called names. As a result, my brother, at the age of six, developed serious social regression. My father had to intervene with threats of legal action against her. As children, we were not aware that we were victims of a tribal conflict that pre-existed the existence of our parents. These teachers used their power as educators to gain advantage over their tribal enemies, except we were just children ignorant of the political battles fought over and around us.

At age ten, I had a male Ndebele teacher, Mr. Hlatshwayo. I hardly remember my other teachers' names, but I remember him vividly. I can still hear his melodic voice as he read to us and I recall his necktie always seeming a tad too tight, like he was choking on the formality required of him as a teacher. I remember his smile and laughter shared often and freely with his students, all his students. Mr. Hlatshwayo was an alcoholic, another factor I have realized in my adulthood. He always reeked of alcohol and cologne, but I liked the smell because he loved reading to us. He read us *Animal Farm* by George Orwell. He was special to me because, unlike my other teachers, he was young and had been to university, not just teacher's college. He spoke to our young minds in a philosophical tone, as if there was much to contemplate in the world. Or maybe it was just to me. I loved reading, and Mr. Hlatshwayo allowed me to explore this love. I would bring in my library books to read whenever I had a free moment in class. My father would take us to the public library on Saturdays and leave us there all afternoon among the books. It was my favorite thing as a child. I often wonder, given Zimbabwe's current economic decline, if the library still has beautiful new books and comfortable chairs at colorful tables for children to enjoy.

*Animal Farm* made an impact on my psyche; I wish I could share this with Mr. Hlatshwayo today. I enjoyed his rendition of the pigs' anthem, which he sang to us rather earnestly. We would beg him to sing it after every hour of reading. It took us weeks to read the abridged version of the book, but it was a class favorite. Mr. Hlatshwayo must have studied the arts in university. Drama class with him was also quite special. I was not a good actor, but I was a good reader, and he seemed to appreciate that more than my acting skills.

My childhood is filled with good and bad memories of school. I loved being in school; the other children I could have done without. In grade three, aged eight, my best friend at the time came first in class. I cried all the way home, until my dad, annoyed and fed up with me, stated, "Well if you don't like your friend getting better grades than you, do better." I remember being surprised that it was that simple. The following term I came first. One of my fondest moments is attending the prize giving ceremony and my father picking me up and putting me on his shoulders. I won several books all shiny and new and could not wait to rub them in my siblings' faces. It was not the only prize ever to grace the family, but it was certainly the only one for coming in first and the only one that was colorful and hard covered.

Throughout our primary schooling, my sister and I competed in creative writing competitions, mostly with each other. We both won several school and provincial awards, but my favorite prize will always be those books because my dad left work early and was so proud of me. As a middle child these moments alone with my father were few and far between. I suffered the typical middle child syndrome, even if my birthday was always the most celebrated occasion of the year—well, thanks to Zimbabwe's independence.

Psychoanalysis, which might be criticized for a propensity toward pessimism, views the human nature and the state of coexistence negatively. Freud (1953) in *Civilizations and its Discontents* states there is an inert tendency toward aggression in us and it is only right to assume it exists in our *others*. This aggressive factor toward others disturbs relations and makes it necessary for culture to institute its high demands (Freud 1953, p. 86). In my work, this is the basis of oppression. Oppression includes racism, sexism, homophobia, and childism among a plethora of ever evolving human deficiencies in relationship. In *Freud and Education*, Britzman (2011) explains Freud's view on human suffering stating that whatever means are available, whatever the external world has on offer, Freud saw psychical reality as mediating fulfillment and as creating an unknown factor, that is, more conflict. Britzman points out that with this insistence, Freud diverted from theories of socialism, religion, programs of betterment, and social eugenics because for Freud, suffering cannot be eliminated as it is essentially the human condition; and that which allows conditions to be human (p. 149).

Aggression, conflict, and human suffering are the precepts of psychoanalysis that make it an ideal framework for the analysis and critique of oppressive human relations. While some might consider it antiquated, psychoanalysis can provide a relatively frank analysis of what lies at the root of oppression in today's social discourses. Freud's overarching intention through psychoanalytic praxis was to find those barriers to his own teaching and learning that resulted in impossibilities. In the same way that Freud's return to early childhood experiences helped him resolve adulthood's problems, a return to the past is necessary to remedy the present and project a better future for social justice in education.

## UNDERSTANDING THE RELATIONAL STRUCTURES OF CHILDREN IN EDUCATION

To develop an identity, a child depends firstly on family and then on wider social circles. Through repetitions in speech, behavior, and interactions a child begins to understand what is acceptable and what is not. One's racial, gender, or sexual identity develops in response to the social opportunities and limitations to which one is exposed. In *Seeing Our-*

*selves,* Carl E. James (2003) explains that individuals have at times been enabled, frustrated, or even in some cases, inhibited by the structures that both collectively and individually—separately and simultaneously—produce these varying results. James makes clear, identity formation complexity, fluidity, and dynamism of relationships exist among individuals. Thus, the premise of this project rests on three fundamental assumptions:

1. Parents and the life of the family are the primary agents of socialization for children.
2. Schooling and education are the secondary agent of socialization and therefore,
3. Education can contain or contaminate what primary socialization has instilled.

To elaborate on these assumptions, I lean on two, also fundamental, systemic theories of family life—the Oedipus complex and object relations—both of which in psychoanalytic inquiry are the bedrock of primary socialization. The significance of these theories in relation to schooling lies in the relational structures of socialization which are either disrupted or further cultivated through pedagogy. Schooling as an agent of socialization has been widely covered (see Davies and Guppy 2010) and includes examinations of the gendering role schooling plays (Phillips 2009; Meyer 2008; Martino 1996) among other key factors of socialization. My work looks more closely at the racialization of children within families; and then within segregated schooling as part of their secondary socialization.

When I was in grade five, my teacher's husband worked with my father, which I discovered after she had reported me for a misdoing to her husband who told my father who "rectified" the situation. That entire year, as a student in her class, my transgressions were addressed both at school and home in a systemic manner that became a thorn in my side. My father would come home well-informed on my activities at school. At one point, I wondered if my father did anything but talk about me at work. I hated her class! My teacher loved threatening me. There was never any leniency or favor toward me, which I witnessed bestowed on other children. I always wondered why she chose not to use her "powers" for good. It would have been great to have a powerful ally in class, but alas for me, the woman reveled in my misery.

Several years later, at boarding school, a similar situation arose. My physical education teacher was married to my father's work colleague, and she attended our church. Like my primary school teacher, she did me no good. This teacher loved to use physical punishment as she forced students to run laps on the field. If we slowed down or stopped, she would come up behind us with a cane and slash our legs. Everyone hated her and expressed it freely. She enjoyed the animosity and seemed to feed on it. Unfortunately, I could not be as expressive as everyone else could because she would tell my parents. I recall her shouting at me to stop giving her the evil eye because she would be seeing my parents long before I did (she went home every weekend but I was stuck at boarding school until the school holidays). She was also not above telling tales, tall tales. Despite this, I enjoyed our relationship because she understood me and I her. As one who had learned to live with an enemy in high places, I had acquired skills of subterfuge and subtle rebellion. I enjoyed hating her. Years later at my wedding, we would laugh at the situation. The connections between my home life and school life in these instances were clear and concise. The lines of communication were always open; and although I hated the tamed lifestyle I had to live in accordance, I was still the beneficiary of a collaborative home and school socialization.

I am aware that I tend to romanticize education. It is my chosen object; the longest and most beneficial relationship to which I have ever committed. I hate when teachers corrupt education because I simply love school. I love its ideals and values. I believe in its promises. Even though I have endured much emotional and physical trauma throughout my schooling, usually perpetrated by teachers who did not understand how or why I value education, I still hold education to be true and good.

I wonder if teachers knew what is direly at stake for each learner in the classroom, would they be more tolerant, perhaps even accepting of the wayward child who does not color within the lines or that student who must try a million times before mastering a task? I wonder if teachers knew that for some children education is the one place where they might not feel rejected or defected, would teachers then go the extra mile in making each day a wonder and adventure of discovery? My love of education probably arose out of being a middle child and finding the one place where I was not a middle child was in the classroom. Of course, I still had other children to contend with, but in class, we were all more or less the same age and knew more or less the same things. I was neither too old nor too young as was often the case at home. The teacher was not my mother or father, so what I viewed as unfair treatment did not cut as deep, and I felt no guilt or shame for hating them or wielding what little power of destruction I had against them. I could also love them and present my gifts of achievement without reservation because I understood my role within the classroom.

Within my conceptualization of socialization is the awareness that it consists primarily of instilling within the child social values and beliefs, including racial, ethnic, and gendered difference. Whether difference presents as positive or negative, and whether received or delivered, unconsciously or consciously, discourses of social difference inevitably become the child's knowledge of the world and others. As children acquire this self-other knowledge, tensions and conflicts arise between what they know or feel from their home life and what they encounter at school. In this book, I use memoir, demonstrated in my personal narrative, to depict the kind of knowledge that one learns, when looking back through social processes that construct social difference. Specifically, I analyze memoirs of childhood in which the struggle for children to think, to be, and to exist consists of understanding, after the experience, the difference between what they knew through family life and what they encountered through pedagogy. This split in their socialization results in unseen psychic trauma with which the child is forced to contend. Naturally, we see that parents want to protect their children from the trauma that comes from the stigma, oppression, and discrimination instituted by government and society through schooling. However, where the family life cannot protect or contain, education as an alternative agent of socialization may be able to intervene.

I begin the narrative case studies with an examination of the education system and social discourses of difference during the children's schooling. I also examine the child's early relationships with primary caregivers, highlighting the disruptions and raptures caused by the overreaching arm of social discourses of difference into the family life. This interaction between society and child, mediated by parental guidance, or, in some situations misguidance, becomes the child's early socialization. The child's primary socialization determines the child's future resistances and tensions in interactions and relational patterns within the education system. This develops into secondary socialization as the child might look to teachers or other key figures within schooling for what was lacking in the family home. For example, Winnicott (1992) states that the duty of a teacher in the child's development is to maintain, strengthen, and enrich the child's personal relationship with the family, at the same time introducing a wider world of people and opportunities (p. 194).

Using memoirs, I examine the deficit created by an undutiful teacher. Children might turn away from teachers and educators because they fail to cover the gap that a disruption of primary socialization created. I highlight what might happen internally to the child whose secondary socialization may further disrupt and injure or what might transpire should education manage to contain and repair by providing the tools and skills to resolve primary disruptions and traumas. As Winnicott (1992) further states, the teacher has a dual responsibility, and a dual opportunity to assist the parent to discover potentialities in parenting; and to assist the child in working through the inevitable psychological problems which face the developing human being (p. 195).

Within the specific education systems depicted in each case study memoir, and through analysis of social values and beliefs recounted in each, I extrapolate education's possible interventions, and discuss education's actual influence on the child's mental and emotional life. In other words, I question how socialization in schooling contributes to the psychic, and by extension, social lives of children. Each memoir as a case study is set during a particularly tumultuous and segregated time in global history. The three memoirs are set in Canada and South Africa, two countries often historically linked together in the structuring of segregation in education. Racialized children were separated from white children into often poor and ill resourced schools run with the specific purpose of instilling social difference and inferiority into the children's minds (Indian Act 1884; Bantu Education Act 1953). Education focused legislation supported these oppressive practices and any revolt was often considered an act of crime and delinquency.

Within these systems even a microcosm of empowerment was enough to make a difference in the outcome of these children and this is what I seek to highlight as the most valued asset of education in relation to social justice. A psychoanalytic reading of the memoirs of harsh and unjust schooling provides a hypothetical way forward through the act of witnessing, thereby implicating the reader of the memoir, and of this book, as accountable to humanity. How we react to these injustices, indeed our response to any injustice, implicates us in the first act.

## THE IMPOSSIBILITIES MADE POSSIBLE THROUGH PSYCHOANALYSIS

> The contact between psychoanalysis and education was established when, in the progress of his work with the adult neurotic, Freud discovered that for an "understanding of his condition or to effect a cure" it was necessary to "trace the determination of his symptoms . . . back into his early childhood." (Kris 1948, p. 622)

Psychoanalysis and teaching have been conjoined since Freud began to formulate the practice of psychoanalysis. Kris (1948) declares that through contact with psychoanalysis, education has extended beyond expert modification of children to include "mental hygiene" (p. 622). "Mental hygiene" implies some cleaning up or sanitization, which in the context of the mental life of children is impossible.[2] Hence, we have the impossibility of both education and psychoanalysis tied to what is contained within, and contaminates the mind. Vanheule and Verhaeghe (2004) explain that there are several professions including education that Freud viewed as impossible, stating that, "According to Freud, in none of these professions can one predict one's ultimate success owing to the large number of uncontrollable factors involved" (p. 498). They further state:

> In discussing the impossible professions, Lacan [1991, 2001] at once accentuates these professions' social nature (in all of these professions the social bond is the pivotal medium through which an agent addresses another in order to effect change) and warns us against making premature conclusions. He qualifies these professions as "hazardous undertakings" and "challenges" [(in French 'gageurs'; Lacan, 2001)].

> The least we can do, he says, is to produce evidence of the impossibility involved. (p. 498)

Following Lacan, Vanheule, and Verhaeghe (2004) think that the concept of "impossibility," on the one hand, requires delineation from adjacent concepts such as powerlessness and on the other hand, professional experiences of impossibility need to be studied empirically to grasp more firmly what signifies impossibility. In social justice education, and in facilitating a socially justice education, impossibility is a crucial concept owing to the emotionality attached to social justice, particularly where diverse subjectivities create a tension in the meaning of "social justice" I will discuss this further in chapter 2.

The impossibilities of psychoanalysis and teaching imply a fundamental deficit in praxis. However, there is a reason two impossibilities continue to make significant impact in the lives of children and why I lean on psychoanalysis to elucidate the effect of oppressive teaching in childhood as both irreparable and reparable trauma. My work focuses on the psychoanalytic possibilities in teaching, both positive and negative. I consider the dehumanization of childhood through education while simultaneously uncovering the restorative possibilities of a socially just education. By applying psychoanalytic paradigms to pedagogy, I look at the trauma of difference, specifically race and sexuality, and the experiences of children who through their schooling develop psychopathologies or relational difficulties for which a socially just education could be an intervention. In this context, "psychopathology" does not refer to psychiatric disorders and mental illness; rather it is the mental and emotional structure that develops through struggle for which a socially just education can be a place of remediation and empowerment. Like the concept of Racial Battle Fatigue (RBF) popularized by Smith (2004; 2010; and Smith et al., 2007; 2011), I view these psychopathologies as social ailments manifest in oppressed individuals requiring intervention through social justice. I argue that attention to the complexities of emotional life as responses to the Other is one way schooling can become restorative.

Education might be something beyond a system of socialization for employment and civil engagement. Education could be an intervention for social justice and by extension contribute to psychic resolution. In other words, education could be more than that which Kris (1948) refers to as the "measures applied by adults, expert or non-expert, teachers, and parents, to influence the behaviour of the growing child in a desirable way" (p. 622). Education, as mental hygiene, could be more responsible and more responsive to social traumas that affect the mentality of learners. These are the possibilities that lie within the impossibility of education.

Referring to the impossibilities of teaching and psychoanalysis, Felman (1982) poses a pertinent question: "If teaching is impossible—as Freud and Socrates both point out—what are we teachers doing? How should we understand—and carry out—our task?" (p. 22). Her question gives an impression of futility in endeavors to educate. Yet despite this futility, Felman (1982) argues, "it is precisely in giving us unprecedented insight into the impossibility of teaching that psychoanalysis has opened up unprecedented teaching possibilities" (p. 22). Felman draws upon Lacan's view that many had reduced the art of teaching and learning into a "functional apprenticeship," and makes apparent Lacan's position that teacher training was destructive to knowledge in alignment with Freud's position which focused on the experience of learning for the analysand. For this reason, I focus on the experiences of children who come into discriminatory and dysfunctional settings of education, where teaching causes unfathomable pain and suffering. I occasionally highlight the teachers' attitudes and ideologies within the dysfunctional environment as complicit to the traumatization of these children. I also seek instances where the dysfunction can also be a space of empowerment and resilience from which the children can find a voice for freedom and self-worth.

I lean considerably on Lacan's work as it allows me to delve further into the Subject of education, who is the child, rather than focus on education itself as a subject. Lacan's return to the Subject refocuses Freud's work with his analysands, who presented Freud an opportunity to conceptualize transference as the key to analytic practice. Likewise, I position transference as a key aspect of pedagogy and in the final chapter I explore Freud's development of a psychoanalytic pedagogy and advocate that the classroom adopts a similar framework.

"In its most massive statements and in its polemical pronouncements, psychoanalysis is first and foremost a critique of pedagogy" (Felman 1987, p. 71). Felman decries the oversimplification of a psychoanalysis of pedagogy that would give the impression that pedagogy must be dismissed altogether. In fact, as Felman points out, there is no such thing as antipedagogue in psychoanalysis. Rather, psychoanalysis is a pedagogical experience granting access to new knowledge, which can benefit the institute of education as it not only critiques pedagogy but also models new perspectives, theories, and practices (Felman 1987, p. 76). Therefore, psychoanalytic paradigms, as critique, for pedagogy bring us to an understanding of the intricacies of the developing psyche within pedagogical spaces. They uncover the underpinning of socialization as a vital part of a child's psychic development. Felman's view justifies a psychoanalysis of education encompassing the institutional structure of schooling, and the pedagogical practices of schooling.

There are some fundamental problems however, between psychoanalysis and pedagogy, which Britzman (1998) highlights stating that at the heart of psychoanalytic work is an ethical call to consider the complexity, conflicts, and plays of psyche and history. According to Britzman, these are the conflicts—Eros and Thanatos, love and aggression—that education seems to place elsewhere; and then these forces seem to come back at education as interruptions, as unruly students, as irrelevant questions, and as controversial knowledge in need of containment (p. 133). The complexities, conflicts, and controversies to which she refers, often result in psychic trauma; and ultimately through this project, I will trace this trajectory as it occurs in educational sites as remembered by adult authors recounting their childhoods at school. As witnesses, we see that where children are involved the foreclosure of the "emotional life of student and teacher" is a cause for concern (Britzman, 2006).

In contemporary schooling, policy makers seek to contain elements of love and hate, which might present as aggression, in tenuous conceptualizations of "safe space." Yet ironically, as illustrated in the memoirs, policy makers used these same passionate elements to establish entire educational systems that instilled feelings of social inferiority in children. I elaborate on the policies and practices in colonial times where trauma, deliberately inflicted on developing minds, achieves the socialization goals of oppressive governments and societies. It is fortunate that we have reached an era in which we feel more compassionate about difference, and yet we still cannot contain our hatred of it in our educational systems, a state of affairs that leads to systemic disavowal in policies and procedures. The disavowal of the psychical dimensions of learning and being in pedagogy results in trauma, an alienating experience for both the learner and teacher, not only from each other, but also from the institution of education and ultimately knowledge. As such, pedagogy becomes a traumatic experience fraught with animosity and debility. Added to this traumatizing pedagogy is the social trauma the child experiences within the scope of a discriminating society. It is no wonder pedagogy seems futile in such circumstances!

I investigate the mechanisms applied to the creation, maintenance, and destruction of social discourses that become psychic reality for children and young people through education. One of the biggest criticisms of the enduring structure of the educational system is the divisive push for tolerant pedagogy taking the form of passivity or neutrality and often sold as "safe space." Paradoxically, for those with privilege and power—the socially dominant passivity is beneficial while those underrepresented remain actively marginalized. Policies and procedures in school systems continue to maintain an active dominance over those who have been historically silenced and oppressed while portraying those who have chosen to be silent while benefiting from oppression as fragile and frightened. Such discourses in educational systems are driven by emotional rhetoric, which is why the subjectivity of both the active and passive must be considered. Psychoanalytic theory generates a subjective analysis of pedagogy that counteracts the status quo that neutrality or passivity upholds in notions of "the classroom as a safe space" (Holley and Steiner 2005).

Ultimately, there is a problem with the formulation of "safe space," which this book critiques as an oppressive idealization of pedagogical space, and which according to research does not actually inspire, or even project, feelings of safety (Holley and Steiner 2005; Stengel 2010; Williams and Evans-Winters 2005). Safety is not possible in teaching and learning because learning wounds. Through my examination of traumatic events in children's schooling, I endeavor to show why safe space pedagogy is a disavowal of difficult knowledge, which is necessary in order to achieve social justice in and through education. There is a dilemma in the practice of safe space pedagogy that acts as a barrier to a full understanding and appreciation of the necessity of violence in order to learn and the necessity of lessening violence in order for someone to *become*. While a safe space is supposed to protect, it inadvertently covers over the trauma that is inflicted rendering the children in our schools victims of an unacknowledged oppression. By doing so, it leaves the traumatic aspects of education, whether necessary, ordinary, or extreme, unacknowledged and dismissed.

Each chapter of this book begins with my personal memoir as a disruption, particularly to the analysis of the three memoirs in chapters 3, 4, and 5. These disruptions serve to highlight the disruptive nature of emotionality, subjectivity, and indeed humanity in the practice of schooling. With disruptions, meanings change, intentions are forgotten, and something else seems to take over requiring that the participants, willing or not, take a position within the space. I elaborate on this in chapter 6.

Overall, my personal narrative informs the reader from what direction I, as Subject, am approaching the literature, both memoir and psychoanalytic. My personal narratives are a working through of the countertransference I grapple with as one who is witnessing the trauma of children thrust into a cyclone of conflict that is dehumanizing. Through my personal narratives, I find identifications that allow me to make interpretations and work through the narratives of the memoirs. While memory and the stories that derive from them may not be a full representation of the totality of actual experiences, as Sonn, Stevens, and Duncan (2013) argue, these provisional truths should not preclude us from making interpretations thereof, as they represent interpretations of reality and are therefore integral to shaping the manner in which social relations are influenced (p. 307). My memoir, then, is not intended to represent the truth of an experience but to support my engagement and analysis of the memoirs I examine in this book. My own upbringing and the education afforded me by a country in transition, privileges me with a unique interpretation of the memoirs of children who went through their own transitions marred by the social discourses of the time. My reality and experiences present a context for which I can begin to work through the matter of what a socially just pedagogy might repair in, and of one's education.

Hook (2013) emphasizes the aspect of working through that is the preceding making of interpretations, as it links to symbolic labor, that is, constant attempts at (re)interpreting, revisiting, resituating "irresolvables" of experience and understanding. He also adds that working through, as it is often projected, misleadingly promotes the idea that conflicts can be definitely resolved, rather than reorganized in an analytic experience. I seek not to resolve my own schooling through my working through, nor do I desire to reconcile the trauma of education to the aspects of it that might be healing. Rather, I seek to offer possibilities and alternate perspectives of social justice within pedagogical spaces by reaffirming epistemic privilege (Harding 1993; Hill Collins 2009; Janack 1997) and pedagogy as privileging. Furthermore, Hook posits that working through is not tantamount to intellectual acceptance or insight; it need not even include the notion of "becoming conscious." He believes the process, based on lived experiences rather than merely on intellectual understanding is liable to halt repetitive insistence . . . of unconscious formations. Per Hook, these contradictions in working through are its raison d'être!

In my interpretations, and working through, I find myself caught up in contradictions of privilege and oppression as the memoirs trigger memories of my own schooling in Zimbabwe. I was privileged but I was also oppressed. I was sheltered but also exposed to violence; I was ignorant but also aware. Moreover, like the writers of the three memoirs, I work through by narrating my experiences, now armed with incisive language necessary to express the absurdity of education. Like the three authors Sellars, Retief, and Mathabane, I gained the "academic" language that enables me to work through my childhood in higher education. My personal narratives, like the memoirs, convey the systemic collapsing of knowledge in childhood. The things I knew as a child, my parents did not know, and what they knew the schools did not teach. The children in the memoirs are assaulted with strange types of knowledge in a segregated system. The memoirs are testimony to the breakdown of meaning that occurs in childhood and education. To these testimonies, I add my own. They are an account of anguish and aggression, of struggle and triumph.

The colonial narratives I explore in my own post-coloniality expose the gaps that time has not covered. There is still unspeakable violence and a lack of safety enacted in school despite ongoing strides in praxis to establish anti-racist and inclusive pedagogy. Looking at traumatic education through a historical lens brings us to an audit of the present and supports us to ask: How far have we come with equity education and why do we still struggle?

## CHAPTER OUTLINES

This book is organized with interrelated chapters that scaffold to a conclusion of the necessity of equipping teachers with the skills to contain the emotional and subjective world of learners in classrooms for the sake of socially just schooling. Although the focus is the experience of the child, the centrality of the teacher in the narrative of the child is not forgotten. There are ultimately two significant groups of educators in a child's life: primary socialization takes place at home and secondary socialization happens within schooling. I juxtapose the lessons learned at home to the lessons learned in educational institutions.

In chapter 1, I discuss the usefulness of psychoanalysis as critical theory in pulling apart the educational system. In my discussion, I heed McArthur's (2010) warning:

> Rather than focus on arguments about whether change occurs at the structural/macro level or at the individual/micro level we need to understand that emancipatory social change requires dialogue between all these levels of change. They cannot be sliced and separated. While critical pedagogy is compelling at a general level, focusing upon a social horizon, it is also important that it never loses sight of the individual, the different, the marginalised, the clusters of disparate groups, beliefs and ideas. The micro, meso and macro levels of an organisation are interdependent and each impacts upon the other. (p. 494)

In relation to this warning, I also consider the insight of Frosh (2010) in *Psychoanalysis Outside the Clinic* who writes that traditionally psychoanalysis is inclined to "'unsettle' situations by revealing the unconscious elements that feed into them (p. 6). He elaborates that this unsettling capacity becomes socially critical when it seeks to expose power situations that rely on the denial of opposition and the pretense that it is necessary to maintain existing patterns of domination" (p. 6). Frosh presents psychoanalytic problems outside the clinic, as a shock of the unconscious that might be too much to bear (p. 8). Considering that education is trauma, it is reasonable that there are aspects that are too much to bear, and yet bearing them is necessary in order to move forward in pedagogy, as both learners and educators. Taken together, these two insights remind us of the limits of examining pedagogy as a knowable or measurable entity. What psychoanalysis aims to uncover is the gap between what is clearly known as fact and what we might wish to know (Frosh 2010, p. 9). I seek to uncover the gap between what is known about education as an agent of socialization and education as an act of oppression. Chapter 1, then, focuses on the possibilities in education through a psychoanalytic lens. What can we gain through psychoanalytic paradigms and how can psychoanalytic paradigms make sense of the absurd in education?

In chapter 2, I address the question: What can the past teach us about our pedagogical practices and the psychopathologies we encounter in pedagogical spaces? Looking to Freud, who was convinced that teaching was not solely dependent on measurable and manifest conditions, I examine the psychical forces at work in the learning mind of a person. Freud (2006) describes the work fundamental to psychoanalysis stating that his academic work set itself the goal of illuminating unusual, abnormal, and pathological phenomena in the life of the mind. He sought to trace mental phenomena back to the psychical forces at work behind them, and to reveal the mechanisms in operation (p. 68). Psychoanalysis offers a critical view of pedagogy, which exposes the sluggish propensity to change in social discourses. To measure the efficacy of contemporary schooling, I begin in the past, sifting through the archives of childhood experiences. As well as examining the psychical dynamics at play in the work of the learning mind, I examine how these dynamics are transferred to, and enacted in, broader social systems. To this end, I discuss the use of memoirs and autobiography in chapter 2; and envisage the possibilities of an active and transformative engagement with life writing to activate social justice. I lean on the identified imperatives of autobiography: the cry of distress and the call to glory (Kristeva 2003).

Chapter 3 analyzes depictions of knowledge that are subjective and generated through power in schools. When children contend with educational projections and subversions of *self*-knowledge the psychopathologies that result in them are long lasting and life effecting. I use the etiology of neurosis through the mirror stage and early identifications to demonstrate how the child internalizes pathologic representations of herself that distort her potential to learn and be. I do so by analyzing the narrative of an aboriginal child in a Canadian residential school. At the most basic level the brute implementation of the Indian Education Act of 1884 in residential schools is dehumanizing. Attempts to rectify the harrowing effects that affected multiple generations of Aboriginal people in Canada have yielded little as attested by the recently publicized work of the Truth and Reconciliation Commission of Canada (2015). Today's schools owe a debt to indigenous people beginning with a recovery of what was lost in the residential schools. The commission's report, *Canada's Residential Schools: The Inuit and Northern Experience*, specifically targeted at revealing the extent of trauma inflicted in the residential schools, shows a lean toward a humanistic approach to counteract the dehumanizing acts of the past. Tied to this, is a commitment to incorporate Indigenous values and knowledge in the education curriculum, which might read as an extension of cosmopolitan trends in education.

Chapter 4 utilizes an Afro-pessimistic conceptual framework to broaden our understanding of oppressive commodification. I focus on the commodification of childhood to uphold the perverse practice of racism and homophobia within education. The impressions of futility in current practices in the art and science of teaching and learning have been a part of education and social discourses for a very long time; chapter 4 shows the complexities and intricacies that continue to prove unresolvable. We already know what humans are capable of, both good and bad, we just need a way to work with both these aspects of humanity; and to face our ambivalence of humanity and use it to cultivate social justice in pedagogy. Unless we face the ugliness in education, society, and humanity, we run the risk of socializing children into perversities from which they cannot emerge whole. Chapter 4 seeks to advocate against the fetishization of children in schools for the maintenance of the status quo.

Chapter 5 presents an example of education as intervention. Through my analysis, I find that when a child develops a race-related psychopathology that drives him to obsessional and continuous searching, the possibilities presented at school might provide him the skills and competencies to find answers. Pedagogy may not give him the papers or award him the prize but it can give him a platform on which he can build his resiliency. Chapter 5 also shows how within the very segregated and oppressive school system, opportunity arises out of accessibility to creating knowledge. For many children, school is the one place where their wounds, deep and festering, are alleviated or further inflicted. The difference between a good school and a school as a badland comes down to the fundamentals of one's experience with traumatic pedagogy (Chimbganda 2015). In this chapter I ask: What kind of pedagogy is valued and cultivated within the classroom? How does pedagogy contain psychic traumas to provide healing or cause irreparable harm that lasts a lifetime?

The conclusive chapter 6 advocates for the adoption of psychotherapeutic technique in the classroom regardless of level—primary, secondary, or tertiary. I revisit some of the difficulties of teaching highlighted in chapter 2 and consider the privileged position of the teacher as instrumental in the secondary socialization of learners. The teacher is the one that provides the opportunities and cultivates on potentialities (Winnicott 1992), the teacher needs to have a skill set that stretches beyond documenting learning outcomes and statistics. I privilege emotional and subjective experiences; and in chapter 6 illustrate how psychoanalysis, also an impossible profession, navigates these crucial aspects of learning and teaching. I draw on Freud's formulations of transference and other key psychoanalytic paradigms to build a privileged space for pedagogy. This space is supposed to provide the ultimate equitable and inclusive learning environment and draws from feminist, emotional, and queer pedagogies. I also briefly project the future dynamics of traumatized learners in higher education.

Overall, a historical analysis of segregated schooling comes at a crucial time in the history of education as it can illuminate some of the disavowed trauma that social difference still inflicts through education. If we examine the psychopathologies of children in segregated schools in the past, can we be sure we will not find the same symptoms in the children in today's crop of segregated schools? Do not the social differences, commodified in colonial times, remain relevant to social stratification and selection in schools today? Even in mixed or multicultural schools, race, sex, gender, and other differences are used to separate and select (Pinar 2010; Pollack and Zirkel 2013; Powell and Barber 2006). The trend continues into higher education.

## NOTES

1. *Colored* was a designation given to children of mixed heritage, mostly mixed black and white. This same designation is still used in much of Southern Africa, with most colored people self-identifying as such.
2. Especially if we agree with Freud's view that children are uninhibited and driven primarily by the id and ego. It is through socialization that the superego begins to instill limits and boundaries (Freud and Strachey 1962).

# ONE

# Psychoanalytic Paradigms for Pedagogy

I do not recall learning math. I can add, subtract, and do basic calculations of multiplication and division, probably a few fractions and simple equations. I cannot solve a quadratic equation or get into the deeper mathematical stuff such as geometry and calculus. More significantly, I just do not recall learning mathematics. I passed my math exams, but not as well as I did other subjects like chemistry, physics, and general science. Chemistry made sense to me. The periodic table was like a family; you learn their names, their personalities and characteristics, and which ones to never mix or burn and which ones are precious and rare. Physics also made sense: for every action, there is an equal and opposite reaction; cause must always precede effect; in a theory of relativity, anything that can go wrong will go wrong. However, mathematics I do not remember learning or understanding. I hate numbers.

I am convinced that my aversion to math is linked to the pedagogical practices of my math teachers. My sense is that my good and bad memories of learning in school correspond with the pedagogical approach of the teacher. My math teachers in boarding school were authoritative figures. They were the three most feared teachers in the institution at any given time. They beat us, pinched us, and scoffed at our failed attempts at solving math problems. One of them, a man of South Asian origin, would pinch girls at the intimate spot between breast and armpit with a creepy grin on his face. Should a girl squirm she risked having her breast assaulted by this man.

It strikes me that I remember the pedagogy of the teachers but cannot remember actually learning math at school. In primary school, one teacher taught us all four subjects: math, English, Ndebele, and social studies. In boarding school, we had different teachers for the twelve subjects. My homeroom teacher was also my math teacher. She liked speaking to me in Ndebele during math classes, always with a sinister grin as she scoffed and ridiculed me in a language to which I could not adequately respond. She also taught my Ndebele language lessons. Needless to say, I did not excel in that class and was often called upon to read aloud so that she could shame me. I did not mind this too much because in my mind, it was not important, and I knew I would not need Ndebele to succeed at anything that mattered to me.

In the third year, we were divided into more concentrated streams—arts, sciences, or a combination of the two. I was placed in the sciences stream. I was good at general science, chemistry, physics, biology, agriculture, and geography. I also took the compulsory English, English literature, religious education, and math courses. The math teacher, also the deputy headmistress, a very tall and robust woman, beat us with all her strength. She was a Shona woman so there were no language barriers between us. There were rumors she dabbled in witchcraft, and that set the fear of her in us. She had a special stick she carried with her all the time. We were unsure if it doubled as a wand. Unlike her two counterparts, this woman did not grin or smile as she raised her wand in swift and brutal strokes across our palms. Instead, she flared her nostrils in the semblance of a facial expression.

Both my female math teachers were at the school longer than most. (The man did not last long.) They had teaching college qualifications where most new and younger teachers had university degrees. Most of the newer teachers also did not beat us as much and were more creative with their pedagogy and punishment. I recall a young expatriate teacher from Canada, Mr. Hilton, made me clean the expansive library walls with a bucket of water and toothbrush for being cheeky in his biology class. Among some of the older staff were two white nuns that had been at the school a long time. They were relics of the British education system, and upon their retirement returned to Britain somewhere to be among their fellow sisters. The nuns also loved to pinch us. One of them, Ms. Lowe, would use the very tip of her gnarled nails, twisting her arthritic ridden fingers so that we were twisting our entire bodies to lessen the pain. The nuns taught us home economics, which included needlework and cookery. I was especially useless in both these subject areas. That was the word most audible to me in those classes: "useless." When the nuns left, the teacher who took over was a rotund Ndebele woman. She translated the term "useless" into Ndebele.

My English literature teacher introduced us to *Jane Eyre*. I fell in love with the Bronte sisters and continue to read all their works periodically. Mr. Mabhikwa was not a particularly good teacher, but he never abused his authority, beat us unnecessarily, or discriminated against us based on our backgrounds. He recognized my love for books and cultivated it. Whenever he was absent, he would leave me his notes so that I could dictate them to the rest of the class as well as guide them in reading the texts aloud. I felt proud of a responsibility for which I had not volunteered. In his wisdom, he probably did this to keep me out of trouble, as no other student would have been able to keep me in line; but also, he knew I was more advanced than my peers in my understanding of the texts. I just simply loved reading. I guided my peers through *Jane Eyre* and *Harvest of Thorns* (a text by a Zimbabwean writer).

Another teacher who nurtured my learning was Ms. Kalenga, who had studied law in university. (She was the sister of my nemesis the physical education teacher.) Ms. Kalenga taught us history and English. With each teacher, my love of learning either blossomed or withered depending on their pedagogy. There were classes in which I paid absolutely no attention, preferring dismissal to do some manual labor outside in the bright sun as punishment rather than sit and pay attention. I was never fortunate to be kicked out of math class, probably because I was too afraid of the teacher's wrath or wand to misbehave, but like I said, I do not remember learning math.

## WHAT IS PEDAGOGY?

> There are places I talked about first: topological places, places that have to do with essence, and then there is your place in the world. You usually get to that place by pushing and shoving. In short, it leaves you some hope. No matter how many of you there are, you will always end up in a certain place, with a bit of luck. It goes no further than that. (Lacan 2008, p. 5)

Lacan's curious, almost whimsical statement might be in reference to the educational system or, to be more precise, the classroom. Parents and caregivers send their children into such places, from the tender formative ages, through the angsty adolescent period, then finally as young adults in higher education to become a part of something bigger and wider: society. Governments enforce this practice as an act of social and economic governance stating that every child has a legal right to an education. A wider sociological perspective may focus on the legal and economic constraints of supplying an education to suit every child; hence, the disparities in achievement as governmental policies are subject to capitalist forces that inevitably trickle down to the very youngest learner in the education system. The government-to-child trajectory often comes up in discourses of inequity and socioeconomic disadvantage, especially as we examine how governments—whether liberal, neoliberal, conservative, or otherwise—formulate their policies. Deficiencies in educational systems correlate to deficiencies in government (Joshee and Sinfield, 2010). In considering the sociopolitical system in Britain, Cole (2012) states: "While the liberal paradigm has been, and remains, multicultural education, the hegemonic form of education in the United Kingdom has traditionally been monocultural education, an education that stresses so-called 'British values'" (p. 178). Like the observation made by James (2001) of the Canadian education system, their perspectives, although relevant, do not consider the psychic effects of social inequality on the children for whom education is a right.

My question to policy makers is: To what kind of education is a child entitled? Every child has a right to social justice if we are to read legislation such as the United Nations Convention on the Rights of the Child (Assembly, U. G., 1989) as a statement of social justice. Therefore, I focus on education in its essence as a promise and act of social justice. It is important, before I proceed, to gain an understanding of education as a place and to clarify the spaces within education where the "pushing and shoving" happens. For it is within these spaces, depending on how one fails or succeeds, that one, hopefully, finds her or his place in the world. These spaces are where the art and science of teaching and learning has to do with "essence"; where I take "essence" to mean elements of emotional and psychic being.

Accordingly, education in a psychoanalytic context extends beyond curricula and widens the scope of pedagogy to include the psychic shaping and structuring of the child's emotional world with the idea of mental hygiene (Kris 1948). Pedagogy is not simply teaching and learning but involves relationships with the broader social systems encompassing parents, administration, and the eclectic community. Pedagogy is social selection, it is social difference, and it is trauma. Ideally, educating—that is, pedagogy—can be both intervention and intrusion, as it causes fractures and raptures within the psyche while simultaneously healing and mending brokenness. The intrusive quality of education is not altogether bad as it can be just what the child needs to develop resiliency and gain independence.

Pedagogy can have the quality of "good enough." The term "good enough" used by Winnicott (1960) to describe the parent that provides a holding environment and facilitates transition through stages of maturation, aptly describes socially just education. Winnicott uses the term to expand on the necessity of care from mother to child to enable a personal existence and as a means of building up what he refers to as a *continuity of being*. Based on this continuity of being, Winnicott elaborates on the inherited potential that gradually develops into an individual infant stating, "If maternal care is not good enough then the infant does not really come into existence, since there is no continuity of being; instead the personality becomes built on the basis of reactions to environmental impingement" (p. 594). To underestimate the value of systemic nurturing, both in the home and at school, means subjecting children to toxic environments in which they are forced to live reactionary lives. A good enough education provides the learner a conceptually nurturing and challenging holding environment and facilitates opportunities for ongoing development. A good enough education provides the learner a conceptually similar-to-home holding environment and facilitates opportunities to *become*.

Another psychoanalyst to use the term "good enough" is Bruno Bettelheim (1987) who speaks of good enough parenting as civilizing to children. Bettelheim illustrates how good enough practices help a child develop moral and civil awareness and explains that when a child acts out this understanding (of order against chaos and good versus evil), the child may begin to appreciate a lesson which cannot be taught to him convincingly in a purely didactic fashion: that to fight evil is not enough. Bettelheim believes one must fight evil in honor of a higher cause and with knightly valor—that is, according to the rules of the game, the highest of which then has become to act with virtue therefore, a good enough system could nurture and promote self-esteem as a potent spur to further integrate id, ego, and superego—that is, to become more civilized (p. 285). In line with the previously mentioned three fundamental assumptions on socialization, Bettelheim's (1987) view requires us to consider how education can contribute to the civilization of children, particularly if civilization is synonymous with social justice.

Unfortunately, the kind of intrusive education to which I refer in this project has the quality of *wild education* (Britzman 2011). Wild education is not child-centered, as it focuses more on the idea of a child being educated rather than the Subject. Wild education is perpetrated through fantasies of a child being educated by the teacher who is an emotional figure standing for authority but dismisses the subjectivity of the emotional child. Britzman (2011) reminds us that because of our psychic functions and dysfunctions, both teaching and learning are typically at odds (p. 127). She suggests that education adopt a psychoanalytic style from which pedagogy may garner a passion for alterity or a desire to learn from otherness:

> Passion for alterity may bring us into a different sense of the teacher's otherness: the vicissitudes of unconscious life, found in the call of dreams, mistakes, sexuality, and jokes. Here uncertainty may signify new beginnings. It may mean interpreting the link between love and loss and presence and absence. It may mean asking the enigmatic question, where is the pedagogue in the pedagogy? (p. 115)

In psychoanalytic discourse otherness is not necessarily, although significantly, based on ethnic, racial, or sexual difference, which gives us leeway to redefine the specifics of difference in a more socially just rendering. Verhaeghe (2008) explains, "in 'Lacanese,' the Other with a capital O indicates both the concrete other and the totality of what the other says to the child" (p. 160). The teacher is both *other* and Other to the child. She/he is Other because of the psychic fantasies and the desire driven unconscious she/he brings into the space and because of the power she/he has (over the child) to act on these fantasies and desires. Thus, we comprehend the significance of the teacher as Other; and why alterity occurs for each person within the educational system where both teacher and child possess and are possessed by the unconscious that speaks. With this understanding of alterity, pedagogy constitutes the relationship of teaching and learning between the teacher's unconscious and that of the child and additionally accounts for what the teacher deliberately imparts to the child. In psychoanalytic terms, this is transference.

If we view pedagogy as the art of teaching and learning, we might take a hypothetical stance of pedagogy as transference, which would lend a way to defining pedagogy as the art of managing conscious and unconscious interactions between teacher and child—countertransference and transference. Pedagogy emphasizes a two-way relationship between teacher and learner, at its least, cooperative, and at its best, collaborative. To begin with, this understanding refines the process of social justice in pedagogy as a reciprocal activity. Both teacher and learner must be willing to engage in the transformative endeavor that leads to social justice. Nevertheless, what is social justice *in* pedagogy, and how is it different from social justice pedagogy? Fundamentally, I believe the difference lies in the criticality of what is being taught and learned.

My overarching focus is social justice in and through education. Critical pedagogy has focused on the improvement of social justice for all (McArthur 2010). With a strong agenda for change—within education, through education, and throughout society—critical pedagogy holds to a belief that education and society are intrinsically interrelated. However, critics of critical theory are wary of the ongoing critical work that brings no change (McArthur 2010). There should be a change that comes with the acknowledgments of wrongs; otherwise, how is it social justice? The inefficiencies in critical theory or critical pedagogy suggest there is a missing element. I suggest bringing the psychic to the forefront of critical pedagogy. I am wary of focuses on structural and political economy that render individuals within these systems invisible. The Subject is critical to critical pedagogy! The cloak of invisibility permits perpetrators to remain unaccountable for the injustices others must live with. Governments, school boards, committees, administrations, and society are made of people. It is individuals who make choices based on their emotional and psychic subjectivities. Therefore, I lean on psychoanalysis to uncover what lies beneath traumatizing pedagogy while maintaining a systemic overview of the resulting mechanisms of resistance to change.

Definitions of *social justice pedagogy* are subjective and often present immeasurable and ideological parameters. For example, social justice pedagogy refers to any teaching and learning experience that drives toward social awareness and transformation in our students (Matthews 2005; Nagda, Gurin, and Lopez 2003). Ultimately, how does one measure an *other's* awareness and how do we quantify or even qualify transformation? On one hand, Kelly and Brandes (2001) explore the challenges of teaching for citizenship and democracy through discussions of social and ethical issues. One might conclude this is social justice pedagogy. On the other hand, Dudziak and Profitt (2012), who examine social justice in social work training and education, illustrate that it is possible for education to generally neglect the foundational knowledge and skills needed to effectively engage in social action and social change efforts. Their definition of social justice pedagogy leans on political and professional action following schooling. Dudziak and Profitt further complicate social justice pedagogy by pointing out that with respect to equipping students with the knowledge and skills necessary for effective social justice work, curricula in training programs are often rooted in assumptions that severely undermine student preparation for social action. They present evidence that the first assumption made by educators is that through adequate and generalist training programs, future professionals in fields such as social work will automatically know how to do social action. "Educators also presume that motivation based on values is sufficient to propel social workers into action. If students espouse a value commitment to social justice, then somehow they will instinctively or magically translate this into action," according to Dudziak and Profitt (p. 236). Additionally, Dudziak and Profitt point out there is an assumption that students will act once they become aware of social injustice; however, we know that action does not automatically follow education or "awareness" (p. 236).

A key differentiating factor between social justice in pedagogy and social justice pedagogy lies in whom the pedagogy serves. Social justice in pedagogy is supposed to right the wrongs for the students within the classroom. It shifts the agenda from a group focus to an individual focus within a classroom group dynamic. For example, including diverse narratives, cultural perspectives, and methodologies in teaching (anything) presents opportunities for all learners to benefit from inclusive education. Within these methodologies, there is room to privilege the individual learner within the group, which is my agenda in chapter 6. On the other hand, teaching about the injustices that learners with learning disabilities encounter in education provides knowledge but not necessarily action and risks lumping all learners with learning disabilities into a group where individual subjectivities get lost or erased. The former empowers with opportunity, the latter empowers with knowledge; and as previously highlighted, knowledge does not necessarily produce action. That is why it is imperative that all subjects, content, and curriculum, regardless of a specified focus on social justice issues, should seek to empower through opportunity for action.

In saying this, I echo a rhetoric I have often come across in education-focused seminars and conferences that seek to address systemic inequities in education for marginalized populations. The resounding statement declares the debt education owes some people, namely Aboriginal, Black, and *othered* racial and ethnic minorities, calling for more than an acknowledgment of past wrongs. Over the years, much has reframed policies and curriculum to be more inclusive and more socially accountable to the wrongs perpetrated against racialized groups. However, much the same criticisms arise at each gathering with no glimmers of hope, at least not in the ones that I have attended. Clearly, something is not working with current models of social justice pedagogy, anti-racist pedagogy, and all the other "solutions" that seem to complicate rather than actually solve the problems we encounter in education. Not that I have the answers, but I endeavor to add my perspective on what is wrong with the system based on the psychic effects of traumatic pedagogy (Chimbganda 2015) on learners. As I mentioned earlier, I criticize the notion of safe space in classrooms in chapter 6.

Examining literature on social justice in education reveals the complications, difficulties, and challenges, particularly in the definition or rendering of social justice in classrooms. The ongoing rhetoric on social justice and anti-oppressive practice at seminars and workshops about education and social justice takes us back to a position of impossibilities and leaves educators with the task of managing what emotions erupt in these gatherings and in the classrooms where Subjects are forced to take binary positions within education. Inevitably we are left with the oppressed and the perpetrators of oppression. I take the position of one who questions and hopefully encounters, through psychoanalysis, a way forward through the befuddlement.

The supposition that all teaching, regardless of subject and discipline, should be socially just becomes necessary when in considering social justice in pedagogy, one may not necessarily refer to accounts of injustice that need to be rectified but certainly rectifies accounts of injustice through a pedagogy that is equitable, inclusive, and takes advantage of diversity.

An example of one attempt at rendering social justice through teaching is in the following example of math education. Math education to the learning child is presented as "fact." "Facts" are a recurring theme in subsequent chapters as they relate to race and sexual orientation; however, mathematics is a different kind of fact. It is indisputable fact, scientific fact, and universal fact. A quadratic equation is a quadratic equation in Timbuktu, Tirana, or Tegucigalpa. Therefore, it should be easy to analyze the efficacy of mathematical pedagogy, *right*? Not if we start thinking about how teaching and learning mathematics can be a social justice measure. Bartell and Carpenter (2008) review Eric Gutstein's *Reading and Writing the World with Mathematics: Toward a Pedagogy for Social Justice*,[1] stating, "Fundamental goals for mathematics instruction are often expressed in terms of individual empowerment and economic necessity: All students need to learn mathematics to become productive workers and informed citizens, and the economy needs citizens who are mathematically knowledgeable" (p. 95). These profound and perhaps idealistic goals for mathematics framed as a social endeavor, must consider that simply learning mathematics does not bring a learner into a position of social empowerment. The way the mathematics is taught has great relevance in where the child can go with the acquired knowledge and skills. In my experience, corporal punishment and fear erased any significant learning or acquiring of mathematical knowledge or skills that might have taken place.

Bartell and Carpenter's (2008) review juxtaposes social justice pedagogy to other fundamentals of pedagogical practice to show that "Instruction in mathematics should help students use mathematics to understand and address inequities in society" (p. 95). They summarize this book as follows:

> Gutstein argues for a reconceptualization of the purpose of mathematics education to include a vision of mathematical literacy as critical literacy for the purpose of transforming society toward equity and justice. Furthermore, he argues that efforts toward equity in mathematics education need to look beyond a focus within mathematics education (e.g., improved test scores, classroom processes, teaching, and learning) to include considerations of how mathematics education is connected with the larger sociopolitical context of society and how teachers and students can use mathematics as a tool to understand and address unjust social conditions illuminated by understanding this larger context. (Bartell and Carpenter 2008, 95–96)

Mathematical skills and knowledge, and the teaching of anything else extended beyond scores and statistics, processes and policies creates imperative opportunities for social justice in the classroom and by extension society. A social justice focus would consider not only how students are performing but also how they are empowered in their life long journey as citizens. The aspect of citizenry is crucial, and later I turn to Rousseau's *The Social Contract* in expand on examinations of social stratification.

There is also the matter of the employability of those traditionally discriminated against when we speak of education as an equalizer. Does having an education necessarily open doors or present racialized and marginalized populations equal footing in the capitalist world? James and Taylor (2008) offer a glimpse of the complications that arise when the act of social justice is separated from idealizations of it in educational discourse by providing a dialectic exploration of young university students who debate the meritocracy of education for racialized students. In their discussions, the students indicate that while considerable strides have been made there are still significant barriers to social elevation or equity for racialized students. Students interviewed by James and Taylor state:

Lewis: Education will get you to the station. While little education will get you near the station [like high school], the more education you get, gets you to the platform. There might be a barrier that won't let you onto the actual train. But education can get you that far. But at least you're there but you have the opportunity to jump onto the train and sure there are roadblocks there, but at least you're on the platform and you're equal to everyone else and you can get on the train.

Tristana: I completely understand what you're saying. But if you think about the increase in education for minority kids before, there was segregation in schools, so white and Black kids got different types of education. With desegregation you're seeing more minorities getting education. But do you see the balance in jobs? Do you see Black CEOs? Do you see women CEOs? Do you see a change in the demographics of who holds jobs?

Several participants remarked at once: But that's changing though . . .

Tristana: But it's not changing drastically in terms of education policy. I understand education can get you to the station . . . but you have no ticket. (p. 568)

If racialized or traditionally marginalized students still face barriers after having attained high standards of education, can we accurately state that social justice has been achieved through education? These questions continually arise when we confront matters of social justice in education and society generally. I doubt anyone has the encompassing solutions; however, we can begin to move toward resolutions that address the aetiology of some of the psychic barriers and complexities that maintain the status quo.

In their previously mentioned critique, Bartell and Carpenter (2008) highlight three points for consideration in examining the efficacy of social justice in pedagogy. First is the teacher's personal and subjective knowledge of social justice inequities, that is, teacher knowledge and pedagogical practice (p. 97). Their second complication is student population—to whom is the teaching presented and for whom is the presentation encountered as social justice? They highlight that white middle class just as all other student populations should engage in social justice through teaching and learning (p. 98). Finally, there is the issue of parents, administration, and community (p. 98). In other words, society will have a word or two to say about the social justice a teacher is seeking to enact through pedagogy. After all, the classroom is not an island unto itself.

Another proponent for social justice through math education, Posner (2010) looks at the equity and authenticity of math education by applying social justice theory and sciences studies to extrapolate a formulation of equity and authenticity in math education. Again, I posit that all material in education should be a social justice endeavor and one way to perceive of this is through a lens of equity and authenticity, like Posner, who seeks to go beyond the dichotomy of structural determinism and psychological theories of agency (p. 129). She seeks instead to show that math education, as social justice, should encompass the language of both the learner and the system. She advocates that students learn the language, customs, and discourse of mathematics in a socially aware practice that allows them to participate in the mathematical community at an individual level.

The "*mathematical community*"? That sounds exclusive! I certainly would not fit in any mathematical community having learned very little of it in all my schooling. So, I question, who are its Aboriginal people and its racialized? Of course, thinking of math in this way presents its own complications, but Posner thinks math education, presented as a social practice that is inclusive and equitable, can be achieved by highlighting one of the qualities of science studies. Stating that early science studies focused on "science in the making," Posner points out that it was through ethnographic style fieldwork in laboratories, that researchers made detailed accounts of the construction of scientific facts which illustrated how scientific knowledge is accomplished through messy work. According to Posner, early scientists found that successful scientific practice depended on multiple factors absent from positivist accounts of science, therefore, scientific facts are neither given nor discovered, but rather are outcomes of complex negotiation processes (p. 131).

Lay people, like me, do not often consider mathematics as negotiable. From early math education, we learn 1 + 1 = 2. We learn that prime numbers are indivisible, but as we progress these facts become negotiable and open to critic. Throughout schooling, we learn many facts about the world around us that we often think are hard and non-negotiable like mathematics. Yet Posner (2010) and others say there is room for negotiation in mathematics and what students need is the right language and an understanding of mathematical discourse to negotiate. What would happen if we viewed all facts presented in education this way? Perhaps we could view education as the development of an understanding of social discourses in order to allow for negotiability. Perhaps I would not have been beaten and pinched so many times by unyielding teachers.

Posner (2010) also draws our attention to "invisible work" as an idea or a concept that has gone through a process of erasure of elements culminating in a "hard fact." Facts are an important element to this book as a rendering of a working through; and indeed to education because of the process of erasure. A pertinent digression, at this juncture, is the erasure highlighted by Black feminist scholars of the participation of women of color in feminist movements and scholarship (Harding 1993; Hill Collins 2009; Janack 1997), which will come to bear on concepts in chapter 6. Something is destroyed, lost, or forgotten in making facts, scientific or otherwise. Posner seeks to remind us of these forsaken elements and opens us to the injustice of the process, "Once an idea is attributed to an individual, we often create a history in which other contributors become invisible and their contributions are erased" (p. 132).

## TRANSFERENCE IN SOCIALLY JUST PEDAGOGY

It occurs to me that there is "something" behind my affection for Mr. Hlatshwayo. I was in his class the year after the malicious tattletale who turned my father against me. Of the many teachers I encountered, to remember a depressive drunk with love might be considered a curious romanticism. Others might view this man as a teacher who clearly violated many ethical issues in his drunken care for minors in a state school. I loved him because he gave words to some of my juvenile feelings of injustice. I have already mentioned I was a middle child. My family struck me as a type of "animal farm." My siblings and I were equal but they more equal than me. I can say this now as an adult with an understanding of my childish self. At the time, I just really loved the teacher that voiced my concerns of injustice through his pedagogy. He indulged my love of books, and *Animal Farm* indulged my taste for revolt and otherness. I wonder if he could perceive my love and if he understood the immense pleasure, he gave to me. Mr. Hlatshwayo gave me hope. In *Pedagogy of the Oppressed*, Freire (2000) states: "Nor yet can dialogue exist without hope. Hope is rooted in men's incompletion; from which they move out in constant search—a search which can be carried out only in communion with others" (p. 91). We could label communion with others as transference since it is through relationship that hope arises. For children and learners in school, communion with teachers and peers brings hope. The message the teacher brings might be one of understanding and knowledge, one that recognizes the incompletion in the child, and one that offers hope through pedagogy, through transference. That is what Mr. Hlatshwayo did for me that year.

To understand the function of hope in pedagogy and psychoanalysis helps us reframe this investigation of social justice in education. Buechler (1995) poses some critical questions that I in turn address to education:

> If hope is an emotion, what gives it its motivating force? Is hope equivalent to the strength of an expectation? Is it a product of certainty about the value and attainability of a goal? How are these (cognitive) qualities related to the emotional experience of being inspired by hope? Can we sustain emotional hope without cognitive certainty? Is such hopefulness contagious in psychoanalysis? How is hopefulness in one partner communicated, or engendered, in the other? How do we under-

> stand hope's absence and its sometimes unfortunate coalescence in the lives of some psychoanalyses? (p. 65)

An education without hope is most certainly one likely to yield a bleak outcome. Hope is curative and the best kind of hope is steady and leads eventually to a realistic understanding of what the future can provide (Helm 2004). To accommodate difference, education should not be claiming to be color-blind or gender neutral. Rather, it should be giving each child a vision of what they can be in their individuality, whatever it may be in the future. Such a role is indeed a tall order for any individual—parent or teacher—nevertheless it is what brings about social justice. Hope is inspiration, and according to Buechler (1995), hope is tied into our emotions. Buechler believes in order for hope to inspire, within a psychoanalytic setting, the emotional analyst must relate with the emotional analysand and from this relationship, the analyst is able to influence the analysand's outcomes. That is, within the transference and countertransference. What then can we learn from psychoanalytic hope and how can educators become the vessel of hope? In other words, how can educators become more skilful at managing transference and countertransference?

Freud's initial contemplation of transference was negative as he felt it was an obstacle rather than a tool in the psychoanalytic process (Robbins 1990), in much the same way that emotionality can be viewed as disruptive to a classroom (Britzman 1998). With time, however, Freud began to understand the relevance and possibilities in this unconscious displacement of feelings of hostility and/or affection and desires. Inasmuch as transference is imperative for a successful analysis in the clinic, it is imperative to education. Freud eventually concluded that transference is an element of any and all human relationships, beginning with encounters in childhood, repeating all the way into adulthood, and across the lifespan. To this understanding of transference as imperative, I add Verhaeghe's (2008) observation that:

> The fundamental fantasy is constructed in and through the first concrete relationships toward the first and second Others. It forms the basis for all later relationships, where it will be repeated with other others. This is nothing but Freud's theory of transference as a general phenomenon. With Lacan (1994 [1964]) we must underline here how this repetition always brings with it the possibility for change. This is why both the diagnosis and the treatment must focus on transference. (p. 363)

Pedagogy, like psychoanalysis, is productive when we focus on transference, especially when we consider psychopathologies within schooling. Transference presents in specific repetitions and patterns the students' experience with the teacher. As with the psychoanalyst, the teacher requires training in the paradigm of transference management.

Due to repetitions, educators are obligated to understand the psychopathological or relational structures of children as important to their education. To begin with, if one perceives the hope contained within the transference (French and Wheeler 1963) as a form of hope for change, one cannot ignore transference as this means killing a child's hope.[2] Hope repeats with each repetition with *others.* If transference is not managed appropriately hope dies or is lost and with it, any chance for meaningful change. In managing transference, words given to breakdowns and disruptions and experienced in earlier encounters with others, process in what we might refer to as *meaning-making* (Eksner 2015). If educators cannot provide intervention, the effects of traumatic pedagogy carry on into adulthood across the individual's life span.

The trajectory of transference and countertransference is traced by Robbins (1990) from Freud to Reich to Horney to Thompson, who finally settles on his own definition of transference as:

> made up of a wish, an illusion, repressed emotion, and character defences, all of which are dynamically related to each other in such a way as to constitute a unified whole. The wish is in the present and is actively effective in present living. (p. 39)

This wish, Robbins states, is for a relationship with a parent or parental figure and it is an expression for a longing for fulfillment based on the real and healthy needs of a child (pp. 39–40). Therefore, I deduce that hope carries forward, through countertransference and transference, the relationship between the teacher and the learner that can be instrumental in enacting social justice. If we consider the impossibility of teaching and psychoanalysis, we might conclude that what makes both possible is transference, which carries *that* repeating hope that sustains pedagogy. It is characteristic in psychoanalysis, per Winnicott (1965), that the analyst does not waste the valuable material that comes up for analysis in terms of the emotional relationship between patient and analyst (p. 117). Borrowing from Winnicott, I posit that the same samples of repetitions (manifesting as relational patterns in the patient's emotional life or psychic reality) that the analyst depends on can be equally valuable to the teacher who by using the cues supplied by the student can interpret that which is just ready for conscious acceptance at any one session. For both teacher and analyst, "[t]he most fruitful work is that which is done in terms of transference" (Winnicott 1965, p. 118).

Fittingly, Dolto (2013) states that psychoanalytic treatment is based on the analysis of resistances and psychoanalytic method aims to circumvent repressive mechanisms and not what has been repressed (p. 10). The denotation is that when we apply psychoanalytic methods to pedagogy we are in effect circumventing the resistance to learn rather than addressing a failure to learn. In other words, we focus on desires in pedagogy rather than the results of pedagogy. The point that Dolto makes is that through transference psychoanalytic treatment is achieved and she defines this transference as the "unfolding of an emotional relation from the patient towards the doctor; it can be positive, negative, or more often mixed" (p. 10). Dolto also clarifies that understanding what of transference belongs to the subjective attitude of either party, to external circumstances, or what attributes to the influences of other individuals blended into the relationship, is an impossible task just as sometimes the waters of pedagogy get murky. The importance of transference is therefore not to whom it belongs or how it transpires; rather it is important because it is a dynamic platform for the expression, cultivation, and realization of desires.

My view of pedagogy as transference brings to the forefront the oft-submerged aspects of ideologies and the technicalities of schooling, namely the emotionality of teaching and learning. I posit that socially just pedagogy reveals suppressed and subverted emotions for both teacher and learner; and what we might judge as recalcitrance on the student's part, or negligence on the teacher's, is after all their transference from which they subjectively teach and learn. The best part of thinking of education in this light is that both teacher and learner are emotional beings and therefore are collectively responsible in creating socially just pedagogy. The teacher inspires; the learner desires; the teacher desires; the learner responds; and the cycle continues. The deep feelings of anxiety and hostility, of love and hate, and of pain and trauma, which culminate in the acquiring of difficult knowledge are of utmost importance. Both parties within the pedagogical relationship have wishes and fantasies. They must work together for justice in a just relationship so that neither remains unfulfilled.

Whether the capacity for thoughtful response is referred to as good teaching or true teaching, the position of the teacher should be to attend to the desire for knowledge that arises in the learner. The desire is expressed within the transference, which is managed as pedagogy.[3] Social justice in pedagogy manifests in a constant cycle of inspiring-desiring-responding, which require ethical maintenance. Ideological notions that view teaching as something technical or efficient without considering the social justice aspect, in my opinion, is harmful and creates irreparable trauma in schooling. Teachers aware of their position as one who inspires and responds, rather than as one who instructs are aware of social injustice and therefore address it in their practice.

## A NOTE ON DESIRE

Desire as an element of humanity, I find, relegates to bad or good, forbidden or embraced. The notion that people are motivated by their desires, regardless whether they are perceived as negative or positive, fascinates me. That is why I rely significantly on Lacan, who throughout his work places subjectivity at the very center of desire. Without desire, we are not.

My own desire in the production of this work is complex. Once I was asked what "made me" pursue doctoral studies. My off-hand response surprised me because despite my psychoanalytic training, it was the first time it occurred to me that this desire might have emanated outside of my ambitions. I answered, "Why go to a movie then leave halfway through the story?" One begins the educational journey (thriller, drama, comedy, or is it a tragedy?) in kindergarten and it makes no sense to leave until the credits starts rolling in higher education. Once I obtained my PhD credits, I would exit the cinema and get a "real" life. Sarcastically, I joked about the definition of "reality." It strikes me now that perhaps one should stay to read the credits as well. In analyzing my response, I realized that at the center of my desire to complete a doctoral degree was the desire to come out with a full story, credits running. I do not know how long I had the desire. My mother says I always told her I would be doing a doctoral degree. I do not remember this. At the same time, I do not remember a time when it was never the plan.

Most importantly, the question was what "made me?" This question implies that even as I performed my doctoral student tasks there was another's desire at play. Something else was making me do this work. An external influence is always making me. This alterity "made me" the doctoral student, writing my story as I experienced it. There is an Other's desire. The question follows: who is my Other?

Lacan in Seminar II states:

> [T]here is no true teaching other than the teaching which succeeds in provoking in those who listen an insistence—the desire to know which can only emerge when they themselves have taken the measure of ignorance as such—of ignorance inasmuch as it is, as such, fertile—in the one who teaches as well. (Lacan and Miller 1991, p. 242)

Lacan's statement considers two significant elements: the desire inspired through teaching; and, the teacher's own (ignorant) position in the relationship. The desire that manifests as transference within a student-teacher relationship is fundamental to teaching and learning. Through pedagogy, the teacher responds to a desire within the student, which drives the student to learn. The acknowledgment and response to the desires manifested in learners is what I consider to be social justice within this context. We recognize the trauma inflicted where the subversion or destruction of a child's desire occurs, evident through the examination of the responses to desires that education inspires within the children in the memoirs. The fulfillment of the children's desires brings them psychic resolution. However, where there is subversion or negation of desires, learning continues to present as irreparable trauma.

Like most doctoral students, I stumbled blindly from one topic to another during my initial years. At some point I had a desire to explore, psychoanalytically, my race and the *other* races surrounding me. This desire at the time arose as a response to the media's portrayal of crime as a black issue in Toronto especially. Outcries from Black community leaders and politicians, responses by Toronto's now infamous former mayor Rob Ford (may he rest in peace), policy makers, and even the tears of mothers who felt the loss of a son, albeit a stranger's son but a son nonetheless, all pressed on my psyche and it "made me" want to study how race works on the psyche. Eventually, my traumatic experiences in university as a black woman "made me" want to seek out spaces where I could learn as a student and teach as a Teaching Assistant (TA) without reservations created by exclusion and inequity based on my racial, ethnic, and cultural background. I found even my psychoanalytic background was used against me by those who felt it did not fit with who or what they desired me to be. I desired a space where I could bring *me* to class and be a part of the learning and teaching taking place.

I have embraced this desire and it brought me to a place where I must understand the desire not only of black people but also of all humanity. I want to know what makes us Black, White, Brown, Yellow, or Red beyond our physical bodies. What makes *us*, especially in our construction and idealization of educational systems? Intricately linked in my racialized desire is a desire to solve the problem of race in education and I know I am not the only one. Nevertheless, is it a problem because we treat it like a problem? There is a thin line between the problem of racism and the embodiment of racial difference. As a racialized woman, I sometimes cannot tell if the problem is that I am black, that I am perceived as black, or that black exists at all in society. I see these complexities in the narratives in the memoirs. I see the desires of the children and of the adult narrators of the memoirs manifest, like my own, in structural psychopathologies.

Added to the complexities of desire are the signifiers of our desires. The unconscious, according to Lacan, is structured like a language (Fink 1995) and as such the unconscious is discourse and within this discourse are specific signifiers, which speak to us. These signifiers reveal much to us about the way an individual understands her own history as well as society's interpretation of that individual's history. Added to the individual's understanding or awareness of self as a social being is the social reality in which the being must operate. For example, in *Seeing Ourselves*, James (2003) examines multiculturalism in Canada, referring to the prevailing social reality in which "culture" is all-encompassing as it shapes and is shaped by intersecting relationships in economic, political, and social systems (p. 42). Along with social reality, there is the psychical reality, which I insist we regard as fundamental in all our educational meanderings. Neglecting the psychical reality is tantamount to neglecting a foundational element to the development of the individual and society.

"The unconscious is also the Other's discourse in a very straight forward fashion: the unconscious is full of other people's talk, other people's conversations, and other people's goals, aspirations, and fantasies (insofar as they are expressed in words)" (Fink 1995 pp. 9–10). Patsalides and Patsalides (2001) remind us that Lacan was evoking Freud when he stressed the importance of analysis as furthering a "restitution" and "reintegration by the subject of his history right up to the further-most perceptible limits," with the understanding that history is not the past," but "is the past [only] in so far as it is historicised in the present" of analysis. They also point out that Lacan underscored Freud's idea that analysis, while being concerned with both dimensions of thought and affect, should ultimately highlight the analysand's own methodology in reconstructing and "rewriting" history through speech, rather than on an affective reliving of that very history in analysis. Conclusively, Patsalides and Patsalides (2001) extrapolate that Lacan was only building on the Freudian idea that the unconscious is structured like a language, and needs to be interpreted as such; stressing the ways in which both thoughts and feelings are "inscribed" and signified through words and "noises of language" (grunts, sighs, coughs, mumblings—all elements of *language*) (p. 202).

It is signifiers that help us understand the language of the unconscious and signifiers that highlight the desires of the unconscious. Within my work, I look at specific signifiers such as "Indian," "Black," and "White" as expressing the unconscious desires of those that are both signified; and speaking. Through signifiers of race, gender, and sexuality, we can understand some of the underlying facts and meanings behind actions. We can also find signifiers where breakdown in meanings, paradoxes, and complexities of positionality occur. When signifiers are lost, we see this in the condition of psychopathology.

Added to the signifiers in the memoirs are the signifiers of education, such as social justice, such as pedagogy, such as child, and such as teacher. These words commonly used within the realms of schooling underscore the desires of individuals acting within the sphere of education. For example, what does the word "teacher" signify in the unconscious? A brief exploration of signifiers in education returns us to Lacan's previous statement on "true teaching" (Lacan and Miller 1991, p. 242). In Lacan's statement, teaching signifies passion for the learner. The teacher is placed in the position of Other and therefore must act within this position as one who inspires. Common rhetoric speaks of teaching as a "fulfilling" career and teaching that "makes a difference." What could be more fulfilling than inspiring within a child or learner an insistence to know? The statement implies without inspiring one is not truly a teacher. Therefore, "teacher" as signifier is "inspiration."

Once the question of desire arises in Lacanian terms, jouissance must be accounted for. *Jouissance* is a word Lacan used to differentiate sexualized or orgasmic pleasure which is enjoyable from the psychic *dis*-gratification of experiencing things one desired (sometimes even sexually). Linked to Freud's pleasure principle (and the unpleasure that Freud defined as beyond pleasure into pain), jouissance "thus nicely expresses the paradoxical satisfaction that the subject derives from his symptom, or, to put it another way, the suffering that he derives from his own satisfaction" (Evans 1996, p. 93).

Exploring the topic of race and racism in education, particularly as a fulfillment of my doctoral requirements, was somewhat satisfying, insofar as it has brought me some level of accomplishment. I remember the anticlimactic feeling that set in a few weeks after my doctoral defense, but I was still unsettled about racial discourse in education. The satisfaction of succeeding at putting together an exceptional thesis brought with it a pain I could not stand. Even now, the more I try to work through racism and its vicissitudes, the more this pain torments me. Any satisfaction at uncovering an intimate detail soon spoils into the pain that detail inflicts. I am left bereft of both pleasure and satisfaction, and yet I cannot stop trying to figure it all out. Jouissance works in a similar way. It is a driving force that brings with it regret and pain even as one seeks for more. Jouissance maintains an illusion of mastery. If I keep writing, if I keep studying, if I keep researching, I will somehow beat racism. The deeper I am drawn into the quest, the hungrier I get for satisfaction; and yet it eludes me. In the memoirs, we see similar quests for power and satisfaction. Within education and society, understanding subjective jouissance is the key to understanding the drivers of exclusion and violence in society, both historically and currently.

## CONCLUSION

This chapter makes a case for psychoanalysis in pedagogy as supplementary to social justice approaches. By wading into the transference that can arise between analyst and patient, we can begin to imagine what is possible between teacher and student. Although often envisioned as an individualistic approach, psychoanalysis is practiced in group settings, particularly in addiction work. In chapter 6, a group approach is applied to psychoanalytic paradigms as a means of resolving the tension between the analyst-analysand dyad and the teacher–multiple students dynamic.

Both my experiences of learning math and studying race have enabled me to begin my argument for psychoanalytic paradigms in pedagogy, particularly as they highlight the personal and intimate experience of learning. Both these experiences indicate the underlying factors that motivate learners. A harsh and cruel pedagogy might instill something but it is not necessarily productive. On the other hand, a pedagogy that responds to desire creates opportunities for a learner to self-discover and self-motivate in the search for knowledge.

Finally, by equating pedagogy with transference, I offer the possibility of managing teaching and learning from an emotional and subjective position. This shifts pedagogy from an exercise of ticking boxes, as criticized by Lacan, to an exercise of responding to desire. Transference in psychoanalysis does not focus on the flow of information from the professional to the patient. Rather, transference in analysis focuses on the production of signifiers, which the professional responds to. In chapter 6, I explore this concept in depth. In the following chapter, I seek a more intimate understanding of social justice in teaching and learning. Having established the precariousness of social justice pedagogy and the disconnection between knowledge and action, I hypothesize, through psychoanalysis, what a linking of knowledge with action might create. I forage once more into the intricacies of subjectivity, emotionality, and humanity to seek the possibilities that may arise from teaching and learning through narrative.

## NOTES

1. Gutstein's book focuses on the pedagogical practices of a math teacher in an urban school catering predominantly to Latino students.

2. Consider Winnicott's (1965) case study with a patient who constantly presented a False Self until the analyst upon realizing this declared to the patient there was no hope but continued with the analysis anyway. In this declaration, the client perceived hope because despite his declaration of hopelessness the analyst continued seeing the patient. The analyst had seen past the façade of the False Self designed to hide the True Self, instigated hope for psychoanalytic work.

3. In chapter 6, I highlight that indivisibility between transference and pedagogy for it is through our interactions and repetitions that we teach and learn.

# TWO

# Why Memoirs?

When I was eight years old, we had a Malawian gardener named Moses. Moses's passion for martial arts and fitness fascinated us. His role model was Bruce Lee. My older brother liked to spend time with Moses who was teaching him how to fight. I was a little jealous of their male bonding because I liked martial arts, too. Moses was a relatively young man whom my father had decided to mentor. For this reason, my father moved Moses into the house to live with us. Then Moses, who was already my least favorite person in the house for his obvious disregard for girls, stole a large amount of money from my parents' bedroom.

When I was a year old, my father found Jesus, or Jesus found him. Either way, with Jesus, we found a better way of life. He began working for the railway company, stopped drinking and smoking marijuana, and distanced himself and us from bad influences. We moved to the suburbs. Life was good. We attended church religiously, and my father became a deacon and treasurer in our local branch. The money Moses stole was the church's Sunday collection my father had yet to deposit at the bank. When my father discovered the money was missing, my father paid it back out of pocket and had a chat with Moses who eventually confessed his theft but was not evicted from the house.

As an activist child, I could not understand why my father did not fire Moses or at least punish him. It seemed unfair to me, especially since my father had been so kind to him. I felt no justice had transpired in the situation and devised my own form of it. Moses received his wages biweekly so I waited for his next payday. I watched my father pay him and Moses sign for his envelope, then followed him to see where he kept his money. When Moses was gone, I moved his money. I understood that stealing was bad, which is why Moses needed to learn his lesson. I did not take it with me, choosing to hide it among his possessions.

For two days, nothing happened. I was on edge and snuck back into his room to check on the money. It was still there. Then on the third day, my father called me. Moses was visibly upset and my father livid. They must have had some exchange. My older brother and sister were standing outside having gone through their interrogation. Before my father could ask, I confessed. I told him I only wanted to teach Moses a lesson. I wanted him to know what my father had gone through when he discovered the church's money was missing. I even scolded my father for not being a little more punitive. I wanted to know how Moses might learn it is wrong to steal if my dad did not discipline him. My father decided I was right: theft was a serious matter. And then he punished me for stealing Moses' money, even when I showed them it was still among his belongings, so technically I had not stolen it.

My childish version of social justice is comparable to some of the wild education that occurs in schools as teachers strive to develop a sense of social responsibility in their learners. One of the most obvious aims in social justice, as stated by Todd (2003), is to arouse responsibility through developing concern for and connection to the lives of *others*, which, like all demands, is by no means innocent (p. 66). My father was wise to teach me that in my quest for justice I was implicated in the transgression of theft. Two wrongs do not make a right. So how can one help another develop social awareness without reproducing the repercussions of injustice?

Recently, young people in the universities of South Africa have begun to revolt against what they refer to as a "glacial pace of transformation" reflected in their country's educational system (Onishi 2015). They look at their historical and social positionality and power and see that very little has changed for black learners in South Africa's higher education institutions. Similarly, in India young women are revolting against gender violence and oppression on campuses based on traditional and cultural regulations that have not kept up with social awareness and transformation. For the enactment of social justice, it is not only the structure of these institutions or structural oppression that we must confront because there are profound underlying and psychical factors that require subjective attention and action. To affect the kind of individual psychical change for which I advocate, it is not necessary to obtain a formal diagnosis from a psychiatrist or educational psychologist in most cases. While education has become more responsive to the mental health of learners diagnosed with disorders, for those subject to social oppression, education might begin by providing a good enough milieu for socially triggered pathologies to find resolution.

We can analyze the glacial pace of transformation through a brief encounter with some contemporary attempts to make sense of the state of education. To this end, I contemplate Mishra-Tarc's (2005) problematization of Westernization in education, Todd's (2008) complication of cosmopolitan education, and Lane's (1998) critique of globalization as I situate the problems I view historically within the present. With the slack in change comes the trauma that leads to the collapse of knowledge, especially when the lived reality contradicts the claims of pedagogy. This is the point of criticism by Mishra-Tarc (2005), who highlights the conservation of social difference in education stating there is a strong need to reclaim, revise, and redefine words in order to resolve the "troublesome, oppressive and exclusive." In other words, we need to work through the past to remedy the present. Calling it "a return to *the Subject*," Mishra-Tarc points out modern Western institutions, like education, continue to rely heavily and often uncritically on unified and universalized concepts of what it means to be human and as a result flawed understandings of subjectivity remain. There is a culture of speaking humanism but not practicing it within education. Within this culture, Mishra-Tarc posits that:

> Those who uphold Western education, often characterized as a "humanistic" endeavour, maintain a non-questioning stance towards classical notions of subjectivity. This stance, misleadingly, renders the foundations of human subjectivity transparent, stable, and untraceable. It is upon this presumed stability of the subject that many educational practices, cognitive and social theories, curricula, and pedagogies depend. (p. 834)

We, therefore, cannot reclaim, revise, and redefine without turning to history to establish a point of correction. As we contemplate subjectivity, narratives help us access an archive of experiences, which we can use to map a way forward. In this chapter, I advocate for the use of autobiographical material in pedagogy to think through the difficulties of enacting social justice education.

Memoirs are useful in teaching abstract values often underpinned in social justice pedagogy. When oppressive and dehumanizing dichotomies are involved, how does one teach the difficult knowledge that leads to empathy and forgiveness? I elucidate on psychic processes leading to social justice by elaborating on Kristeva's (2003) identified imperatives of autobiography—the cry of distress and the call to glory. This chapter also introduces the three memoirs analyzed in subsequent chapters as I explore the educational experiences of children in the context of social difference.

I began to share my own narratives through my personal memoir from the beginning of this book. As previously explained, the object of my memories weaved into this exercise of psychoanalysis serves the purpose of informing as well as disrupting the reader so that it is possible for the reader and me to share this experience of constructing possibilities. (Although asked repeatedly by reviewers of this book to include a psychoanalysis of myself within this work, I have declined the suggestion so that the reader (you) have the opportunity to interpret my musings in our transference (yours and mine) in the same way that patients might want to analyze their analyst and indeed students might try to "read" their teachers.) Edwards (2013), a writer and psychoanalyst, examines the role of the analyst's memoir in the therapeutic space:

> What psychological transactions does a person thinking and then writing about childhood make with her own childhood? In "Creative Writers and Daydreaming" (1908) Freud considers that a writer uses aesthetic form in order to allow readers to view their own daydreams and memories through the lens of the writer's creative work "without any self-reproach or shame." So, it becomes a shared enterprise, melding reader and writer at a subconscious level. (p. 392)

This chapter extends the circle of sharing, through my memoir, through the analysis of the three memoirs, through the work of my book reviewers, and through the reader (you). In other words, the result is not limited to what I have typed as an official document but it includes the readers', writers', academics', and educators' views of their own daydreams and memories through the social justice lens I offer in these pages.

In this chapter, I offer a psychoanalytic perspective that makes it possible and ethical for the teacher to recognize ego-syntonic and/or ego-dystonic desires and fantasies. Here, the teacher's subjectivity not only appears and manifests but will also simultaneously bear the trace of its own interruption and destruction in the face of the other. The definition of "subjectivity" in this chapter encompasses subjection and openness to the other as well as the thematization, thinking, and knowing, as consciousness and as ego (Zhao 2012, p. 669).

We might conceptualize the import of emotionality in pedagogy through Freire (2000) who states in *Pedagogy of the Oppressed* that as teacher and student attain a knowledge of reality through common reflection and action, they discover themselves as permanent re-creators. Freire points out that in this co-creation, in this collaboration, there is no pseudo-participation, rather a committed involvement (p. 69). Regardless how we might conceptualize the emotional dynamic in the classroom, there is need for instruments that provide opportunities for emotional learning. My suggestion is the use of memoirs in teaching and learning as a way of navigating, acknowledging, and utilizing emotionality in pedagogy.

In my conceptualization of the *afterwardness* afforded to both learners and teachers through memoirs, I highlight the affective qualities necessary to effect social change and cultivate social awareness and transformation. The work begins with the teacher creating a facilitating space, which I will expand on in chapter 6. In this chapter, I lay the foundations for a perspective that privileges the writer as teacher and reinstitutes the teacher as an affective partner in the dialogical development of social justice. Beyond the dialogue, I advocate for action as the imperative that results in actual transformation.

## THE TEACHER'S EMOTIONAL LABOR

> As the dialectic of being and not-being, Levinas's subjectivity is a historical process of becoming that is formed and reformed, regenerated and regathered, for the purpose of justice and that is constantly being disrupted, suspended, and inverted by the presence of the other. The essence of subjectivity is not only situated in sociality; it is also at its core temporary and historical, at the edge of its own destruction. It will never reach a norm, an invariable nature as the humanists envisioned; subjectivity is not one essence, but rather a movement of events of essencing. (Zhao 2012, pp. 672–73)

Memoirs as tools for pedagogy may provide a space in which the individuals involved in pedagogy can confront the disruptions and antagonisms that come from intricate or guileless, imperceptible or overstated, rigid or flaccid, volatile or placid expressions of transference. For the teacher, especially, it affords a space for emotional teaching without exposing one's personal narrative to the sometimes destructive and callous responses of the resistant learner. In line with this view, Lewkowich (2013) speaks of teaching as a space of deviation and learning through the uncanny. In this space of vulnerability, it is possible for the teacher to teach as well as learn. In this space teaching is constructed with the arbitrary, "tangential reasoning," and things a "long way off" to stumble upon what is significantly insignificant in memory and presence (p. 63). Lewkowich uses the concept of "remembering spaces" to recall his own fantasies, desires, and emotionality. As social spaces, inhabited by the teacher, the other, and what is absent and therefore present, classrooms, as stated by Lewkowich, enable the witnessing of repetitions—resistances and resemblances that bring more to the story of teaching than what maybe obvious. We might think of memoirs as remembering spaces. In this space, fragmentation and distortion might bring about "distress and a feeling of being unhinged" (p. 64). Also, possible through memoir is a method of (self) analysis through writing, interpretation, reading, and remembering. As I stated, pedagogy is traumatic meaning, as Lewkowich speculates, teaching requires "guttering" and "learning in the margins" (p. 65).

Affective overloads require *facilitative environments* (Winnicott 1965) that I believe teaching through memoir provides. While working with memoirs can stir emotions, it also creates a screen through which the emotions can be mediated and understandings negotiated so that what is learned is more than the factual or academic detail but the deeply crucial aspects of relating emotionally with one's *other*. For the teacher, negotiating with learners the use of power that comes with knowledge is an important aspect in pedagogy, especially in the field of social justice pedagogy.

In an attempt to demonstrate the messy and often arbitrary condition of teaching and learning (if we are to be honest about what really goes on in the psyches of teachers and students in the classroom), Lewkowich endeavors to *free associate* with the reader as he goes through his experiences of teaching. He hopes that his illustration will inspire teachers, as professionals, to seek a degree of freedom and deviation from what has been the acceptable way to teach. The teacher comes to the space with a kaleidoscope of anxieties, fears, desires, and wishes that are colored with memories, affects, and past relational strategies from encounters at school in their childhood or days of learning (p. 67). It is these uncanny moments that Lewkowich suggests teachers should not only acknowledge but also embrace as what constitutes the present emotional position which is, from time to time, passionate and out of control. He elaborates that it is when we are brushed brusquely against this threshold that the uncanny emerges in our very self, at the moment that we also witness its undeniably outside appearance; like some kind of passionate, demonic double, moving forever further as we chase it away, remaining always outside our grasp (p. 70). Lewkowich also discusses the *burden of feeling,* which he describes as "an affectively persistent encumbrance that is charged and disposed through human and non-human relations of meaning, interdependency, and reliance" (p. 65). This burden, which he says accompanies every educational act, motivates unconscious movements of love, hate, authority, and desire. He uses the word overabundance which implies excess in affect and emotion, which Lacan would have labeled *plus-de-jouir*, the excess of jouissance (Fink 1995).

Lewkowich's (2013) article was somewhat difficult to follow as most free associations might be. In the clinic, the analysand may muse in any direction and often takes the analyst along and both hold on to a seemingly precarious hope that their jaunts will take them somewhere. Sometimes things seem out of control and the analysand looks to the analyst to reign in the freedom and deviation from "the problem" that brought the analysand to the clinic. But what if it is the analyst who remains unbridled? What if it is the teacher who is out of control? Without the necessary skills and competencies, pedagogy that addresses the ugliness of society, can become quite ugly in itself. Through a lens of anti-oppressive practice in education, Kumashiro (2002) addresses the tension between idealistic teaching and psychic realities within a social justice framework and examines how repetitions and resistance play out in the classroom. He states that the complicity of teachers to the status quo, against anti-oppressive ideologies, is neither intentional nor explicit but often plays out due to psychic identity associations that can privilege some over others. Educators cling to notions of authenticity, tradition, and nature which offer a sense of identity, belonging, and normalcy which means they unknowingly cling to desires which are oppressive to their learners (pp. 68–69). These desires do not dissipate due to an awareness of issues of social justice, suggesting that there is an emotional conflict that occurs within the educator. This conflict requires that the teacher possess some emotional resources to reach a resolution that allows for social transformation while relieving the anxiety that comes from going against one's self-preserving desires. Without these resources the repetition and resistance continue to play out in the studio of human nature resulting in wild education (Britzman 2011).

As he examines his own experiences as a teacher educator and classroom teacher, Kumashiro (2002) draws on the work of Butler to illustrate how teaching ideologies have become so entrenched in education that educators find themselves working against social justice while trying to rectify situations of oppression. In these patterns of fantasies and desires, transferences and projections are repeated and emotionality becomes a key factor in teaching outcomes. He argues that "our desire to work for social justice often contradicts and is superseded by our desire to repeat only certain ideas of what educational work is 'supposed' to be" (p. 69). He sees this as a hindrance to teaching and learning and elucidates on resistances to the interruption of personal desires in what is perceived subjectively as "good" teaching.

The condition of being *out of control* and the idea of excess is taken up by Ramvi (2010) who discusses the teacher's experience of losing control over his or her own feelings. As she brings us back to the fantasies and expectations teachers have about their work as educators, Ramvi draws attention to the shattering of idealistic fantasies due to emotional excess and how that can make teachers feel more than just incompetent, but out of control. Ramvi (2010) identifies moments of excess as reenactments, stating that transference between teachers and students that manifests as power struggles is really more of an internal struggle the teacher has with fantasies and different conceptions they have of themselves (p. 339). She suggests that teachers learn from these experiences to accept, tolerate, and forgive themselves.

The culminating fear of emotionality in the classroom scaffolds onto anxiety-ridden self-expectations of being a responsible and responsive teacher and then ties into subjective fears of teachers as individuals. The vicious circle is enough to collapse any semblance of safety for the teacher who is supposed to be providing a "safe space." When we consider the social justice imperatives teachers are passionate about but must hide in a bid to maintain a professional persona, we see how conceptualizations of the classroom as a space are a critical element to pedagogy.

Often juxtaposed to emotionality, "rationality" is perceived as definitive of the freedom from egoistical constraints that prevent the individual from communing fully with others. Within education, rationality means conformity and normalcy at the cost of negating all things ego-syntonic including affective expression. Teachers suppress their desires, or rather an acknowledgment of their desires and fantasies, as irrational and adhere to ideologies that make them "good teachers." The desires and fantasies are dismissed as "unscientific or prescientific," as "mere perception, mere imagination, mere worldliness, and mere duration" (Zhao 2012, p. 665). The result is a paradoxical tension where emotional resources are circumvented in emotional crises. Similarly, Kumashiro (2002) concludes that student teachers often desire learning that affirms their beliefs that they are good people and resist learning anything that reveals their complicity with oppression (p. 73).

There are rules to emotionality in curriculum and teaching, which Zembylas (2002) suggests are ideologically based on discursive, political, and cultural economy. He looks specifically at the *structures of feeling* as an approach that views emotionality as cultural material that is ever changing with zeitgeist in form and value as well as possession—an everyday commodity that is an intersubjective lived experience not necessarily in its temporal occupation but as occupied by the participant (pp. 192–93). For a teacher, this view enables a position of self-consciousness and emphases that the term "feeling" is used to make a distinction from ideology as "worldview," and identifies the meanings and values that are actually lived and felt and the relation between these and formal or systematic beliefs (p. 193). Zembylas explains that a structure of feeling is a social experience still *in process,* often not yet recognized as social but taken to be private, idiosyncratic, and even isolating. He elaborates that it is also a cultural hypothesis, derived from attempts to understand such elements and their connections in a generation or period. Thus, structures of feeling name the simultaneously cultural and discursive dimension of our experience but do not negate these experiences as also felt and embodied. In other words, "structures of feeling" permit a bridge between language and embodiment. The notion of "structures of feeling" describes the ways in which ideologies reflect emotional investments that remain unexamined during our daily interactions, because they have been woven into what is considered common sense (Zembylas 2002, p. 194).

An understanding of emotionality becomes relevant when teaching ideologies must be examined as counterproductive to the mission of social transformation and social justice. The use of terms such as emotional labor, emotional management, and emotion work show that there can be no teaching without emotion and as such it is imperative that teachers acquire and maintain emotional resources if they are to be "good teachers." Emotion work involves resisting and vulnerability, which emerge when teachers are challenged with new knowledge through experience and language. Emotions are invoked but depending on one's emotional management they can either result in a positive or negative outcome.

That is emotional labor. Structures of feeling are, therefore, examined against the backdrop of school structures and norms which often are indicative of ideological structures of pedagogy. Within this framework, teachers must operate to educate learners while saturated by their own emotionality which is subjective. This living world of the teachers cannot be ignored as they must often yield to forces beyond their control.

The concept of structures of feeling is crucial to the critical study of emotion work with teachers because emotion work acts to saturate teachers' affective elements of consciousness and their relations, so that the world they see and interact with, and the interpretations they put on it, becomes their actual living world. This theoretical position provokes a study of emotion work with teachers that considers the vulnerabilities of the teaching experience; the clash between one's views of how teachers should act and the actual enacted practices within a school context. Emotion work, in teaching, aids in negotiating the meanings of roles and relations rather than in conforming to predetermined norms. Finding out "where feelings break down, take a detour, reverse their content, betray understanding," and hence "where affective meanings become anxious, ambivalent, and aggressive" opens possibilities of identifying particular elements within the school culture that subvert the social order (Zembylas 2002, p. 197).

An analysis of power relations and structures of feeling enable us to investigate the emotional rules in teaching: "Emotional rules reflect power relations and thus are techniques for the discipline of human differences in emotional expression and communication (Zembylas 2002, p. 200). There are specificities in language, ethical/emotional territory, attributions, pitfalls, and goals that must be confronted. Ultimately, these designate and police emotionality for teachers, teaching them what they should or should not value. The specificities are used to dismiss teachers' emotions such as anger, anxiety, and vulnerability while expecting teachers to offer emotional expressions of empathy, calmness, and kindness regardless of circumstances. These ironic rules are disguised as ethical codes, professional techniques, and specialized pedagogical knowledge, which for the emotional teacher could be quite debilitating and ultimately negates the psychic realities of the teaching profession. The conflict that arises is not only external (between individual and school) but also plays out in the psyche of the individual who must self-regulate as a professional teacher.

The stances these educators—Lewkowich (2013), Zhao (2012), Ramvi (2010), Kumashiro (2002), and Zembylas (2002)—take implore us to examine the tools and resources at our disposal in teaching about social justice and teaching in a socially just manner. The question then becomes how might teachers deal with the emotional anxiety that comes from discovering or even acknowledging their complicity, their desires, and their fantasies? How can they successfully disrupt repetitions and let go of their resistance to learning, and therefore teaching? What emotional resources are available to student teachers and even experienced teachers to help them resolve psychic conflict?

To begin with, we might examine our responses to emotional crisis, which Kumashiro (2002) lays out as ethics of emotional crisis in education. For example, when a teacher is confronted with the anger, sadness, anxiety, and guilt of students confronted with new knowledge. Like Kumashiro, I believe it is more ethical to learn through crisis than it is to maintain harmful repetitive patterns that leave students ignorant of the happenings in society. I believe it is carelessness that drives a teacher to dismiss or negate the emotional reactions of students to anti-oppressive pedagogy by invoking "safe space." Forbidding emotional work in the classroom curtails both social justice and social justice pedagogy.

## WORKING THROUGH

Subaltern studies have presented us with the dilemma of the subject that cannot speak because the legal and/or structural terms of discourse are not equipped, designed, or able to hear and/or give voice to her experience. Spivak (1993), a renowned scholar on the field, speaks of the silenced subject of history, subordinate to imperialist subject-construction and epistemic violence. Invoking the works of Spivak, Swartz (2005) offers us subaltern psychology as an opportunity for the subaltern's story to emerge as clinical case study. Swartz states, "Psychoanalytic case histories have a particular claim to representing 'the Real' (Lacan), 'the true self' (Winnicott), the 'I' before the structuring and alienation of self from need/desire through the intervention of language" (p. 514).

Psychoanalysis provides praxis that enables empowerment through free association and through language, which is why Spivak's (1993) question, "can the subaltern speak," extends our understanding beyond the silencing of voices to the very core of the power that is language, and in turn, the question of who yields this power. Swartz (2005) takes a critical stance in forwarding the idea of subaltern psychology, stating that it broadens the parameters of the subaltern quest to include the interrogation of everyday activity of clinicians making historical subjects of their clients in case records, sewing them into a patchwork of clinical theories and techniques (p. 507). In this sense, Swartz proposes that the most significant contribution of subaltern studies in postcolonial historiographies lies in the prominence it gives to who speaks or writes and for whom, when, and in what representational context (p. 509). She states: "Voice, the capacity to speak, and to command an audience, and the possibility of inventing a language that will rupture the steady appropriation of experience into hegemonic meanings, has a central place in postcolonial studies" (p. 509). Therefore, if we focus on the intention of writing we identify two intentional beneficiaries to the subaltern's memoir—the subaltern himself, who works through his writing and the reader who also accesses a working through by way of transference.

Apart from offering clinicians and scholars pedagogical material, the writing of the subaltern's experience offers the subaltern catharsis, which is why therapists often recommend and encourage their clients to write. Edwards (2013) clarifies the writer-reader relationship by bringing together Freud's concept of *internal triangulation* and Melanie Klein's interpretation of the internal world's development of ideas around subjectivity, objectivity, and triangular space in relation to an internal acceptance of the primitive oedipal situation. Edwards elaborates on the *third position of the mind* as that space where thinking evolves, and posits that it is vital in order for the subjective self to have a relationship with an idea. To Edwards, subjective and objective points of view can thus be correlated as nodal points for the triangular space; and what might be called an internal spaciousness grows as the result of seeing oneself objectively as well as subjectively, in the Oedipal triangle (p. 393). Ultimately, Edwards (2013) suggests that in reading a memoir, especially a memoir majoring on childhood, reader and writer join forces at an unconscious/subconscious level where reader projects part of the subjective self into the experience she/he is reading about and sees it from this "third position." The reader also extends the triangular internal space available for reflection about childhood in general, and importantly, about her/his own experience juxtaposed with the childhood being described by the writer of the memoir. Through this intimacy and communion, I urge for a thinking through of social justice.

The cathartic benefits of journaling are well-documented and the purgative act of writing allows the writer a privileged space in which to abreact through evoking and reliving traumatic events. Lewis (2010) who examines creative art forms of therapy believes that when someone enters into a therapeutic process with any of these approaches, he or she learns to tell a new story about his or her life (p. 272). "Whether one tells the new story in terms of psychic conflicts, cognitive distortions, family dysfunctions, patriarchal oppression, spiritual exile, or insufficient neurotransmitters all of these approaches help people tell a new story" (Lewis 2010, p. 272). It is clear that the psychic act of working through allows the writer to express and discharge those affects which originally resulted from traumatic experience but which have undergone repression immediately.

Sometimes it is not simply what has been repressed that requires working through but also, what has been prohibited and what has been circumvented. In the memoir featured in chapter 4, *The Jack Bank*, Glen Retief (2008) works through the blocks of repression of thoughts and feelings he could not tolerate as a white gay child growing up in segregated South Africa. Retief tells us of the wickedness surrounding him and acknowledges that in this situation so much was still unknown to him. He writes:

> This is the treasury of cruelty that has opened its doors to me, at twelve going on thirteen, in this redbrick school in that jacaranda-lined valley town: the opportunity to buy into a reservoir of evil and violence, whose annual returns seem steady and lucrative, or to look elsewhere, for as-yet-unknown dividends and profits. (p. 127–28)

Several times in the memoir, Retief alludes to his incapacity to express and comprehend the things he knew but could not tolerate about himself. He spent his entire childhood hiding away from himself, which he confesses as an adult, expressing the melancholia, the indignation, and the umbrage that become his psychical state of mind. He does this through the writing of his memoir. Through this deferred act, he fills the emptiness that he once felt with knowledge. The memoir is a catharsis not only of what was done to him but of his own shortcomings and his self-denial.

According to Kristeva (2003), the art of writing for some provides a motor dimension, muscular and anal control, an aggressive appropriation of the body of the other as well as one's own body, and finally, a masturbatory and narcissistic gratification. Further, she states that writing allows an evasion of judgment of the other and protection from phobic affects. "Though it enables them to reconstruct their psychic space, it shelters them from reality testing. The psychological advantages of which are obvious" (p. 137). Self-loathing and self-denial both of which are elements of melancholia are common affects in people who suffer oppression (Domenici and Lesser 1995; Prager 2009). Retief's internalized homophobia was something he needed to work through. Writing his memoir was an opportunity to do this therapeutically. As the subaltern speaks he works through to a point of self-justification and by giving voice to his struggles he makes affordable to the rest of us valuable pedagogy for social justice.

## A PEDAGOGY OF VALUE

Educators tasked with teaching values such as empathy and forgiveness might use narratives of trauma as teaching material. There is a level of emotional engagement in social justice pedagogy that cannot be measured in learning outcomes or stated perspicuously in lesson plans. For example, in examining anti-racist pedagogy as emotional pedagogy, Zembylas (2012) affirms:

> the call for a "fragile pedagogical space" or a "pedagogy of discomfort" should not be assumed to be always already transformative, and beyond question. So many things can go horribly wrong misunderstandings of the purpose, the surfacing of troubled knowledge and a suppor-

> tive space for this and then perhaps disruptions preventing the issue being resolved. It needs to be recognized, then, that while this approach may potentially move us beyond the us them of critical pedagogy, it is no simple recipe for dealing with issues of racism in the curriculum. (p. 120)

Whether we call it troubled knowledge or (my preference) difficult knowledge, the value of these lessons lies in their resonance with one's affective, social, and psychic experiences. If we focus specifically on empathy and forgiveness in social justice pedagogy, we can explore abstract human values such as suffering, peace, and reconciliation, using memoirs. The psychoanalytic formulation of difficult knowledge offered by Britzman (1998) can help educators confront the deeper aspects of pedagogical practice. Memoirs as part of curricula, particularly in higher education, advance the strivings of abstract pedagogies and enables the sharing of difficult knowledge, which brings insight concerning the acknowledgment of discontinuity from the persistence of the status quo, and hence asks something intimate from the learner (Britzman 1998). The efficacy of autobiographical material in social justice pedagogy lies in the *deferred action* or what Laplanche and Pontalis (1974) call *afterwardness* made available to learners through the psychic process of acquiring difficult knowledge. Simply, deferred action is a psychic rendering of the past in the present as a means of emotional, social, and spiritual growth. When learners make use of memoirs to engage with social injustices beyond their personal experience they gain the opportunity to experience social justice in the form of empathy and forgiveness.

Helene Deutsch's autobiography as observed by Kristeva (2003) "resisted" the two dramatic imperatives that are often inherent in autobiographies—the cry of distress and the call to glory (p. 189). However, many memoirs as autobiographic literature make use of these imperatives, which is why I suggest they are especially productive and useful in pedagogical endeavors for social justice. "The cry of distress," easily heard in the memoir, draws us to the experience of emotional and mental catharsis that comes through reading. Keeping in mind the social justice endeavors, however, requires the learner to move beyond what can sometimes be a superficial identification with the protagonist to a more intimate revolt. I label the inspired intimate revolt, "the call to glory."

Both writing and reading, as Kristeva (2003) posits are "an intimate revolt" that is keenly different from speech. To Kristeva, intimate revolt is a return, a turning back; a change on which the future depends as it is a questioning and displacement of the past, and this return is a simultaneous recollection, interrogation and thought, which presents the possibility of questioning one's own being and searching for oneself (pp. 5–6). Further, Kristeva refers to literature as an act of revolt that opens psychic life to re-creation, continues, and recurs, even at the price of errors and impasses (p. 6). A simplistic interpretation of Kristeva's perspective: one can re-find self through another's experiences. A myriad of examples of memoirs might personally, and significantly, influence social consciousness. For me, the memoirs bring to heart education's complicity in the dehumanizing commodification of childhood. Children were unfortunately pawns and victims to the power struggles and oppressive ideologies of adults. These memoirs highlight traumatizing pedagogy on societies' most vulnerable. The most powerful and persuasive memoirs elicit awareness and implore readers to be witnesses to the writer's testimony. Memoirs bridge the difference in time and space to an experience where intimacy crosses lines between subject and learner. Felman and Laub (1992) make the case for testimonies of traumatic experiences in literature highlighting the value in these testimonies, which lies in what they can teach, more so, as it brings from the external into the internal, that which we would often consciously and unconsciously come to know as *other*.

Through reading, there are opportunities for communion between the writer and learner, the internal and the external, the past and the present as well as in creation and destruction. Further, Felman and Laub (1992) state:

> The emergence of the narrative which is being listened to—and heard—is, therefore, the process and the place wherein the cognizance, the "knowing" of the event is given birth to. The listener, therefore, is a party to the creation of knowledge de novo. The testimony to the trauma thus includes its hearer, who is so to speak, the blank screen on which the event comes to be inscribed for the first time. (p. 57)

When we read the memoir, we are in essence listening to the cry of distress echoing from the past; and we are obligated, at the very least, to acknowledge, as witnesses the trauma of the writer. The memoir reminds us by bringing to our consciousness the atrocities we would rather negate or relegate to history. The connection between writer and reader is highlighted by Coen (1994) who points out that a reading of a text can evoke within a learner fantasies, wishes, and desires previously denied but brought to light by the writer's disclosure. Essentially, Coen states that in reading a text we obtain gratification and even work through some of our own pathologies. This connection is the catalyst that drives the psyche to act and re-act to the testimony of trauma, which is difficult knowledge. If, however, the learner denies the testimony of the writer, she/he denies their connection, therefore her/himself.

Sometimes learners forget. According to Freud (2006), "The forgetting of impressions, scenes, and experiences comes down in most cases to a process of 'shutting out' such things" (p. 392). *What things?* Things that make us feel shame, guilt, complicit, and most importantly, powerless. I believe that this shutting out results in a guilty society that neglects the remediation of injustices, and therefore protracts the trauma of the oppressed. However, the memoir seemingly far removed from current existence, forces the learner to relocate to where the writer is situated. There the learner has a conscious choice to make between forgetfulness or intimate revolt. The act of reading engages a consciousness that actively engages pieces of the unconscious that inspire intimate revolt. In much the same way that writing functions psychically, reading "reveals that which has been suppressed, covers over that which has been disclosed, and more generally breaches the very oppositions that are brought to sustain it" (Dimitriadis and Kamberelis 2006). Reading the memoir acts as an uncovering of things learners could not otherwise access.

Teaching about trauma through memoir requires more than critical analysis and social theory. Simon (1992) states, "If we wish to help articulate counterdiscursive positions from which students may begin to define practices that challenge existing social forms, more than insurgent readings are necessary" (pp. 115–16). He elaborates on the necessity to contest the provision of meaning based on institutional authority, indicating students should be able to interpret and work through their own meanings in texts as a way of disrupting the status quo of hegemonic relations often constructed through institutionalized connotations. *Meaning making* is an encounter that occurs between writer and reader, which cannot be institutionalized in any social justice endeavor. Simon also insists, "The practice of pedagogy cannot be developed in a formulaic manner, for teaching is, first and foremost, a practical activity that must respond to the contingencies of particular classroom encounters" (p. 117). Reading memoirs for social justice does not call for an intellectualization of the experiences of the writer rather it is a call to break through the repetitive cycles that make social justice impossible.

## EMPATHY AND THE CRY OF DISTRESS

Featured in my third chapter, in the memoir *They called me Number One,* Chief Bev Sellars (2013) states:

> I asked myself, "Is it possible to make other people feel what I once felt and understand my message? Is it possible to make others realize the damage they are doing to themselves and to their loved ones? Is it possible to help others by writing about my experiences, or will it only create tension with others who shared those experiences? Should my memories stay just memories?" (p. xiv)

Sellars wonders what empathy she can garner from readers so that they move beyond a superficial response to her cry of distress. Empathy is a word society, whether through parenting, formal curricula, or clinical intervention strives to teach children, as soon as possible, in the hope that it makes them better people. An elementary definition of empathy is "the ability to walk a mile in another person's shoes." Being empathetic means that you can sense and identify with what another person is feeling. As children get older the meaning becomes more complicated. For older learners, especially within higher education, we begin to speak more sophisticatedly about emotional intelligence (E. I.) as a humanistic value in society. To Halpern (2001) empathy involves discerning otherwise unrecognizable experiences of another person, which requires a level of cognitive and affective function. In relation, Zembylas (2013) uses the term "empathic imagination," referring to both Halpern (2001) and Hollan (2008) in his construction of a pedagogical understanding of empathy.

In truth, the definition of empathy as a dialogic process generates a number of interesting pedagogical questions, which Zembylas (2013) attempts to tackle:

> What enables a student to imagine well and accurately the emotional perspective of another individual, especially someone from an "enemy" community? Is it "appropriate" to teach children about/for empathy at the elementary school level, particularly when a conflict is still unresolved? How does the political, cultural, and educational context shape the process of teaching about/for empathy at schools in a conflicting society? Does a student who gets to "know about" the "enemy's" life experience necessarily empathise with the "other"? All that said, it seems clear that complex personal, interpersonal, historical, and cultural influences are always at play in the process of constructing empathetic imagination. (p. 23)

The pertinent questions presented by Zembylas concern the pedagogical goal of uncovering the meanings and values that individuals construct about the past, themselves, and the *other*. In other words, they concern the signifiers individuals, communities, and society attach to life experiences. Zembylas maintains studies in peace education emphasize that to construct a unified society in the aftermath of loss and conflict, empathy, that is, understanding the other's perspective and imagining how the other might feel, is an important part of the peace process (p. 19). However, a deeper examination indicates that the notion of empathy is easily lost in the politics of the day and countless other affects and factors that tend to circumvent the ability to feel another's pain. The most obvious barrier to empathy is pain, which as a human condition, is immeasurable and unquantifiable, whether physical or emotional. Hence, so that I might begin to cultivate a more fruitful exercise in social justice pedagogy, I privilege the voices of the oppressed as the first significant step in any construction of empathy and by extension, social justice.

Reading the memoir should do more than elicit sympathy for the writer. It should garner historical empathy, which Farley (2006) describes as an identification. The identification is not based on superficial and outward markers, but on the psychic alteration, that comes with difficult knowledge, perhaps found in the famous words of Michael Jackson, "the man in the mirror." De-historicized empathy rescues social justice from the archives of the past and enlivens our attention to present relationships. Farley offers a succinct actualization of the process of learning through history for children, which I extend to the act of reading the memoir. Extrapolating on the significance of learning history and from history, she states that read through the lens of identification, educators can view students' efforts to learn history as fulfilling any or all of the following fantasies: to consume the past, to be watched over, to be watchful of others, to be invisible, to be seen, to escape death, and to participate eternally in the present (p. 1029). Also focusing on the pedagogical espousal of history by students in classroom presentation projects, Farley analyzes the demonstration of a pedagogy that encourages not only the learning of technical details such as dates and chronological occurrences. Instead, she turns our attention to the intimate value of history as a fantasy able to fulfill a temporal void in participation. Through space and time, history brings those that *were* to those that *are* and amalgamates into a working through.

Similarly, as pedagogical material, the memoir is beneficial in its therapeutic capacity to work through feelings of guilt, helplessness, and complicity that might arise when one encounters historical acts of oppression through reading the writer's testimony. Reading, as deferred action, creates empathic opportunities for social justice, which comes through positioning oneself to stand against a repetition of the injustices of oppression experienced by historical *others.* It is not necessarily a call to aggressive or even violent action; rather, it is the decision to acquire, actively and mindfully, difficult knowledge. "To make relevant experiences beyond one's own, indeed, even within one's own realm, means that one must work through the remittances that primary identifications put in place" (Britzman 2000, p. 38). I use Britzman's statement to explore the possibilities of an empathy that extends beyond the victimized or oppressed to insightfulness about the *other*'s experiences of trauma and society's oppressive practices. In other words, empathy considers all members of society as responsible for the injustices against all *others.* To include one's self as guilty through social complicity requires a level of social consciousness, social concern, and social knowledge that the memoir aids the learner to develop. For the learner who is willing to work through the injustices, an understanding of what the writer experienced results, but it goes beyond what I view as a superficial empathy to a place where identification reveals one's complicity in history. An *in-the-present* encounter with one's self in the past is difficult knowledge. Further elucidating on the parameters of difficult knowledge, Britzman (1998) deems that it requires one to do more than confront the difficulties of learning from another's painful encounter with victimization, aggression, and the desire to live on one's own terms. Difficult knowledge calls one to risk approaching the internal conflicts, which learning brings (p. 117).

A psychoanalytical paradigm of social justice pedagogy realizes that the learner will come face to face with his/her own internal conflict of ignorance. The writer's cry of distress echoes in the learner's own frustration with the status quo. To confront one's internal conflicts, the learner begins with an acknowledgment of injustice and gains knowledge through trauma, experiencing a pedagogical kind of empathic pain and suffering. Through deferred action, the learner "must be willing to both confront outside knowledge as a mode of address that demands the learner's transformation of memory and to tolerate psychic or existential time, the time of the belatedness of understanding" (Britzman 1998, p. 118).

Difficult knowledge accessed through the writer's memoir is socially deferred action; and there's hope that the psychic alteration of the learner might lead to acts of social and self-transformation. As Farley (2006) invokes the work of Freud and Levinas' to explain psychic responsibility through identification, she posits Levinas has a critical lens on the responsible subject who feels accused in innocence, stating:

> For Lévinas, responsibility emerges from a pre-linguistic, or we might say, pre-critical experience of being. Levinas's sense of responsibility is, then, something one feels before the decision to perform a duty and before the effort to strike just enough emotional distance in empathizing with others. It begins, but does not end with the surprising discovery of the self as always already constituted in relation to others. (p. 1033)

For the learner, there is a moment of clarity, a discovery that what the writer experienced occurred in the same world he/she inhabits, and therefore relates to him/her. Through this identification, the learner sees him/herself as a crucial part of the cry of distress. Farley also states that Lévinas constitutes the self in others: "I am 'in myself' through the others," a space in which we can read identification not as a narcissistic consumption of the past, but as a sign of the vulnerability that constitutes being as responsible for others in times and places before the self (p. 1033). Understood through Freud's (1932) concept of fetishism, narcissistic consumption, in this context, ties into the previously mentioned afropessimitic view of commodification. (In this working through, *afropessimism* moves us toward authentic freedom, while psychoanalysis helps us find a language that can express adequately the complexities of race.) Freud believed that fetishism, a form of narcissistic consumption, was a mechanism in which the subject can both mentally give full value to reality while simultaneously denying, repressing, and forgetting unwelcome consequences. Hence, through a narcissistic consumption of history or the writer's experiences, the reader gives full value to the reality of oppression but "scotomizes" his/her own complicity, social responsibility, and pedagogical empathy.

Coupled with Britzman's (2000) statement on the remittances that primary identifications put in place, Farley's statement means not only those who feel the guilt of complicity during the time of oppressive occurrences would benefit from memoirs but also generations in the distant futures will have much to learn from the writer's narrative. Hence, autobiography is an essential tool in social justice pedagogy as it helps readers step out of their self-consuming guilt and shame in primary identifications to a space where they see themselves in others regardless of *when* these others might have *been*. The memoir acts as a cautionary tale against the repetition of history and offers a way forward through valuable lessons from the past by maintaining the identified pain and suffering in all temporality.

On teaching trauma through literature, Britzman (2000) asserts that to study the difficulty of others is to in fact, to study how one comes to relate to the conditions of difficulty expressed by others, as opposed to somehow attempt to reacquire the felt experience of the other. Likewise, as she explains, to be receptive to the difficulties of the other is different from feeling another's pain as that is actually impossible, because instinctively, when confronted with another's expressions of pain, one tries to attach by imagining how one would feel in similar conditions (p. 38). Thus, reading the memoir should not be about feeling the *other*'s pain and suffering because empathy, as it has popularly been psychologized as "walking in another's shoes," is a fruitless endeavor. Rather empathy, particularly in social justice pedagogy, is witnessing the cry of distress and responding to the call to glory.

## FORGIVENESS AND THE CALL TO GLORY

I feature the memoir *Kaffir Boy* in chapter 5, where Mark Mathabane (1986) makes clear his pedagogical objective, stating:

> The white man of South Africa certainly does not know me . . . so my story is intended to show him with words a world he would otherwise not see because of a sign and a conscience racked with guilt and to make him feel what I felt when he contemptuously called me "Kaffir boy." (p. 3)

Mathabane discloses his difficult childhood during South African apartheid in the 1960s–1970s, a time some might choose to forget as history. However, reading it today makes it, perhaps more so, a call to glory for social justice. The autobiographies and memoirs that come from those who suffered the injustices of South African apartheid do not simply give a subjective account of what happened; rather, they issue an atemporal call to glory to engage actively against the tyranny of discrimination, racism, and genocide.

As Mathabane details the atrocities of his childhood, he challenges the ignorance of inexperience. In social justice pedagogy, ignorance is not an acceptable excuse because as Felman (1987) states, ignorance is a desire to ignore, not simply a lack of information but the incapacity—or refusal—to acknowledge one's own implication in the information:

> Ignorance is linked to what is not remembered, what will not be memorized. But what will not be memorized is tied up with repression, with the imperative to forget—the imperative to exclude from consciousness, not to admit knowledge. Ignorance in other words, is not a passive state of absence, a simple lack of information: it is an active dynamic negation, an active refusal of information. (p. 79)

Indeed, the instinct to avoid pain and suffering is human however, this insistence on remaining ignorant is a denial and subversion of justice, and it is the very thing that Mathabane (1986) seeks to unsettle. The pain and suffering he hopes to provoke in the readers is what brings change. It is a necessity that the learner cannot justly shirk. Insight or true understanding is change. Insight is the generation of something new through a process of reflection where something takes place within the learner that signifies social justice. The learner might not need to join the ranks of those fighting for social justice in the trenches, but this difficult knowledge, this shift from ignorance to insight is social justice because it propels one, through identification, to seek forgiveness.

In letting "the white man of South Africa" know, Mathabane helps those socially complicit face their conscience, and unconscious, and to reach a place of forgiveness. Some white South Africans, like Straker (2004), admitted to their complicity but felt helpless against the apartheid regime. There were those who wanted to live in a different society but still benefited from the system that gave them privilege over the oppressed. In Straker's (2004) words, "emphasis is placed on the experience of white South Africans who were progressive and against racism, and our feelings of shame and guilt arising from involuntary forced association with the corrupt apartheid regime" (p. 407). To address these feelings of guilt and shame, one must acknowledge the cry of distress; and out of witnessing and admitting one's complicity, come to forgiveness, and an ability to respond to the call to glory.

Such forgiveness is what Kristeva (2003) refers to in her exploration of literature as an experience that deploys intimacy and is timeless and strange in its forgiveness (p. 12). In elaborating, she explains that:

> Forgiveness does not absolve acts. Under the act, it raises the unconscious and makes it encounter another, in love, another who does not judge but hears "my" truth in the availability of love and for this very reason allows rebirth. Forgiveness is the luminous phase of the sombre unconscious atemporality, the phase during which the latter changes

> laws and adopts the attachment to love as a principle of renewal of the other and the self. (p. 20)

Kristeva makes an important statement in that forgiveness is not given by another; rather, one forgives oneself with the help of an *other* just as one must find one's position within the discourse through the *other* (p. 19). Forgiveness, therefore, could be whatever psychic formation ends the cycle of guilt and shame, accusation, and animosity, by establishing an intimate identification between the writer and the learner.

Sometime ago, I had the fortune of meeting Dr. Frank Chikane, a South African political leader who wrote his memoir at a young age. People do not usually write their memoirs in the early thirties, but for Dr. Chikane the oppression in apartheid South Africa meant his life was in constant danger. During an interview with Dr. Chikane, he made the observation that for South Africa to move forward as a nation, everyone, on both sides of the historical divide, needs to forgive each other and themselves. He spoke of some of the atrocious acts perpetrated by white South Africans and in turn pointed out that black South Africans were also guilty of heinous acts. As a nation at war within itself, everyone was caught in a culture of death and destruction until at some point, it didn't seem to matter whether it was a black man or white man wielding the weapon, someone was suffering.

The question of forgiveness of self, let alone *others*, bears great weight. For how can those born after the end of apartheid but still living its consequences forgive when everyday they endure the vicissitudes of apartheid? How can those still benefiting from the inequitable distribution of land and wealth seek forgiveness? Whether we are talking about black people forgiving white people, or white people forgiving older generations who passed down a legacy of privilege through oppression. Dare I say, white people need to forgive black people?

In classrooms, memoirs present opportunities for us to move into a space where forgiveness through pedagogy is possible. Kennedy (2011) advocates for such pedagogy that yields forgiveness, through the work of Arendt and Derrida:

> Forgiveness offers hope for the possibility of reconstituting sociality after a breakdown has occurred. Or, put differently, forgiveness affirms natality—that term Arendt uses to describe the capacity of each of us to act anew without being locked into the determinations and conceptual fixities of the past. (p. 381)

Expressly, forgiveness is the awakening of the capacity in learners to respond to the call to glory. Forgiveness moves beyond political and social barriers to a collective intimate revolt against oppression. Unfortunately, forgiveness cannot be legislated and it cannot occur through policies and procedures or lesson plans and learning outcomes. Even in exercises such as the South African Truth and Reconciliation Commission or the recently published Canadian Truth and Reconciliation Commission report, we see that when the oppressed are asked to forgive it is difficult, as one cannot adequately express to *the other* the pain that forgiveness would require. In South Africa, Archbishop Desmond Tutu's response to refusals of forgiveness made it plain, forgiveness always comes at a price where one seeks reparation. Then, how is the cost of reparation calculated? How, and who, can accurately summate the cost of trauma? When one cannot pay the price of reparation, is the relationship between oppressor and aggressor not inverted? Once more, the need to go beyond the structural and economic to the psychic so that we can move forward by some degree, confronts us.

In any account of social justice, we need to understand the inversion of power, as explained by Swartz (2007), who highlights the intricacies and complications of the work of forgiveness facilitated through the Truth and Reconciliation Commission in South Africa:

> The act of forgiving in a conversation between perpetrator and victim issues from a position of power, however momentarily it is held. This unsettles the free flow of dialogue, invokes uncomfortable notions of who after all is "innocent," and never allows the sentence "I forgive you for being my victim," thereby creating another layer of subalterns, "the forgiven," ironically shackled in the very moment of release. (p. 519)

The shackles make social justice impossible by resisting forgiveness through shame and guilt. Social justice cannot transpire in the face of accusation and animosity. We simply cannot teach social justice in a classroom cloaked as "safe space" yet tainted with silenced guilt, shame, animosity, and accusation. Then again, can we say that empathy or forgiveness has occurred if social justice pedagogy is reduced to what Kennedy (2011) describes as an educational approach to social breakdown focusing on either critical analysis or rectifying material histories of injustice and inequality? Clearly, we need an intimate revolt that breaks away the shackles in the moment of release so that individuals are able to become active respondents to the call to glory.

From the paradoxical position of both victim and perpetrator, Straker (2004) confesses, "In regard to guilt, because of the corruption of the law, we judged ourselves, not in legal terms, but in ethical and moral terms (i.e., in terms beyond the law)" (p. 410). The laws that perpetrated trauma could not bring the healing required for those who were complicit in oppression and yet felt themselves oppressed. The memoir offers learners in these paradoxical spaces the opportunity to forgive themselves and thereby let go of the guilt and shame associated with privilege. Intimate revolt, beginning with forgiveness, does not absolve acts of social injustice but offers a way to break through guilt and shame to acts of reparation that are attentive to the past without erasing the testimony.

## LOVE IN PEDAGOGY

We could also define forgiveness as a change in law that brings love (Klein and Riviere 1964). Klein stated to be genuinely considerate implies that we can put ourselves in the place of other people; we identify ourselves with them and it is from this capacity of identification that love develops as we become able to disregard or to some extent sacrifice our own feelings and desires in the interest of the ones we love (p. 66). The law in this context is the status quo of victim versus perpetrator. Through this kind of love, learners see that even those complicit through privilege are victims and even those oppressed hold the power to which Swartz (2007) refers. In the status quo, hate, defined by Riviere as a destructive disintegrating force tending toward privation and death (Klein and Riviere 1964), maintains social injustices but love, gained through social justice, cultivates harmony and union tending to life and pleasure (p. 3).

Perhaps we do not often think of love as necessary in the classroom but it is certainly worth considering when we aim for social justice. When we consider that social justice in education is supposed to make inclusive what has been exclusive, and the ongoing challenges that endeavor encounters, it makes sense to lean toward the radical. Love might be considered a radical measure in the classroom, maybe even unprofessional but if love is the measure that makes the difference between harm and help then perhaps it is time we exposed classroom spaces to more affect and affection.

The definition of love in pedagogy requires we re-evaluate what we understand of love. Analysis of love in relation to empathy aids us in re-evaluating what we understand about education as a human endeavor as per Todd (2003), who broadens the terms of social justice education to include love, which takes on a distinct difficulty that demands something far greater of us in terms of commitment, concern, and responsibility because the feeling of love, unlike empathy, is a seemingly rare attachment that the self holds for a unique Other. In addition, Todd affirms that love is supposed be reserved for only a few people in our lives, as opposed to empathy, which is presumably more far reaching, meaning in education, love is deemed a much too narrow and exclusive feeling to be of any value. She further extrapolates the aspect of love that would be required to move forward a social justice agenda, stating that "one of the most obvious aims in social justice education is to arouse responsibility through 'developing' concern for and connection to the lives of 'Others,' which, like all demands, is by no means innocent" (p. 66). Like me, her point is not to romanticize education but to communicate concern by taking responsibility, so she says:

> Rather than defining love as an unequivocal good that should be pursued in developing moral concern, my intent is to read the communica-

> tive effects of love that underlie our attempts at being-for the Other, and to what degree they allow for a learning from the Other. This means turning to the risks embedded in such communication and evaluating the degree to which such risks hold promise for conditions of non-violence. (pp. 67–68)

When a learner chooses to heed the call to glory that choice communicates a commitment to social justice, and that commitment in turn requires responsible action. Love, in terms of pedagogy, is not simply affective. Love is active partnership, collaboration, and connectivity. We could view the call to glory as an issue of love, which gives us a way of inspiring within students love for *others*. In the final chapter, I shall return to the necessity of love within a privileged space.

## A WAY FORWARD

> While teachers in social justice education have long relied on stories of suffering to encourage students to take on social responsibility, what marks human rights education as different is pressure from the force of law itself. Human rights education demands that students recognize and adopt a sense of universal duty from their very singular experience of the ethical encounter with another's suffering. (Sliwinski 2005, p. 222)

The question of affect and the complex dynamics that may interfere with learning from human oppression and suffering requires that we do away with distinctions between human rights and social justice. In my use of memoirs, I explore the dehumanization of childhood through education, most definitely as an abuse of human rights, as well as a matter of social justice. Social justice education for me encompasses both an examination of the violation of human rights as well as an acknowledgment of social inequalities and injustices. As I stated before, the question is not just whether or not a child is receiving the education they are entitled to as a human being but also, what is the quality of education the child is receiving?

My rationale for the use of memoirs in social justice pedagogy as stories of human suffering advocates for more than just learning *about* the suffering of children in segregated education, rather we should learn *from* these narratives of human immorality. Sliwinski (2005) wisely states that knowledge of human immorality does not, in itself, change people (p. 222) and I strongly support this view as important to recognizing the two imperatives I have outlined—the cry of distress and the call to glory. When one witnesses the human immorality portrayed in these narratives of human suffering, one becomes a part of that history and occurrence. When one acknowledges the call to glory, one becomes instrumental in the resolution of the history. One has learned from, not about, the writer's account.

With each of the memoirs in the following chapters, I listen for the cry of distress and interpret the call to glory, offering a psychoanalytic reading of these identified imperatives of autobiography as constituting social justice. If social justice is to be more than a mantra in educational rhetoric, the terms and problems involved must be explicit. Without a deep understanding of psychical life and its evolving nature and without attentiveness to the cry of distress—emotional experiences of social violence—the idea of social justice remains an empty signifier.

My autoethnographic methodology renders social justice an acknowledgment of the child's cry of distress and the narrator's call to glory. The analytic reading takes a clinical stance, particularly in terms of psychopathology as I apply psychoanalytic paradigms to understanding race and difference within pedagogy. This psychoanalysis relies heavily on transference and countertransference, with both the child in distress and the narrator issuing the call to glory. My interpretations, therefore, are the cry of distress that I hear in these memoirs of social trauma inflicted through pedagogy, and the call to glory is at the narrators' insistence, also made possible through pedagogy. The usefulness of this methodology lies in the availability of transference and countertransference with the narrative in what I regard as privileged space; a concept I shall expand on in the concluding chapter. To distinguish between transference and countertransference outside of actual clinical or classroom interactions might appear to be somewhat convoluted; especially in this methodology. Transference might be easier to identify as the reader's reaction and/or response to the memoir. Nevertheless, the memoir is hardly going to respond or react to the reader holding the book.

To explain my discernment between transference and counter transference, I'll use the book *Jane Eyre*, which I have read countless times. Each reading presents a new facet, a new dimension, a new trigger to my emotionality, as I have grown and matured from my first encounter with the book at age fourteen, to the most recent reading just before I began my doctoral journey. At each stage, I uncover a fresh and often new rendering of what others might refer to as humanity. I have read *Jane Eyre* as a young girl, who can only fantasize about the romantic love affair between Jane and Mr. Rochester. I have read it as a young woman who has loved and hated a man. I have read the book as an academic, as a social activist, as an educator, as a mature woman, as a postcolonial scholar, and as a black feminist. This shifting and new rendering by the same narrative at each encounter is what I view as countertransference.

My evolving subjectivity, at the insistence of the narrator, perceives a new call to glory with each rendering of the narrative. Farley and Mishra Tarc (2014) suggest that countertransference be considered on the grounds of its effects that can be put to work in the symbolic realm of thought and representation. They clarify that:

> Inside and outside the clinic, interpretation of childhood testimony carries traces of both social and psychic conflicts associated with witnessing its difficult content. In adult and child alike there can be wishes for certainty, fantasies of power and victimization, and desires to be cured and cared for against the terror of both helplessness and rage. The fact of the child's transference and its counter in the adult makes it difficult to know the meanings of trauma belonging to the event and its retelling, and those belonging to the adult's "deeply held fantasies" about "children" and the analyzed child. We suggest that analytic attention to currents of social and psychic countertransference opens the adult witness to what Hans Loewald (1979) terms "self-responsibility" [p. 760]. (pp. 844–45)

I distinguish between transference and countertransference as I have distinguished between the cry of distress, which is my witnessing of the child's story and the response to the narrator's call to glory as self-responsibility. This self-responsibility relates to forgiveness and love as previously discussed. It is social justice. Farley and Mishra-Tarc (2013) further state in their analysis of adult countertransference to a child's artistic expression of his trauma, that there is a question on how an adult, as belated witness, can represent the conflicts and associations embedded in the enigmatic details of the child's testimony. Further, how can they attempt to bear witness to the unseen and unthinkable quality of traumatic experience, a radical helplessness born of the adult's abject failure to prevent its occurrence (p. 847)? I find myself in the same position with these memoirs. Faced with a call to glory, I attempt, ethically and justly, to present an academic rendering of the trauma the children experienced. In this position, I find myself working through my complicity and indeed helplessness in preventing past, present, and future traumas in education. As an educator, the countertransference is magnified. I am aware of the trauma I inflict as part of an educational system in denial of the traumatic social differences we perpetuate even as we struggle and rally against them.

In this project, I consciously resist aestheticizing the memoirs. There is a danger of getting lost in the artistry of the account and reducing my reading to a fetishistic consumption of "the story." It is possible to be "touched" and "moved" by the narration to the extent of shedding tears, and then simply getting up and returning to "real life" without having been affected in any way that counts. I have already revealed my tendency to romanticize education and in an effort to curb this aspect of my own subjectivity in my interpretations, if it is at all possible, I resist seeing the exquisite in the pain and the wonderment in the trauma. In the memoir chapters (3–5), I distinguish between child and narrator by using the child's name where I hear a cry of distress, and the narrator's name where I identify a call to glory. These narratives, through the memoirs, present an accounting of the past in a way that creates, for me as reader, the author's subjectivity. In this sense, memoirs are not the same as raw events but cast their lot with the power of the symbolic by presenting the Real, the Imaginary, and the Symbolic.

There are multiple complications in this work, just as we might encounter in the clinic and indeed in the classroom. I explore these representations of complications and attempt to make "sense" of them through psychoanalytic paradigms. The more significant of these complications, by number of occurrence across the three narratives, and by implication in current educational and pedagogical praxis include paradoxical identifications, facts, complexities, breakdowns in meanings, and the collapsing of structure both systemic and psychical. I explore these within the Symbolic register, and use them to expand on the aetiology of psychopathologies—neurosis, perversity, and obsessionality—in the children and in the structural systems in which they develop as social beings.

As stated earlier, I leave the psychoanalysis of my childhood up to you the reader. I also implore you to seek within the next three chapters your call to glory and your forgiveness of others and of yourself. I refrain from sharing my own experience of the call to glory from Chief Bev Sellars, Glen Retief, and Mark Mathabane beyond what is in this book. Although we have embarked on an intimate journey and are connecting through shared memories of my childhood, I feel, as a psychoanalyst, that the call to glory rendered by these three people to you (through me) (although you would benefit more from reading the memoirs yourself) must be something you heed personally as I have done.

# THREE

## Bev Sellars: *They Called Me Number One*

When I was twelve, I wrote my first major state exam. This exam determined the caliber of school into which a child progressed for secondary schooling. I was dying to go to the same boarding school my older sister attended. I had already written the entrance exam for the school and passed. Now I had to pass the state exam. To register successfully for the state exam, we had to bring in our birth certificates so that our names were recorded correctly. I asked my parents for my birth certificate and took it to school without looking at it myself. At school, I handed it to my teacher who would return it to me when she had inspected my records.

As in many formerly colonialized countries, we had English names but we also had ethnic language names, which we often used at home and in "informal" settings. Using the English or Christian name was associated with formality, business, and social class in some circles. My family called me Tapo at home. At school, they called me "Gloria." That is until at the age of twelve, I discovered that my name is Glorie. I was livid. I went home and demanded an explanation. It turns out, as with my birth story, my naming story was not quite clear either.

My father and mother, despite having two small children by the time I was born, did not have their lives "sorted." Dad indulged in drink and marijuana undependably. Mama was a young mother with three children by the time she was twenty-two and five by the time she was twenty-six. They met when they lived in the same neighborhood in (what was formerly) Gwelo. She, while living with her older sister, met a man twelve years older than her. A match made in heaven, except he was an irresponsible drunk with a pushy family and no income to rely on. Dad was an intelligent man who had missed many opportunities due to his recreational habits. He won a scholarship in his younger days to study aviation in America, but turning up drunk during the orientation program resulted in his dismissal from the program. He similarly lost other educational and career opportunities over the years. I am not sure what he was doing in Gwelo at the time. My mother's brothers were his drinking buddies; and then she was pregnant with my older brother. When I was born, my father was unemployed and my mother tells me it was so bad they had no money for diapers for me. Dad was responsible for the naming misfortune. Thus, for twelve years I was Gloria. He must have intended for it to be Gloria because he seemed to discover Glorie around the same time I did. I cannot say, and I cannot recall the explanation provided in response to my outrage. It took a while for Glorie to catch on. When I went to boarding school, Mama would write me letters with my name misspelled "Glory."

A few weeks after the name "correction," I was on the playground with some friends when a schoolmate provoked us. I am not sure what the argument was about but somewhere during the verbal exchange the girl called me "Gloria." "It's Glorie! I! E! Not Gloria!" I shouted at her. She responded, "Well whatever your stupid name is." I launched myself at her in a blaze of fury wanting her to take back her words. I think it must have been building up for weeks—this anger at having to become someone else. Our friends pulled us apart and we went back to class. News of the fight soon spread across the school.

I was a prefect, as was she. Prefects were the law keepers of the school. I had broken one of the cardinal rules, no fighting! Everyone was sure of our demotion. It would be humiliating to stand on the assembly hall stage and have my badge stripped from me. I would have to wear a different uniform and give up my striped blazer. Yet all I could think as I anticipated the humiliation was, "I hope they say Glorie, not Gloria." I was not demoted or reprimanded. I guess the authorities did not hear about the fight. But since then, I have fiercely guarded against mispronunciations of my name.

For some reason people resist the name Glorie. I recall talking to a white woman once at Service Ontario who asked me if I was sure my name is Glorie not Gloria. My scathing response was, "Are you sure you are asking me if I am sure what name my parents gave to me?" Her shrug made me wish I was back in the primary school playground so I could launch myself at her with full force. At some point, I started underlining the "ie" at the end of my first name anywhere I wrote it. When I started my doctoral studies, I stopped using the name Glorie in preference for an abbreviation of my middle name.

Todd (2008) discusses current trends in education, particularly, cosmopolitan education, which claim a commitment to humanistic pedagogy. Also analyzing cosmopolitan trends in education, Pinar (2010) refers to the acknowledgment and affirmation of specificity and difference, pointing out that it is precisely this line of thinking which is reflected in the current turn to a cosmopolitan direction in education, with its blending of concerns for world citizenship, human rights, democracy, and cross-cultural understanding. Both Todd and Pinar view the cosmopolitan project as one that seeks to educate for global awareness and positions a shared humanity as a condition of global justice beyond the narrow borders of national identities. However, Todd warns that this turn to cosmopolitanism and humanism for better education might become the negation of the trauma and injustices cosmopolitanism seeks to address. The problem is including a subjective account of history does not necessarily address the trauma, which is apparent in notions of "safe space" where difficult subjectivities are presented as "history" as if a rendering of oppressed subjectivity in past tense makes it more palatable. The expectation for learners to be objective about these accounts means the negation of personal experiences in favor of standardized knowledge.

The key aspect lacking in education is the account of those presently suffering the injustices now archived in history books and, by extension, education's accountability in marginalizing presenting suffering. In current trends of cosmopolitanism, humanity becomes an ideological capacity to care that does not translate into actual caring. That is why Todd's (2008) call to face our humanity and the social injustices that humanity leans on for its very existence is particularly relevant in my work. She states that humanity creates inequality and social difference, humanity causes the trauma of difference, and this trauma, must in the very least, be acknowledged as existing in pedagogy.

Sometime ago, I presented an interpretation of Fanon's *Fact of Blackness* at a conference. My view was critical of the flaws in racial discourse that advocate for equality without recognizing how everyone leans on and relies on difference. This psychoanalytic view was not well received. During the question and answer period, which was marked with a rebuffing awkwardness, a male stood up and asked me about my humanistic view of race. Much to my amusement, his question received applause from a relieved audience. I gathered from this, the idea of humanism makes people feel safe and this comes at the price of muting the things that make us uncomfortable and awkward about difference but are critical to our development both in the university and in humanity.

Vital to the understanding of the injustice of racialized schooling, Sellars's (2013) experiences of the Indian Residential Schooling system remind us of the need to audit current systems and practices in pedagogy, as we need to account for education's commodification of racial difference. As we continue to witness the resurgence of segregated schooling based on social and cultural differences, Sellars's testimony reminds us of the risks that lie in separating children based on their differences from the dominant society, especially when it empowers those that fit in by disempowering those that do not. The likely psychopathologies that arise from such practices have underpinning effects, not just on the children that develop emotional and mental difficulties as a result, but also on future generations, and the future of our educational systems. This chapter will illustrate oppressive segregation on the grounds of difference does not solve any problems but further complicates them as long as they are dependent on the dehumanization of children. It is clear from Sellars's account that the system depended on the mental enslavement and physical domination of children who became confused about their identity and worth, and eventually lost any sense of meaning through education.

## THE MIS-EDUCATION OF THE "INDIAN"[1]

My analysis of working through trauma in Sellars's (2013) *They Called Me Number One,* encounters the psychopathology and mis-education of Bev Sellars as representative of the trauma inflicted on Canadian aboriginal people. Experiences of schooling for Sellars triggered neurotic psychopathologies that resulted in amnesia and episodic fugue among other things. Sellars (2013) tells us that many of the people who endured Indian Residential schooling along with her, before her, and after her, lost significant memories of incidents that transpired during their oppressive schooling (p. 40). Pedagogy for these aboriginal children in Canada consisted of brutal colonization and oppressive marginalization. There are instances and episodes of her childhood she cannot recall, which renders efforts to heal redundant. How can one heal when one cannot remember the traumatization but still suffers its effects? In this chapter, I tackle the practice of pedagogy that subjugates and oppresses through "facts" presented as education. Like the oppression of Australian aboriginal people (Grant 2016), the education of aboriginal children in Canada began with the cruel act of denying the child her given name and replacing it with a label for the sake of "expediency," resulting in a split in the psychic being that eventually widened into a chasm where amnesia seemed the only rescue from oppression. Sellars's memoir offers us a glimpse into the mental life of a child who loses her *self* because education was inflicted upon her. I use "Bev" to distinguish the child from Sellars, the adult, who through the memoir stands in testimony to the trauma experienced by aboriginal children in education. The account of Bev's experiences provides a witnessing of the insistence of agency that has been squashed in childhood.

To help us understand more critically the power "facts" can have on one's psyche, I draw on Woodson's (1933) *The Mis-Education of the Negro.* Woodson analyzed the American education system, designed at that time, to keep the Negro in a place of disempowerment (the same methodology employed by the educators in Sellars's memoir). He wrote:

> If you can control a man's thinking you do not have to worry about his action. When you determine what a man shall think you do not have to

> concern yourself about what he will do. If you make a man feel that he is inferior, you do not have to compel him to accept an inferior status, for he will seek it himself. If you make a man think that he is justly an outcast, you do not have to order him to the back door. He will go without being told; and if there is no back door, his very nature will demand one. (p. 71)

Woodson's statement is fundamental to understanding the effect of domination through education as it elucidates on the psychic power bearing down on individuals through systemic constructions of racist "facts" that are detrimental to their welfare. The profound effect of mental subjugation imprinted as servile identifications on the unconscious through signifiers of the Other's desire are not physically apparent to the eye but manifest in daily actions of self-invalidation.

In the ongoing process of socialization, the supposedly "fact-based" identifications that become the determination of boundaries, statutes, and limitations endured by children is crucial in understanding the conditioning that turned children into "Indians" through the Canadian Indian Residential Schooling system. The system produced generations bound in lifelong neurotic subordination to the Other, even after they left the school so that even without invigilation they were seeking the backdoor. As Verhaeghe (2008) states, "Identity concerns the way psychological reality comes into being" (p. 151), meaning, for those under an oppressive educational system, what comes into being—their identity—comes through the psychological "facts"—signifiers—that are the desire of the one in a position of power and authority. For those racialized into positions of inferiority, the psychological imprinting of this identity is a traumatic experience resulting in the racialized either striving to defend against it or succumbing to continually seeking the backdoor.

A focus on racialization as the psychological reality presented as "facts," formulated to keep specific bodies in a place of inferiority and servitude to white supremacy and privilege is also crucial in evaluating our current educational systems. I view racialization as a form of psychopathological identification imprinted on the psyche of the oppressed to maintain governance over their bodies and their minds. Through systemic racism, the Subject becomes alienated from self by the Other and ultimately separates from the Other becoming an isolated Subject incapable of existing outside of the Other's discourse.

The children were presented with "facts" about "Indians." They were systematically conditioned to function according to these "facts" on who and what they were. Verhaeghe (2008) explains that psychological reality bends the Real into so-called "facts." Constructions of the signifiers of the Other's desire are translated into "facts" that through psychic subjugation make the Subject, in this case "the Indian." More specifically, "facts" are made for and by the subject in its relation to the Other, that is, the children in relation to their educators. Education for these children could be seen as a form of introjection and internalization of racist constructions so that what the Other says became the basis for the child's self-identity as evidenced in Sellars (2013) statement:

> What a terrible thing for vulnerable, young Aboriginal children to hear. There were plenty of derogatory remarks about Indians in western movies, and we saw many westerns. . . . I cringed and the shame I felt at being Indian went deeper and deeper each time I heard a derogatory comment about Indians. The flipside to that, of course, were the "perfect" White families shown on TV. They were perfectly manicured, their homes were immaculate. Everything about them seemed perfect and, because I did not know any White families, I assumed this to be the truth for all White people. (p. 82)

Based entirely on the "facts" presented to her during her schooling, Bev's psychic identity was a largely unconscious representation of racist constructions that depicted her as inferior and as less than animals in relation to white people. As any child might do, she tried to reconcile what she thought she knew about her people and her family with what she consistently heard and learned at the residential school. As an illustration of the Subject's and the Other's identities, along with the relationship between the two, Sellars's account exposes the oppressive systematic representation that juxtaposed "Indians" as degenerate and white people as perfect to justify the oppressive relation between the two. The oppressed children could not even respond to the cruelty of their oppressors with animosity, as we might expect. Feelings of animosity, rage, indignation, or anything else implying agency on the children's part had been demolished through punitive acts of violence and degradation. Throughout her education, we see manifestations of an oppressive dichotomous subjectivity.

Chief Bill Wilson in Sellars (2013) describes the duration of the Indian Education Act as one of the darkest periods in Canadian history. Bev's family was already fragmented and disrupted by racial oppression and violence. Sellars discloses Bev's stepfather was an alcoholic given to domestic violence, which resulted in an abusive and unstable home. Her mother, whom she describes as beautiful, fell victim to the lust of a white man and spent some time in prison for defending herself against rape. Consequently, Bev's grandparents stepped in when her parents were unable to parent. Her earliest memories of care by her grandmother are an element she refers back to repeatedly as she tries to convey the details of her traumatic schooling. Sellars recalls feelings of contentment in her grandmother's house up to the age of five (p. 12).

"Between the ages of 2 and 5, a number of changes take place that have enormous implications for a child's psychological function and identity formation" (Verhaeghe 2008, p. 166). We know that Bev spent these significant years surrounded by a loving family where she learned from her grandparents and significant others (Sellars, 2013, p. 21). In this family with strong community ties, systemic harmony, cultural values and beliefs, her identity formation was secure as it allowed her to navigate her early childhood in (what might be called) a normal way. At home, in a loving environment, she was presented with images, first, and then words, with which she could formulate an identity in relation to her family, who were her first Other. It is then, according to psychoanalytic theory, that a child is normally going through the Oedipal process and acquiring signifiers that affect her psychic development.

At age five, Bev fell sick and spent considerable time at a hospital. During her hospitalization, she forgot her family. One could say the loss of primary signifiers that helped her construct an early psychic reality left her traumatized to the point of fugue. In a place where she could only identify with one nurse who unceremoniously disappeared, her primary socialization suffered disruption. With this abandonment, another attempt at identity formation was lost to her, and Sellars describes it as one of the biggest hurts of her life and a severe blow (p. 25). Bev's first impressions of education were in this hospital where she learned to feel shame, hurt, and frustration because of childish inabilities (p. 25). Eventually, Bev returned home after about two years but she had no time to re-acquaint herself to the signifiers she lost. Bev was enrolled at the school three weeks after returning from the hospital.

Due to her experiences at the hospital and later at the residential school, in her young mind, and with her limited vocabulary, Bev could not figure out who she was and where she and her people fit in, except in relation to white people. "The words 'invisible' and 'undesirable' in this context hadn't yet made it into my vocabulary" (Sellars 2013 p. 81). Infants, in particular, according to Verhaeghe (2008), experience tension that they rely on the Other to ease and contain (p. 158). Where the Other is absent the tension continues but when the Other can and does respond, even if it's not a perfect response it should be good enough, so that the *lack* (the impossibility of ever answering the tension of the drive in full) of the child is not unbearable (p. 158). In Bev's experience, at the hospital and later at the school, there was no easing of the tension in which she was submerged. A constant state of tension undermined her attempts to self-soothe. All she received in her education was unpleasurable, and eventually she developed a neurotic psychopathology.

A child needs to be able to cast out the unpleasurable and internalize the pleasurable, but for Bev there was no balance that could allow her to develop a healthy desire for self. For the child internalizing destructive signifiers during identity formation, the desire to desire ego-syntonic images and words develops becomes the child's lack. The child desires to desire something other than what Other has allowed her to desire. Bev lacked a self-identity; all she had was what the Other said she was. Sellars (2013) writes:

> Messages I was getting from everyone around me at the Mission told me that I was inferior to White people. Messages I got from my family were telling me the same thing. My grandmother had gone to the school for nine years where she was brainwashed into believing she was inferior to White people, and she relayed that message to me in different ways. Some of my uncles and brothers who had gone to the school relayed that message to me. . . . The schools and other agencies that were created to look after the Indians also relayed that message. Everything in society told me that I was not good enough because I was Indian. (p. 83)

Her residential school education, facilitated by oppressive colonial systems, was continually ego-dystonic, therefore traumatic. Enrolled in the same residential school that had been the mechanism for her family's destruction for several generations she ceased to be Bev. Her grandmother, mother, extended family, and immediate community had attended this school, and all possessed the psychological scars as uniform. Though her grandmother had suffered abuse at the school, she had no choice but to send her children, and then grandchildren, to the same system, knowing what it would do to them. Sellars testifies to Bev's grandmother's powerlessness against laws that dictated how she cared for her family.

## "INDIAN" PRODUCTION AS EDUCATION IN CANADA

Before the scourge of colonization, Indigenous people in North America lived in tribal societies where a strong sense of community meant family extended beyond blood relations only to include people of the same clan. Social development was facilitated by individual figures within the clan who took on the role of teaching and maintaining the education of children through daily activities, which included play and the completion of community oriented tasks that instilled a sense of accomplishment and contribution to the collective.

> In summary, the clanship system provided the structure necessary for a tribe to maximize cooperation, which strengthened the tribal social system. Also, it is important to point out the advantage of this system to an individual's sense of identity from a psychological, emotional, and social viewpoint. (EchoHawk 1997, p. 61)

Then the Europeans settlers came. They viewed the practice as primitive and therefore inferior. The settlers subsequently destroyed and devalued the communal system of Indigenous education using the Indian Education Act. The result was mass separation of young children from their families and communities to labor-intensive industrial schools. Haig-Brown (1991) explains that these residential schools were meant to teach young aboriginal children how to be white, with the statement that the country, [European] Canada, owed it to "the poor Indian" to give him all that will afford him an equal chance at success in life with his white brother, by whom he was supplanted. The value of the clan life and family to the education, moral development, and cultural continuance of traditional Indigenous society was lost to these children, replaced by the moral and social values of English dictatorship.

The Contract School System facilitated by the church and financed by the government is described by Buetow (1971):

> It offered to provide board, clothing, lodging, tuition, etc., to Indian pupils if in return the government would provide a fixed annual per capita compensation. This proposition was accepted, and Catholic Indian schools became more successful. (p. 381)

Sold to the Indigenous communities as a provision for a brighter future for its community, the education system was supposed to honor their traditional values and culture but allow them to live in harmony with the settlers (Carr-Stewart 2001). The superficial harmony covered over the commodification of the Indigenous people by the white community as Sellars (2013) illustrates:

> At Christmas, we put on a concert for the White people around the area. I'm not sure who they were, but they packed the playroom and we did a show for them every year. Our Aboriginal parents were not invited. (pp. 47–48)

It would not be fair to say the primary goal of the church in operating residential schools was economic. Many missionaries, as EchoHawk (1997) states, risked their lives and well-being in the belief that they were indeed saving lost souls. Buetow (1971) provides some insight into the role of the Roman Catholic Church in particular, in the education of Aboriginal children during settlement and colonization in the Americas. To begin with, he outlines the tenets of the catholic faith, which included service provision, care, and indoctrination of the poor into the Catholic faith. This work began within Europe then spread as the European nations sought after new lands and resources during the period of colonization. Buetow states, "As for the Indian, the ideals of the missioners were to discipline him, make him self-supporting, and bring him the truths of Christianity" (p. 378). This management of "the Indian" did not regard the tribal teaching of aboriginal culture and values as education. The missionaries managed them, trained them, and taught them, setting them up in village clusters as they saw appropriate, generally destabilizing Indigenous society, its languages, and values. The disintegration of the Indigenous way of life preceded the formalized Indian Education.

Left up to missionaries who despised the Indigenous way of life and its primary socialization of the children, the secondary socialization of the aboriginal children took the form of violence. Everything the children learned as infants, during their early development, was disrupted and disparaged resulting in the development of internal conflicts. It is not possible to realize fully the many cruel acts perpetrated in this secondary socialization but the effects of this school system are evident in Sellars's (2013) memoir as she explains Bev's grandmother's parenting choices:

> I was so surprised to learn that when she was taken to the Mission she spoke only Carrier. I asked her why she didn't speak it now and she said angrily, "They whipped us when we spoke our language!" Once she and her sister, Annie got to the Mission, Gram said they had to learn English quickly. . . . Like so many Aboriginal parents who were fluent in their Native tongue, she did not pass on her language to her children. She spoke only English to them. When speaking the language always resulted in being strapped for it, I imagine it would be hard to now just start speaking it in cue. (pp. 44–45)

Bev's grandmother knew discipline in the schools was usually harsh, so to protect her loved ones from the threat of corporal punishment, she raised them ignorant of their language and cultural values. As a colonial measure, aboriginal children were systemically alienated from their language, culture, and families through brute force and constant abuse.

Consequently, with education came a rejection of Indigenous values as pagan, in favor of what seemed safer and acceptable to their oppressors. EchoHawk (1997) states that many Indigenous children rejected the values and lifestyles of their parents and converted to Christianity, which produced factions within tribes, clans, and even between spouses.

Sellars (2013) expresses her thoughts on the abolition of their language:

> The kids at the Mission were not allowed to speak their Native languages, but the irony of the nuns speaking French to each other was not lost on some kids. Although we would never tell the nuns to their faces, many of us resented not being able to speak our languages freely when the nuns openly spoke the language they had learned as children. (p. 45)

Those who did not reject their language out of a questionable "free-will" had no choice but to follow English customs and values. Within this fractured society, English became the main language of communication and with it came certain signifiers that we see illustrated in the account of Bev's fragile psychic reality in the residential school. Viewed as "facts," the images and words used to format the identities of these children led them to become what the Other wanted them to be. Sellars (2013) discloses Bev's struggle to integrate the constructed "Indian" to a self-identity based on her early upbringing. The adverse disintegration of Bev's inner being was the result of this struggle.

## ABSURDITY: COLLAPSING OF MEANING

The meaning of a lot of educational rituals and schooling practices can appear absurd in hindsight, but often when decision and policy makers introduce new measures meant to rectify social issues with educational they act out of subjective desires they might not be aware exist within them. Armed with good intentions and unacknowledged biases, fears, and prejudices, educational authorities can do significant damage that can have resounding effects in the individual lives of children who are not consulted but must live by the verdict. For example, Le Blanc (2013) presents a critical discussion of the controversy surrounding the Saskatoon Public School Board's retraction of a proposed policy change,[2] and the provincial government's scrutiny of provincial assessment policy in public schools. He posits this drama exemplifies the tacit understanding on the part of the public of the socialization purposes of school in preparing students for the world of labor.

Particularly relevant is Le Blanc's (2013) positioning of the absurdity of the situation in the realm of ideology:

> The success of any ideology is dependent upon its capacity to filter core ideas to a broader population, to define the terms of discourse in any given subject, to become a kind of "common sense" among a population so that the "feel for the game" of a particular ideology is acquired by that social group (Fairclough, 1989). This can often be expressed through the articulation of core values for a population—ideology's task is to set the baseline for discussion. (p.17)

Caught in this controversy and political back and forth were the children, required to comply with whatever decisions were made then retracted by the adults. Educators and policy makers insist that children follow "guidelines," which are hardly ever explained to the children. When the policies and dictated structures fail, learners in their suffering are used to make sense of the failure. Issued unconsciously with the absurd guidelines is an oppressive insistence that learners prove the decision makers correct and useful, which forces them to become creative in order to maintain the absurdity. Instinctively, most children play along, making jokes of the rituals as a method of coping and self-preservation.

In Sellars's (2013) memoir, religion was a key instrument used to formulate oppressive practices and rituals in the European sanctioned education system. Missionaries and clergy were intimately involved with the daily administration of the schools, meaning the perpetration of many atrocities committed against Indigenous people in residential schools was done in the name of religion by people purporting to be doing God's work. Sellars testifies that the Christian religion was not explained to them, therefore, they had no choice in what they could learn or believe, which made the conversion into Christianity redundant. She states:

> We practiced until we got it right, with proper pronunciation of the Latin words and when to say them, but the meaning was not translated into English for us. We were, as usual, just little robots programmed to do everything on cue. We were not at residential school to get a well-rounded education. (p. 45)

The Bible was a central text in the education of children who often learned English through the memorization and quotation of the Bible, without any real understanding of the religion itself. This replaced the oral history of the Indigenous peoples, which the children would often have inherited from their families and community educators. The aggressive civilization of the Indigenous children through religion was sold as beneficial, not only to the crown but also to the church, which gained much in the way of land and economic resources from the industrialization of the children (Davin and Early Canadian Online 1879).

Ironically, for Bev and her schoolmates, all the religious seriousness was a comical mystery to them. As children are prone to do, they played at religion garnering whatever logic they could while attempting to mitigate the impact of the absurd situations to which they were the Subject:

> Going to confession was equally comical. In fact, some of the comical things we did at the Mission were usually during times we should have been the most serious. We made up sins because there was no way the priest would believe we hadn't sinned, and we probably would have been punished for lying if we said we were free of sin. . . . At the trial investigating sexual abuse charges against our principal, Father Hubert O'Connor, a woman from Sugar Cane testified that young girls who had no idea what adultery was nevertheless would confess to it. They heard adultery was a sin, so it seemed logical to confess to it. I'm sure none of us were ever sorry, but we went through the motions that were required. Things said in the confessional were not punishable by the strap. We were given prayers to say and everything was forgiven. (Sellars 2013, pp. 46–47)

Using comedy and play, Bev and her peers made the structural meaninglessness of their lives something tolerable. On the absurdity of ritual, specifically religious habits, Zuesse (1983) states, "It is extraordinary how all ritual, even that most personal sort called 'habit,' grows from and memorializes the encounter with the Other" (p. 41). The priests signified authority and therefore stood as Other to the children. Similarly, in educational systems today teachers, as Other, take authoritative positions within schools in relation to children. Zuesse also says that "Behind habitual actions, then, is an audience, an Other and a studied mode of giving up the self to the Other and to already defined transcendental meaning" (p. 41).

I recall a ritual in my early schooling that commenced with the entrance of the teacher into the classroom. It took me a while to comply with the imperative that we stand when the teacher walked in and stayed standing until he or she sat down or gave us permission to sit down. We were expected to greet our teachers in unison, wait for the scripted response then answer in chorus. Every school day begun and ended with a show of reverence to our teachers. I hated it and a few times faced the wrath of authority for not complying. I am not even sure how little four and five year olds were taught to act and speak in perfect unison but somehow it happened.

The Other demanded a performance of rituals and tasks beyond the comprehension of Bev and her peers, but the children recognized the relevance these rituals held in meaning making and socialization. The children recognized their roles in the meaningless ritual were the key to any semblance of community between them and their oppressors, so they played along. In doing that, the children gave meaning to their oppressors' actions, notably satisfying the desire of their Other. The act of confession to Bev and her peers was a ritualistic subservience to the desires of the Other, who without the children's cooperation could not rightly justify their educational system.

We might make sense of the rituals Sellars (2013) describes through Zuesse's (1983) explanation:

> An interesting characteristic of such thorough ritual universes is the playfulness and humour of the ritual, for here the bodily bridge between self and other is fully accepted, not denied, and so there can be an easy movement from shame to shamelessness, self to other, inward to outward, solemnity to humour. (p. 45)

Within the dichotomy of Subject and Other, sinner and pious, "Indians" and whites, it appears only the children in their innocence could make the easy movements as they were able to see the absurdity in the religious practices forced upon them. The priests and nuns took these rituals quite seriously but the children played with the ideas and concepts in a form of creativity they could not exercise anywhere else. Zuesse (1983) also talks of the "relatedness" that religious rituals allow, pointing out that religion allows everyone to be human and to relate to each other within that commonality. For the children, the confessional was the one place they related to their abusers as humans. In the confessional, all was forgiven and punitive acts were negated through ritual. The children's innocent confessions allowed the abusive missionaries absolution. The absurd ritual of confessions of adultery and wickedness by mere children justified for the priests the dehumanizing acts they perpetrated against the children daily. The religious words and acts performed in the confessional collapsed into meaningless rituals.

I remember my own absurd experiences of Anglican boarding school where we had Mass several times per week. The Masses were repetitive, so after a couple of terms at the school, without realizing it, I had memorized the entire service. When we could get away with it, my friends and I often entertained each other during the long Sunday Mass, especially during the dreary hot summer days. Students caught dosing off or not paying attention were reprimanded and given manual labor as a punishment. Sometimes Mass started in the afternoons. Hundreds of sweaty girls, in a post-lunch meal daze tried desperately to stay awake. Masses were compulsory attendance. Only if one was knocking on heaven's door could one get out of attendance.

At one such Mass, I did not realize I was reciting the Mass aloud along with the priest who solemnly delivered the lines I had heard a million times by then. My neighbor nudged me out of my recital and pointed at a prefect who was looking at me threateningly. Unfortunately, not just the prefect was angry with me, as a few locals attended our Masses and some of our teaching staff. The consequences were dire. I had desecrated the holiness of the Mass by making (what presented as) a mockery of the solemnity of the words only the priest should say. It was not intentional; nevertheless, I was branded sacrilegious and ungodly. What I had done was viewed as transgression against God, the priest, and everyone else. I really did not mean to disrespect anyone; the words of the Mass had come to mean nothing to me as I had heard them so many times. They held the same value as a nursery rhyme. Well, I remember nursery rhymes more fondly than my Anglican Masses.

Within the Indian Residential Schooling system, ideology was driven by notions of white supremacy and the drive for colonization. Religion was instrumental in filtering core ideas of what was good and bad, what was right and wrong, what was desirable and undesirable, what was white and what was "Indian." Religious language was used to turn the "facts" created in the Other's mind into the lived experience of children. At the school, the signification of "sin" rested upon children who had no concept of it.

Zuesse (1983) states:

> The chief difference between merely personal rites like habits and more universal rituals of a culture or religion lies in the profounder assumptions of the latter: in them is a vaster horizon of existence, no longer idiosyncratic and accidental but a form of being or becoming far more elemental and necessary than the greatest personal finesse, more true than any personal "sophistication," for it is held in common with all other human beings of the greater community. (p. 41)

Within the greater community of colonization, Bev, and Indians in general, played the role of "sinner." They were required to confess even where they had no sin to speak of. The level of the importance placed on the ritual of confession and forgiveness was absurd. Also absurd was what was required of the children, treated as a rule as less than animals. Yet in the confessional, the meaning of the ritual relied heavily on the children's actions. The absurdity for these children lay in the forgiveness of whatever their creative little minds could come up with for the priests without punishment. In the confessional, their creativity was encouraged, even nurtured, as long as it meant they were sinners. Outside the confessional, with the same people, their "sins" incurred brutal and consistent punishment.

## THE "INDIAN" CHILD'S MIRROR STAGE

Lacanian psychoanalysis teaches us that it is the function of the Other to install within the Subject the signifiers of desire. Through language, spoken by the Other, the Subject comes into *being*. The Other speaks his desires and the Subject must either yield to her own lack to take up the desires of the Other or resist this installation to become a perverse subject locked in the Imaginary realm. To resist means to forgo the Symbolic. Outside of the Symbolic, desire becomes symptomatic in repetitive cycles that do not allow for mental hygiene. The child caught up in a repetitive cycle in the Imaginary presents with symptoms that we witness in neurosis. To enter the Symbolic, the desires of the Other must be good enough.

At a seminar presented in Zurich, Lacan (2010) speaks directly to the *Cogito* relating this to *situational apperception*. He elaborates on the phenomena of the *mirror stage* as an identification whereby the child recognizes and masters *self* and he explains "the transformation that takes place in the Subject when he assumes an image" (p. 2). Lacan claims there is jubilation in this stage for the infant still beyond language, not yet Subject, meaning:

> This form situates the agency of the ego, before its social determination, in a fictional direction, which will always remain irreducible for the individual alone, or rather, which will only rejoin the coming-into-being *(le devenir)* of the subject asymptomatically, whatever the success of the dialectical syntheses by which he must resolve as "I" his discordance with his own reality. (p. 2)

At this stage, the child is free from the constraints of subjectivity, and from the oppression of the Other. However, according to Lacan, the function of the mirror stage, through the function of the *imago*, is to put this *un*Subjected being in touch with his reality (p. 4). The reality referred to is psychic, and as Verhaeghe (2008) explains, it is an idiosyncratic construction in and through the primary relationship of Subject and Other (p. 161), and thus "facts" are created. Further, Verhaeghe clarifies that the external and internal worlds develop simultaneously in the same process of reciprocal mirroring.

For impressionable children, elements received and perceived from the outside world are not easily differentiated from their internal world. "The foundational layer of identity boils down to the image presented by the Other that the child takes in and which forms the base for the ego"

(Verhaeghe 2008, p. 163). Children tend to operate at primordial levels; therefore, they rely on the Other to reflect or present the images with which they can identify. Constantly presented with *unpleasurable* (Bell and Lacan 2014) images of themselves in school, Indian education traumatized children like Bev. The signifiers given to them were like a mirror image that caused them shame and degradation.

For Bev, it was easier to yield to the Other's desire, which unfortunately, was not good enough but wild. Sellars (2013) gives us a glimpse into the enduring effects of a wild education:

> The message of "don't try to be better than anyone else" had an effect on me for years. The more invisible I was the better. The more mediocre I was, the better. Don't strive to be the best, strive to be the least! And it was seen as okay to be the least. (pp. 49–50)

Through the installation of "Indian" as signifier, the missionaries constantly uncovered the children's psychic lack. Struggling to mitigate the unpleasureable, children in the residential school turned on each other. Sellars (2013) illustrates this by stating that anything "different" was cause for some sort of attack and the kids needed to put down other kids because they didn't feel good about themselves (p. 51). She believes Bev's education, and the education of all Aboriginal children in Indian residential schooling, was a breeding ground for dysfunction.

The scripting on the Subject's unconscious by the Other begins as early as birth, explains Lacan (1998) who further states, "If he is apprehended at his birth in the field of the Other, the characteristic of the subject of the unconscious is that of being, beneath the signifier that develops its networks, its chains and its history, at an indeterminate place" (p. 208). He posits that from the onset the Subject must always be negotiating and responding to the Other in order to *be*. As the Other installs signifiers on the Subject's being, the Subject is both conscious and unconscious of herself, and she becomes the split subject. The [self] ego and the Other are what divide the Subject. Where the ego struggles for self-identification and self-fulfillment, the Other forbids and imposes lack.[3]

> Does the subject not become engaged in an ever-growing dispossession of that being of his, concerning which—by dint of sincere portraits which leave its idea no less incoherent, of rectifications which do not succeed in freeing its essence, of stays and defences which do not prevent his statue from tottering, of narcissistic embraces which become like a puff of air in animating it—he ends up by recognizing that this being has never been anything more than his construct in the Imaginary and that this construct disappoints all his certitudes? For in this labour which he undertakes to reconstruct this construct *for another*, he finds again the fundamental alienation which made him construct it

> like *another one,* and which has always destined it to be stripped from him *by another*. (Lacan 1981, p. 11)

Bev had to grapple with her Indian identity, not as she saw herself but as her oppressors saw her. Generation after generation, Indigenous children experienced an education that bound their self-identities in knots from which they could not extricate themselves. Sellars (2013) explains how they tried to cope with the images presented to them:

> We had a saying at the Mission if we did anything stupid. We excused ourselves with the line, "Oh well, I'm just an Indian." Mom remembers being called "Dirty Indians," "Stupid," and other derogatory names by the authorities at the Mission. I don't remember being called names, but we got the same message. What a messed up world in which to raise an impressionable child. What a messed up world in which to raise whole Nations of impressionable Aboriginal children. (p. 50)

The "Indian" child, while trying to negotiate her racial identity, was always struggling against the imposition of it by the Other. Bev was alienated not only from her *self,* but also from the Other as they simultaneously, and in tangent, constructed her reality. Tangency occurred where from time to time they might have been some congruency on the characterization of "Indian" but inevitably the meaning would collapse and once more conflict would arise.[4] Within this dichotomy, the missionaries, as Other, functioned to forbid and impose. To break this oppressive dichotomy, the "Indian's" function would be to continually resist and reconstruct. However, in early childhood, the capacity to resist and reconstruct was beaten out of the aboriginal children, consequently producing many aboriginals prone to self-medicating through alcohol and drug misuse. We must stand as witness to the psychological impact of residential schools across Indigenous communities in Canada today.

Where Lacan referred to questioned subjectivity, I consider the inner conflict of racialization:

> Is the place that I occupy as subject of the signifier concentric or eccentric in the place I occupy as subject of the signified . . . the point is not to know whether I speak of myself in a way that conforms to what I am, but rather to know whether, when I speak of myself, I am the same as the self of whom I speak. (Lacan 2006 p. 430)

To ponder on such a question: "Am I the same as the self of whom I speak?" means there are inexplicable or contradictory versions of self the Subject must know in order to know of whom she speaks. In knowing these *selves,* the Subject, if in a socially just relationship with the Other, can negotiate, reposition, and reconstruct herself through the relationship; taking on new signifiers produced as the situation requires. Bev, unfortunately, was not in a position to negotiate, to resist, or to reconstruct. Given the violence that met any form of self-actualization, Bev and her schoolmates learned to be obedient even to the falsehood of whom and what the missionaries said they were.

The conflictual dynamic of racism within the learning environment results in paradoxical identifications in minds too young and vulnerable to process the facts from "facts." Even as she questioned the truth in the oppressive identity forced on them, Bev was not sure of anything different because they were continually told who and what they were as "facts":

> . . . The Silent Enemy (1930), showed an elderly Indian woman who had been thrown out of her teepee because she was too old to help with the family. The rest of the tribe did not want her around anymore. One scene showed her fighting with the dogs for scraps of food that were tossed her way. At the time, I couldn't differentiate between fact and fiction. Even though I knew that did not happen in my community. I believed somewhere in my "Indian" world we were that cruel and I felt such shame. (p. 81)

Myths, especially mythical creations, play a significant role in the expression of desire. The mythical "Indian" contained for the oppressors all the signifiers of wickedness and immorality in humanity. By projecting these characteristics on the "Indians," they could justify their dehumanization of the "Indians" as already not human. "Given the wide gulf separating the cultures, Europeans have tended to imagine the Indian rather than to know the Indigenous people, thereby to project onto Indigenous people all the fears and hopes they have for the New world" (Francis 2012, p. iv). In *The Imaginary Indian: The Image of the Indian in Canadian Culture,* Francis clarifies the role of the "imaginary Indian" in the creation of a Euro-Canadian identity. The savagery and brutally ascribed to the Indigenous people ironically masked the aggression and brutally enacted by the colonizers upon the Indigenous people, in much the same way the evil and immorality ascribed to the children in the school masked those attributes in their educators.

Evans (1996) clarifies Lacan's cogito, stating that, "this concept of subjectivity refers to what Lacan calls 'the subject of science': a subject who is denied all intuitive access to knowledge and is thus left with reason as the only path to knowledge" (p. 27). Thus, we see that reason is an essential part of any conscious and unconscious development of self. Without reason, the children were unable to develop an integrated sense of self. What was given as fact was unreasonable to them, and what was expected of them came out of the Other's reason. The colonizer's "Indian" was an unreasonable creature to those who had to embody its signification. In Bev's schooling, we see that "firstly and primarily the child quite literally receives the images and words for its internal experience from the Other" (Verhaeghe 2008, p. 155). Separated from family and protective community, and repeatedly exposed to images and words that maligned her identity, Bev suffered guilt and shame for the mythical "Indian" she embodied, not for something she had done. Her paradoxical identification meant guilt for feeling guilty and shame for being ashamed. These are burdensome affects for any child to work through.

Psychoanalysis teaches that a child's subject formation comes through relations with the Other; thus, when a child experiences anxiety or depressive reactions, it is the Other who must contain this situation and provide a psychological identity by mirroring what the child is experiencing internally. In other words, the child must find expression through signifiers—words and images—that the Other provides. In Bev's education, the signifiers that were supplied by the Other were destructive of any self-worth or recognition. What Bev learned triggered psychic disintegration, which caused her to develop anxiety and depressive reactions that are symptomatic of neurotic psychopathology.

## THE SPLIT SUBJECT

The "Indian" signifier was not the only one Bev had to contend with in her education. Sellars (2013) shares some common practices used in residential schools:

> Another thing that happened soon after we arrived at residential school is that we were given a number that would become our identity throughout our years at school. I became Number 1 on the girls' side. Although the other kids all continued to call me by my name, "Bev Sellars" ceased to exist for most of the nuns and priests. (p. 32)

Perhaps the most obvious signifier of all is the name of a person. Fink (1995) explains that the name of a child, often chosen long before the child is born, or even conceived, inscribes the child within the Symbolic. At the time of naming, the Subject and the child are unrelated but as the child grows into the name given by the Other, it becomes the signifier, which according to Fink,

> more, perhaps, than any other—will go to the root of his or her being and become inextricably tied to his or her subjectivity. It will become the signifier of his or her very essence as subject, standing in for him or her. (p. 56)

Through naming, the child becomes a part of the family and community. In other words, it helps constitute the child within the Symbolic Order. In society, surnames and ethnic/religious names are specific and immediately identify us in most circles as belonging to a distinctive family, people, or nation. Fink elaborates that a name is a rigid designator, always, and inflexibly, designating the same thing—a primordial signifier (p. 57).

Fittingly, a child's failure to assimilate a primordial signifier may result in psychosis. Such a failure leaves "the child unanchored in language, without a compass reading on the basis of which to adopt an orientation" (Fink 1995, p. 55). So, what happens when the child is robbed of her primordial signifier? Imagine the horrible trauma of a rigid and inflexible element of a vulnerable and still developing child's subjectivity yanked out of her very being and replaced with a nondescript designation. They called Bev Sellars Number 1.

Like many colonized peoples globally, ethnic and native names were dismissed in favor of English/Christian names. Within the Indian Residential Schooling system, many children already had Christian names but for the sake of expediency, these were stripped from them and they were numbered like objects (as part of the larger Indian Act put forth by Canadian government and in turn utilized to record status). The erasure of people's names was a dehumanizing act that resulted in the breakdown of psychic structure. Number 1 and Bev Sellars became the split subject, a condition profoundly illustrated through the Subject's alienation from self in Sellars's memoir. Repeatedly, Sellars attempts to reconcile her early childhood experiences under the care of her grandmother and family to the "Indian" called Number 1, whom the nuns created through pedagogy.

The significance of names in the Symbolic Order is as Fink (1995) elaborates:

> The name of the Other's desire must be set into motion—from the mother's partner, to teacher, to school, to police officer, to civil law, to religion, to moral law, and so on—and give way before the signifier of the Other's desire of subjectification is to take place, that is, if the subject is to become the Other's desire, leaving the signifier to its own devices. (p. 66)

The child's name is equally as important in the Symbolic Order as the *name-of-the-father*. *Le nom du père* is crucial but it is the child's given name that signifies the child as a subject in the Symbolic Order and without Subject there is no Other, just as Francis (2012) indicats, without the Imaginary "Indian," there was no Euro-Canadian. While the Other's name signifies authority, the child's name signifies a desire that differentiates child from Other. Therefore, in *un*naming Indigenous children, the organically installed Symbolic Order was disrupted and the children became Subject to a new oppressive order.

One's given name also gives meaning to individual subjectivity within the social order. We see this illustrated when Sellars (2013) begins to recognize the differences between Bev Sellars and Number 1. The child's identity became Subject to a social order that dictated through names, what she should think, feel, and desire. From the first day at the residential school, the desire of the Other took over and the new signifier "Number 1" deleted Bev, making her a stranger to her *self*. Bev arrived at the school with a different identity, which although still acknowledged by other children (as a form of resistance) ceased to exist with the simple *un*naming—Number 1. Number 1 signified a different object altogether—the Imaginary "Indian."

The essence of a name is further grounded in Lacan's (1987) statement: "the name, I demonstrated to you, is a mark already open to reading—for which reason it will be read identically in all languages—imprinted on something that may be, but not necessarily, a speaking subject" (p. 88). Fundamentally, the name, whether the Subject speaks or not, has meaning wherever that Subject goes, the name speaks for her. We, therefore, can conclude that taking away the names of these children, *un*naming Bev, was an act of silencing the Subject. Through Sellars's (2013) testimony, we understand the erasure of the children's desires as effectively dehumanization.

We might then define dehumanization as the erasure of one's subjectivity. Sellars gives us two examples (among many) of punishment for daring to speak; not because silence was expected but because she was expected not to think as a Subject:

> "You're in my class," she said. "No, I'm in grade three," I told her. She didn't believe me and tried to force me into her classroom. I resisted. Thankfully, I had not been at the school long enough to know that I should blindly obey everything I was told to do. (p. 35)

The act of thinking was an indication of non-compliance, which was not expected of Number 1. In this defiant speech and act of non-compliance, we catch a glimpse of Bev, not yet entirely erased by Number 1. Sellars offers another example:

> One night I went down and, instead of telling the nun the position of the clock hands, I told her what time it was. She looked at me with total disgust and sent me back downstairs again. "I told you to see where the hands were!" she barked. . . . I learned that speaking my mind or questioning anything would only get me into trouble. Using my mind was even more unacceptable. . . . I felt dumb when I thought I knew how to tell time and the nun made me question myself, and I felt dumb that I didn't know how to do something I should've known four years earlier. (pp. 37–38)

Number 1 is obedient only through oppressive conditioning. Bev, on the other hand, was a child eager to please, happy to participate (p. 26); essentially, a thinking and speaking subject. There is a stark difference between Bev the child from a loving and nurturing home and Number 1, the ideal object of the Other's desire. Sellars describes a morning ritual that began soon after she arrived at the school. The physical beatings with a leather strap became part of her education, teaching her to take and accept pain as something normal or necessary.

Aside from the obvious physical trauma sustained daily, these beatings served a psychic conditioning of the children to positions of lowliness. Sellars (2013) records the memorable initiation Bev received on her first morning at St. Joseph's Mission stating the child's immediate obedience was quickly established (p. 32). A child's immediate compliance to unfamiliar rules indicates a violence that threatens. Children rely on their survival instincts in unfamiliar environments. Therefore, Bev's first day of school required she depend on her survival instincts to navigate education. A threatening pedagogy does more than trigger a physical need for safety; rather it touches a psychic aspect of childhood development. Social justice requires that educators be aware of the threats that pedagogy issues.

The idiom "knowledge is power" means knowledge yields a threat to those too young, inexperienced, and ignorant to know. In education, pedagogy determines whether knowledge empowers or threatens. Pedagogy instructs affect, either it wrenches and disturbs or it builds and empowers. Sellars (2013) highlights the effects of a violent education on the psyches of the children who soon learn to repress their feelings to circumvent more violence: "It did not take long for the new kids to learn to bury their feelings no matter how scared or lonely they felt. It took the nuns only two to three nights to stop the crying" (p. 34).

Bev's schooling had long lasting detrimental effects. The Other in her life left her "crippled" and dispossessed of herself. Sellars (2013) discloses some of the inner struggles Bev experiences from her childhood into adulthood, stating that even as an adult she would go out of her way to avoid encountering white people. Being around white people made her uncomfortable and she felt unable to look them in the eye and could not challenge them even when she knew she should. Sellars explains the anxiety, the phobias, and the low self-esteem that Bev suffered:

> I couldn't handle even the slightest compliment or criticism with any grace. . . . I enjoyed the feeling of being hungry and at one point was very skinny, even borderline anorexic. In a nutshell, I was emotionally and socially crippled in my ability to deal with the world. (p. 112)

The psychic relations between abusers and their victims are outlined by Young-Bruehl (1996) in *The Anatomy of Prejudice*. She refers to the abuse of victims (like Bev) as labor, explaining that:

> But socially the victims supply the need for a specific kind of labor: they support from below the life and the lifestyle of those who rule over them. They do "despised but essential labor," labor the prejudiced will not do themselves because doing it would make them feel lowly, beastly, and unclean. They do whatever the rulers, by reason of religion, custom, and mores consider dirty and fleshly. (p. 373)

Therefore, apart from serving the nuns and priests, these children made them feel better about their positions. Children acted as fetishistic objects to the desires of the Other. In one instance, Sellars (2013) asserts the fetishization of these children as quite blatant:

> The older ones who attended the school during my sister Dolly's time said there was a nun who they swore had an orgasm when she would strap kids. They said her face got all red and you could tell she really enjoyed giving the strap. (p. 87)

Intrinsically, Bev's educational outcome was a neurosis that lingered into adulthood and set the tone for the rest of her life. We witness similar symptoms of racialization in Fanon's (1963) account of the "Fact of Blackness."

## FANON'S FACT: RACIALIZATION AS NEUROSIS

Neurosis is a concept often used in a very general way to describe the subjective effects of psychological distress. However, in my analysis of Sellar's testimony, I use the psychoanalytic understanding of neurosis as an inability to physically represent or elaborate internal pressure that results from inadequately repressed internal impulses seeking expression or blocked due to an external traumatic event (Longhofer 2015). Racialization from Dalal's (2002) perspective is a process of socialization through identification with racial classifications such as "black," "white," or, in Bev's case, "Indian." In my reading of Sellars's memoir, I concluded that racialization could present as a neurosis when it cannot be embodied in any way other than that constructed by the Other. Racialization, subsequent to repeated sanctions by the Other, develops into a neurosis because there is no relief from the tension created by repression. Any defense against external traumas at the hand of the Other is negated and the racialized subject lives in a constant state of oppression. The racialized individual comes to see that they cannot be outside of what the Other presents through racist signifiers. As Fanon (1963) expresses, "not only must the Black man be Black; he must be Black in relation to the white man" (p. 110).

Racialization develops as a neurosis in the mirror stage where the Other self-aggrandizes by producing signifiers (words, images, and symbols) that demean the Subject's identity, thereby binding the Subject into a subordinate racial classification. We witness in the outcome of Bev's education (and countless others worldwide who have struggled with racial identities) that racialization negates self-actualization. The tension racialization produces between Subject and Other triggers neurotic symptoms in the Subject, supported by stereotypes attributed to particular racial groups. Within education, the adverse effects present as predictors of failure and ineptitude on the part of the racialized child. Contemporary awareness prevents education from disadvantaging racialized children further by compelling us to reexamine the mechanisms of racialization within our schools and pedagogy.

When stereotypes are used to predict the outcomes of students there is evidence of teacher biases, selective resourcing, and most detrimentally, psychic subjugation. For a cultural analysis of stereotypes as a mechanism affecting the educational outcomes of young Black boys in Canada, I turn to James (2012) who offers a critical analysis that exposes how stereotypes in educational contexts are in fact racisms against specific cultural and ethnic groups to justify a systemic disavowal of race and racism as factors influencing students' gendered schooling and educational experiences. James also points out Anglo-white middle-class structures, ideals, norms, roles, values, and expectations, for example heterosexual masculinity, derive from conceptualizations of difference. However, it is not just difference; it is difference in relation to whiteness, which essentially amounts to stereotypes. Sellars's (2013) understanding of who Bev was and the stereotypes constantly used to signify Indians were always in relation to the ideal and values of whiteness.

Racialization is where Bev's experiences, Francis's (2012) "Imaginary Indian," and Fanon's (1963) narrative of the "Fact of Blackness" converge. Fanon, like Bev, examines shame and self-contempt instilled through his relations with white people. Due to his psychoanalytic background, we are able to grasp a firmer understanding from his testimony of the disintegration that occurs when interiorizing racialization. Fanon possessed the diction that Bev states took her a long time to attain (p. 81). In his self-analysis, Fanon also alludes to education's inability to mirror for him so that his self-identity was ego-dystonic. One important revelation we gain from Fanon is the ever-looming threat of castration that renders the racialized servile and seeking the back door (Woodson 1933).

At the intersection of psychoanalytic theory and Afro-pessimism we gain an understanding of race as a psychic condition of difference. R. L. (2013) explains the Afro-pessimistic view that black non-existence forms negativity against which white liveliness and freedom defines itself positively. Lacan viewed castration as something beyond prospective figure and symbolic disability, and beyond phantasmatic possibility or introjection; something based on more than a fleeting glance, and read as a [sexual] difference. However, an Afro-pessimistic view considers Moten's (2003) definition as the proper name to give an oft-repeated literal, historical, and material event against people of color (p. 177). This event results in racialization. It is what the missionaries set out to do and accomplished by mirroring words and images that destroyed the identities of countless children like Bev, reducing them to neurotic subjects seeking the backdoor.

The pathogenesis of racialization as a neurosis begins with the rise in tension between what the individual desires as a subject and the accompanying experience of unpleasure that results from a sanctioning of this desire through racist "facts." Fanon (1967) views the dilemma thusly:

> The Black man has no ontological resistance in the eyes of the white man. Overnight the Negro has been given two frames of reference within which he has had to place himself. His metaphysics, or, less pretentiously, his customs and the sources on which they are based, were wiped out because they were in conflict with a civilization that he did not know and that imposed itself on him. (p. 110)

With no recourse to oppression by the Other, tension rises, and as Verhaeghe (2008) states "its cause internal; it is in the subjects' own drive, which seeks an answer in the Other" (p. 190). In racialization, this vicious cycle of seeking and sanctioning between the Subject and the Other results in neurosis. Bev's experience of education was one where any self-directed thoughts or behavior based on her primary socialization were sanctioned. As a measure of self-preservation, she was conditioned to seek direction continuously from her oppressors; an education that resulted in a number of phobias in her childhood (p. 112). From psychoanalytic theory, we gather that phobias are a result of representations that cannot be integrated into the ego (Bracher 1994; Verhaeghe 2008).

A notable symptom of neurotic racialization is the repeated relational patterns between the oppressed and the Other. Fink (1995) states, "The castrated subject is always presenting itself to the Other, looking to win attention and recognition from the Other, and the more it presents itself, the more inescapably castrated it becomes as it is represented by and in the Other" (p. 73). Sellars illustrates this when she makes reference to Bev's impressionability causing her to view herself as inferior to white people, and consequently withdrawing from white authority even after leaving the residential school (p.112). Bev repeated her relational structure with every white person she came across. "This repetition is entirely bound up with the relation and can be given different names depending on the theory one is using: fundamental fantasy, cognitive schemas, attachment style, or reciprocal patterns" (Verhaeghe 2008, p. 194). I choose to call it racialization.

## CONCLUSION

In this chapter, I have illustrated the mental ramifications of neurotic racialization through the imposition of a colonial education. Over time, the pain and hurt of an oppressive pedagogy becomes something with which the child identifies; even where it is replaced with something good or complete, oppressive pedagogy presents as something bad and inferior anyway. The effects are imprinted on the child's internal working model; the psychopathology is long lasting. Such relational structures are typical in the relationship between student and teacher. Children strive to impress their educators hoping to gain from the Other signifiers that can help them formulate positive self-identities in the classroom. Compliments, encouragement, and opportunity from educators go a long way in the psychic development of children. The difference between this normal childish behavior and the racialized subject, such as Bev, is that each repetition results in more trauma and further sanctions based on "facts" like "an 'Indian' child cannot tell time." An audit of current expectations, teacher bias, and teacher selection alerts us to this cycle of racialization in our classrooms.

The relational dynamics between racialized children and their teachers are pertinent in terms of so called "multicultural education" discussed in the concluding chapter. In early childhood, especially, children encounter new races, cultures, and languages only at school, where they cannot retreat to the safety of their family and home when pedagogy raises tensions. It is at school that they first encounter any significant social difference and where they learn how their individual subjectivity sets them apart from their peers and teachers. The other side of my argument, as illustrated through Sellars's (2013) account, concerns what education should be: a space where the tension can ease through signifiers in which the child can find some healthy identity formation and resolution. Where education does quite the opposite we are presented with a neurotic child, like Bev, with a disintegrated psychic reality.

When educational ideology sanctions the self-identification of children based on their race and origin, the result is learners who are unable to self-direct or to function independent of the Other. Racialization defeats the previously discussed objective of education as mental hygiene. Conclusively, mental hygiene cannot result from ego-dystonic images and words presented to learners as "facts" on which they formulate their inner worlds. The facts presented to learners should be integrative of all the things they desire as well as what the Other desires, which is mental hygiene. A required balance allows the child to develop and learn positively and exercise one's agency.

To be able to tell one's narrative is to act on the insistence of one's agency. Sellars (2013), through her memoir, tackles much of what she could only experience as absurd in childhood. The contradictions and paradoxes we witness in her narrative allow us to interpret the cry of distress of aboriginal children in residential schools at the time, going through horrific rituals, their agency negated and beaten out of them. In adulthood, Sellars is able to give us an account through her own working through. We witness in her memoir the difference between knowledge as power and knowledge as a threat. We learn how the psyches of children can disintegrate when adults cause meaning and meaning making to collapse through oppressive rituals in education. Deep things that affect must be narrated, but if they cannot be narrated, if meaning cannot be (re)interpreted, revisited, resituated, and reorganized as per Hook (2013), we witness the psychic disintegration.

In the memoir, the meaning of the symptom, which the narrator recognizes by instituting herself as hero, comes through the cry of distress. Attribution for heroism belongs to the one who tells the story because they navigate the murky waters of collapsed meaning, violent pedagogy, and dehumanized childhood, to offer us an opportunity to learn and thereby halt the repetitive insistence . . . of the unconscious formations (Hook 2013). As readers, we have the option to take up the mantle and as co-heroes work through the history of Indian Residential Schooling in Canada.

## NOTES

1. Chief Bev Sellars (First Nations in Williams Lake, BC - frin Xat'sull (Soda Creek)) uses the designation "Indian" in her memoir. I use the term in reference to the aboriginal children and people oppressed and racialized through the Indian Education Act. Essentially, I view the act as a mechanism of producing the split subject who is "the Indian."

2. The Saskatoon Public School Board was changing their assessment guidelines regarding late assignments and plagiarism, the response from the public and the provincial government was swift and condemnatory. Though the board claimed they were promoting classroom practice resonant with contemporary research and the Ministry of Education's assessment policy, the public reaction, as expressed through television news, talk radio, and the Internet, was a veritable landslide of popular resistance (LeBlanc 2011).

3. This is referred to as *alienation*, which is a form of frustration. The condition of frustration is between the Imaginary (of the ego) and the Symbolic (of the superego).

4. Stereotypes are a prime example of such tangents. As they at some point represent a truth but eventually are perceived as ego-dystonic by the Subject, or they become an egocentric taboo that the Other begins to forbid.

# FOUR

# Glen Retief: *The Jack Bank*

I went to boarding school when I was twelve, three months before my thirteenth birthday. On the first day of class, our homeroom teacher asked for a volunteer interim class monitor to serve until we, as a class community, were better acquainted and able to hold proper elections. I volunteered. I figured it would not be very different from being a prefect; and everyone else seemed either too afraid or not interested. Two weeks into my volunteer position, I came to class late, having attended the clinic due to feeling somewhat under the weather.

As I walked into the room, welcomed by a tense sinister silence filled with anticipation, I handed the teacher my note from the nurse before sitting down. As soon as I sat down my deskmate leaned over and whispered, "You're in trouble." I was confused. I looked to the teacher for clarity. "Yes," she began, "it's good you are here." She sneered. I can still remember the scene to this day, quite vividly. She always had chewing gum in her mouth, and as she spoke, she moved the chewing gum around each enunciated word, for a change delivered in English rather than Ndebele. She continued, "There have been some allegations against you. It seems you are using your position as classroom monitor to bully your classmates." Her cruel smile indicated she had already sharpened the guillotine for my beheading. She had a ruthless disciplinarian reputation. I was a little afraid. More than that, though, I was very confused. I did not respond right away even as she stared at me, the chewing gum churning deliberately in her mouth. Finally, I asked who had made these allegations and when was I supposed to have bullied these girls. Satisfied with my obvious powerlessness she turned to a girl I had never spoken to before: "Betty?"

Betty was a tiny child. I was small but she was even smaller. She spoke with a voice that I might say suited her frame. I did not know at the time that Betty was also quite devious and a practiced liar. She told a story about my threatening to beat her up for speaking out of turn. My deskmate sat beside me, clearly fighting an inner battle whether to show her solidarity or stay neutral. She chose to stay neutral. No one supported Betty's story and no one supported me. In an audience of fearful classmates, there were only three of us in this drama; and I was not going to be the victor. Nevertheless, I went down with something of a fight. I raised the point that for the last week I had been arriving late because I was ill and attending treatment at the clinic. I also pointed out that we had only been at school for about two weeks so I hardly knew the names of most girls in my class and certainly had never talked to Betty. I was telling the truth. I spoke in English.

My teacher switched back to Ndebele, a practice she used to disarm those of us she clearly despised. Foreign students did not suffer this humiliation—we suspected it was because their parents paid more in fees—therefore, their children were privileged. The school policy was an expectation that all activities conducted must be in English, unless it was during French or Ndebele lessons. I could not respond in Ndebele but little Betty could. As it turned out, her father was Shona but her mother was Ndebele, so little Betty was fluent in both languages. I was not. The teacher carried out her interrogation in Ndebele, I responded in English; and Betty counterattacked in Ndebele. I lost the battle and spent two weeks watering the vegetable gardens from morning until lunchtime during class hours for being a bully. I missed several classes and received little to no support to make up for the lessons. Betty was also promoted to class monitor within two days of her professional sabotaging of my short-lived career as a good student.

After that episode, I spent every Saturday of my four years at boarding school serving some punishment or the other. I was notorious and became part of the orientation and induction material for new teachers and staff. Over the years, I became the most punished girl in the school's history. I was an average student, not putting much effort into studying. When others were studying, I was either breaking a rule or serving punishment for breaking a rule. One time, I was suspended for something in which I had absolutely no involvement, as it had occurred in my absence. The school authorities just assumed I was involved and put me down as the "ringleader." I did not deny my participation or set them straight on my whereabouts during the hours in question, mostly because I should have been in my dormitory when the incident occurred. History had taught me claiming innocence was futile; I was going to go down for something no matter what. I served my sentence and carried on with my rebellion.

In my third year in boarding school, we had a new English teacher, Mr. Wilson, who taught us geography and science. On his first day, he walked into the classroom and asked, "Which one of you is Glorie?" I did not volunteer myself and none of my classmates gave me up. He decided to ask us one by one, I told him I was "Alice, from Zambia," hoping the diversity within our school would shelter me from this man's scrutiny. I convinced him Glorie was not in class that day. The following week, however, Mr. Wilson was wiser. Someone must have told him the truth. He decided to focus the day's geography lesson on Zambia. For two hours it was battle of wits as he threw questions about Zambia at me, none of which I could answer but somehow I managed to bluff my way through the class. Finally, he forced me to confess, which I did, unapologetically. My punishment was to do a poster presentation on Zambia the following week for the rest of the class. Mr. Wilson and I became great friends. His hobby was snake hunting, and I joined him on his excursions several times after serving punishments on the weekends.

When I wrote my ordinary level exams, I did well enough to return to the same school for advanced level. However, the school would not take me. My uninformed father could not understand why, so we drove the three hours to the school in order for him to meet with the principal, Mrs. Beardall. She was a kind, gentle woman who never raised her hand against a student but her deputy, Miss Samushonga, was especially vicious and enjoyed beating us. She was also my math teacher, the one with the wand. She was unaccommodating, rude, and dismissive of my father. Miss Samushonga told him that the school would never welcome me back because of my "bad record." My father was heartbroken and drove me home in a sad "disappointed in you" silence that lasted the entire three hours of the journey. It was the first time since the day Betty hung me out to dry that I regretted my behavior in school. Throughout my boarding school years, my parents had remained blissfully unaware of my troublesome lifestyle as long as I was not failing my course work. My sister, who was at the same school for two of my four years, knew about it; she avoided me out of shame during the school term, but she never told my parents. What happens at boarding school, stays at boarding school.

In this chapter, I lean once more on Todd (2008) to express my intention to face humanity through my project:

> My task here in these brief pages, then, is to sketch out a reconsideration of the idea of humanity for cosmopolitan education, one that neither is a plea for a new humanism, which states unequivocally what counts as human 'flourishing' and 'fulfilment', nor is it a call for an antihumanism which would similarly reduce persons to the abstractions of social systems or power structures. . . . I suggest that a renewed idea of humanity must account for human limits as well as human possibilities and needs to be read in relation to the very violence and antagonism that inheres in the specific contours of *human* interaction. The primary question I therefore address is how do we imagine an education that seeks not to *cultivate* humanity, to borrow from Nuss-

> baum (1997), but instead seeks to *face* it—head-on, so to speak, without sentimentalism, idealism or false hope? (p. 3)

One might read Todd's statement as sharing the same values as Afro-pessimism, which states the sentiment of the irreconcilable differences between the world and Blackness and has become a movement driven to expose the perversity of race symptomized by the commodification of Blackness.[1] This chapter expands on the conceptualization of Afro-pessimism to include other forms of oppressive commodification. I focus on the commodification of childhood to uphold the perverse practice of racism and homophobia within education. The impressions of futility in current practices in the art and science of teaching and learning have been a part of education and social discourses for a very long time. Chapter 4 shows the complexities and intricacies that continue to prove unresolvable. We already know what human beings are capable of, both good and bad. In education, moving forward requires a model that cultivates social justice in pedagogy while working with both good and bad aspects of humanity, and as a means of facing our ambivalence of education, humanity, and our individual selves.

## APARTHEID AND THE EDUCATION OF WHITE BOYS IN SOUTH AFRICA

The psychoanalysis of racism is a dynamic and relatively new application for Freudian theories. Generally, psychoanalysis views racism as a form of perversion based on the jouissance of the Other, which results in the alterity of those who are racialized (Bracher 1994). Miller (in Bracher 1994) elucidates on the internal conflict between self and Other when we attempt to logically erase racism maintaining that what we are attempting to see is what makes the other *Other* (particular and/or different), and how in in this dimension of the Other, we find war. In accordance, racism, to Miller, is precisely a question of the relation to an Other as such, conceived in its difference. To Miller, it seems none of the generous and universal discourses on the theme of "we are all fellow human beings" has had any effectiveness concerning this question. The question cannot be effectively tackled, points out Miller (1994), because racism calls into play a hatred that is directed precisely toward what grounds the Other's alterity. In other words, the jouissance of the Other constitutes one's alterity and it is that perception of the Other's jouissance that validates racism. He explains, "If no decision, no will, no amount of reasoning is sufficient to wipe out racism, this is indeed because it is founded on the point of extimacy of the Other" (p. 79).

Extimacy, a term used by Lacan, draws our attention to the elements of our inward or intimate selves that are attached to the Other, or as Miller puts it, the extimacy of the Subject is the Other. The underlying motivations for oppression still lingering in today's schools are exposed through a fundamental understanding of the perversion that became the education system of South Africa during apartheid. The desire and hatred of an *other's* perceived jouissance became the legacy of white boys in South Africa. Their education centered on achieving their own jouissance by destroying the perceived jouissance of black people. During apartheid, sexuality and racism were, as Ratele and Shefer (2013) make clear, intricately enmeshed. In Shefer's (2013) words, sexuality was powerfully imbricated in apartheid policies, practices, and ideologies.

My discussion on the education of white South African boys centers on the psychoanalytic fundamentals of racism. I examine the ways in which the atmosphere of hatred becomes legacy to white South African children who, as adults, recount their paradoxical positions during apartheid. In what Sonn, Stevens, and Duncan (2013) refer to as "dominant history," narratives such as Retief's remain hidden and ignored. In colonial discourse the focus has been on the oppression of black South Africans, however, the public transcript conceals the workings of power and oppression over time and in different contexts. Hidden from much of apartheid rhetoric is the trauma of schooling for white children subject to the laws of a racist government and society. White children raised in South Africa might stand accountable for the acts of violence perpetrated against black people, yet internally they struggle with the trauma of their indoctrination into the apartheid system (Shefer 2013).

Emerging research and literature sheds light on the psychic oppression in the education of white children in apartheid South Africa (Hook 2011; Hook and Long 2011). Sonn, Stevens, and Duncan (2013) state that decolonizing methodologies are informed by critical theoretical approaches in their commitment to examining and transforming power relations. These methodologies value standpoint, that is, they highlight that there are no value-free positions from which to engage with knowledge construction and social transformation (p. 301). The standpoint of white children in apartheid South Africa engages discourses of power in the efforts of decolonization. Education must consider the oppression of all children.

The narrative of Glen Retief in *The Jack Bank* exposes readers to the perversity of a system that thrived on the disavowal of lack. With a continued focus on social justice, I examine Retief's (2011) narrative as a depiction of the consequences of a perverse society on the emotional and mental health of vulnerable children. Caught at the intersection of racial and sexual difference, Retief's memoir raises concerns about a perverse legacy handed down to children through enactments of sexualized violence. This resulted in the dehumanization of children who could not comprehend the injustice inflicted upon them but compelled to carry on the tradition. The children consequently turn on each other. The disavowal of their subjectivity occurred through oppressive acts. Their objectification was by Others who deemed it acceptable to instil patriotism and citizenship through violence. Retief writes:

> This whole experience is supposed to unite us. "Work together, Standard Six!" . . . But sometime during those ten weeks, in fact the opposite of solidarity develops. We stop trusting each other. We become vicious and feral; start proclaiming half in jest and half in seriousness—"Him!"—when John asks. (p. 107)

Retief's use of the term "feral" brings to the forefront the depravity of the acts of perversion against these boys; and of course, black people. By age twelve, he is beginning to understand that apartheid is violence that must and can only endure as patriotism. His education preordained him as connoisseur of violence against black bodies. This cycle causes emotional and mental trauma for him. State sanctioned violence, school condoned violence, and unbridled authority perverse the structures of society by dehumanizing its vulnerable members.

Black people and all children in apartheid society were dehumanized in order to maintain the status quo and assuage the anxieties of those who felt they had much to lose. As a rite of passage, dehumanization prepared traumatized children to live as perpetrators of violence against black people. "The biological vulnerability and the developmental position of natural aggressiveness in young children make them particularly susceptible to dynamics in which power is operative" (Twemlow 2000, p. 755). As such, violence was a cultural artefact in apartheid South Africa. It stood as an emblem of power and domination. In order to dominate, one had to suffer domination, passed on through pedagogy as institution.

I look at the violent acts as "childism," which Young-Bruehl (2012) has described as centered on the oppression of children, bringing into account children's treatment by adults, and the difficulties of acknowledging adult oppression of the young. Young-Bruehl defines childism as follows:

> a prejudice that rationalizes or justifies acts that harm children or fail to meet their basic needs. But at the more fundamental motivational or fantasy level, childism can be defined as a belief system that constructs its target group, "the child," as an immature being produced and owned by adults who use it to serve their own needs and fantasies. (pp. 35–36)

Young-Bruehl's view of child oppression is poignant where educational systems make decisions that do not consider the rights of the child. In Retief's (2011) testimony, the perverse ideology of white supremacy required children to be subordinate to the extent of performing perverse acts against each other. Their participation in the cycle of oppression, enforced through violence and abuse, was a measure expected of children in order to maintain their government's perverse belief in white supremacy. A refusal to participate by either hurting or being hurt met with corporal punishment.

Based on the psychological and scientific "findings" of the time, black people were labeled all manners of wild and sexually immoral (Lambley 1974). These oppressive views of race determined the education of all of South Africa's children. Ratele and Shefer (2013) point out that apartheid was entrenched through laws and discourses that went further than the imposition of geographical separation, and insisted on placing taboos on sexual intimacy and bodily (dis)connection between subjects of different race. Deviation from this ideology, viewed as anti-apartheid, could result in punitive measures (Harvey 2000).

Within this system, white male entitlement took on the role of regulator (Ratele and Shefer 2013) and hegemonic masculinity took on its power through disempowering, devaluing, and marginalizing "other" masculinities in particular gay and "feminized" men (Shefer 2013). These statements provide a basis for viewing the eroticized discipline and education of Glen and his peers as victimization of children by the government. At an all-white boys school, the children's constructions of masculinity were distorted by fantasies of dominance over the "imagined other," namely, blackness. Retief (2011) writes:

> In that week we have been assigned skivvy masters: seventeen-year-old matrics for whom we must play black South Africans, making their beds in the morning, polishing their shoes, and taking their clothes to the laundry room, where Swazi and Shangani maids will launder, iron, and fold them. (p. 103)

The pedagogy within the institution focused on eradicating the perceived jouissance of any white people who did not measure up to the regulator's ideal of whiteness and therefore represented blackness within the space. Through impressions of blackness, caricature and the sexualized oppression of blackness, the white boys established a shared understanding of incompetence, stupidity, inability, and so on (Shefer 2013, p. 178). From the apartheid papers, Shefer analyzes a white man's testimony of his schooling in South Africa: "In short, a series of racist stereotypes and bodily evocations became part and parcel of the repetitive play of white adolescent boys, vital instruments in the ongoing in-group/out-group identity practices of who was cool and who wasn't" (p. 178).

Also subject to the regulator's punitive gaze, black women were the most vulnerable adult group during apartheid; therefore, it is not a coincidence that the smaller, younger, and more vulnerable boys were cast into the disempowered roles of Swazi and Shangani house cleaners and forced to act as fetishistic objects for the establishment of the white male as ideal. The role vulnerable groups played in maintaining the ideal of white masculinity in South Africa is explained by Moffett (2006) who states that rationalized intimate violence was a "control mechanism."

However, the underlying need to control stems from the dominator's feelings of anxiety according to Moffett, who elucidates on the narratives of social control over [black] women before and after apartheid. She states:

> The pernicious and overtly racially ranked hierarchies endorsed and enforced during South Africa's apartheid regime continue to have profound implications for women and their experience of gender-based and sexual violence, even after these forms of social stratification are apparently dismantled or transformed in line with rights-based principles. (p. 131)

Similar to the white people running the Indian residential schools discussed in the previous chapter, the majority of white South Africans ironically trusted the people they debased to make sense of their daily lives. Power gained through domination can be disarming as it insists on the labor of the oppressed in order to thrive. The comforts and privileges desired by the oppressor makes him wholly dependent on his victims.

Retief's (2011) testimony examines the mental struggle of a child to comprehend the social system in which he inhabited a paradoxical expectation of privilege and subordination. In Glen's experience, he was *an other* to both whites and black people because of his English heritage. More than that, he was *an other* morally and sexually because of his orientation, a fact he denied for as long as he possibly could until it shattered him. Whatever the terms of his childhood, there was a socially and state sanctioned practice of trauma dealt against him. Retief writes:

> Afrikaners dislike black people: there is some bad blood there I do not altogether comprehend. Miss Jeanette, when she talked to us once about the tensions between the races, said it had to do with the fact that both the blacks and the Afrikaners love land and cattle—hence the battles of circled wagons against the spear throwing warriors. But my own hunch is that there must be more to it than that. In the way some of the playground boys joke about dropping an atom bomb on Mozambique or putting poison in the Soweto water tower, I sense a vast, toxic reservoir of superiority and contempt. (p. 27)

Glen's education did little to clarify the differences beyond superficial histories. The violence of racism and oppression coated in religiosity reinforced ideologies of legitimacy. These messages created an emotional tension calcified by efforts to make sense of his sexuality. Glen grew up with the notion that anything that was not Afrikaner was deviant. Black people suffered for it, and the English, though tolerated, were illegitimate. Trying to comprehend and accept his sexual difference was something he could not begin to grapple with given the complexities in the social discourses of difference surrounding him.

## RACISM AS PERVERSION

Let's return to Miller's (1994) assertion that even when scientific proof is available to indicate that "we are all fellow human beings," we still, as a society, cling to notions of difference and depend on superficial measures to justify our segregation. In fact, a social construction does not motivate us; rather, the stakes draw on the instinct to hate what we perceive as another's jouissance at the expense of our own. What we perceive is not skin color or ethnic markers; it is signifiers of the other's jouissance, which proscribed as deviations from what we deem "normal," encounter punitive judgment. Miller's statement significantly clarifies and underpins the psychic properties of race that make irrelevant any scientific or biological properties we might draw upon to explain the social phenomena of racism.

What then is race? Race is a signifier of perceived jouissance. I support this definition with Spillers' (2003) view that race speaks through multiple discourses that inhabit intersecting axes of relations that banish, definitely, the illusion of a split between "public" and "private" (p. 378). In other words, race is that thing that the Subject happily flaunts, daring to flout the Other's conditions of relationship. Race is shouting obscenities from the rooftops instead of keeping private that one is defiantly different from the Other. South Africa's response to the dare was to beat the black man until he became "essentially flimsy or ephemeral . . . more heard than seen" (Retief 2011, p. 24). Spillers further states:

> While we are confronted from time to time, with almost evidence that the age of the postrace subject is upon us, we are just as certain that its efficacies can, and do, move from one position to another and back again. (p. 379)

I understand the temporal traveling of race through Lacan's conception of metonymic signifiers: "diachronic movement from one signifier to another along a signifying chain, as one signifier constantly refers to another in a perpetual deferral of meaning" (Evans 1996, p. 117). In his book, *My Teaching*, Lacan (2008) states:

> The subject is manufactured by a certain number of articulations that have taken place, and falls from the signifying chain in the way that ripe fruit falls. As soon as he comes into the world he falls from a signifying chain, which may well be complicated or at least elaborate, and what we call the desire of his parents is subjacent to that very chain. (p. 44)

Our understanding of race as an identity draws from articulations of signifiers. "Black," as a racial designation, articulates certain details, as do "white" and "Indian" from the previous chapter. Race as a signifier, therefore relies on the history of race to evolve. Included in the history, is the desire of those who brought the Subject into the world biologically. As part of the process of secondary socialization, Others bring the Subject into a world that uses and misuses race as a signifier of jouissance. The roles that all these others and Others play in the Subject's experience of race means we cannot leave the history of race and it's pain in the past.

I have often heard younger generations—the millennials—dismiss racism as an obsolete social evil. In classrooms, students insist that learning about racism and oppression perpetuates the trauma and cancels out the progress that has been made. In several academic conferences and contexts, I have heard it said that "we are not where we should be but thank God we are not where we used to be." It is true, significant progress has been made socially and justly for men, women, and children who have historically been oppressed. I know as a student and as an educator, talking about racism has left me feeling raw and pained. It is tempting to insist its history and all is well because I have managed to achieve some level of success that was not possible in the past because of colonialism and oppression. However, if we bury the signifiers of our current social discourses in the past as history, we are not getting rid of the pain. We are repressing it and eventually our unconscious will present the consequences. Our unconscious will speak.

Calls for reparation in efforts of truth, peace, and reconciliation prove that the history of race still has great power over our understanding and perceptions of race today. A post-racial subject is not possible where the history of race determines the commodification of race. We still order our relationships based on perceived jouissance. Therefore, race is complicated inasmuch as jouissance is complicated. The complication lies in its illusory quality wherein the promise is denied and yet perceived as fulfilled in others. The quest of jouissance issues from a promise of pleasure that is never delivered. What monetary value can we put on the promise of jouissance and how can we say when reparation has been made if we still perceive this illusive jouissance in the *other*? Worse still, how can one let go of the perversion that results from the pursuit of jouissance if it means one can no longer enjoy the privilege of the Imaginary realm.[2]

In *Psychoanalysis and Literature: Perversion, Racism and Language of Difference,* Yanaginio (2008) describes racism as a form of perversion because it is an expression of resistance to difference. Calvo (2008) advocates mindfulness when examining racism in psychoanalytic terms, asserting that fantasy drives the subject into the perverted position. Calvo also expands on the racial fantasies in which subjects engage, essentially seeking to answer basic questions about racial identity in relation to our others. *What does she think of me? How is she like me? How is she different from me? What kind of relationship is possible between us?* In turn, Hook (2013) states:

> The ambivalence of such imaginings—providing a gratifying relief from anxiety and yet also potentially raising affective levels of hate—would simply be following the usual course of fantasy. That is to say, following a Lacanian perspective on fantasy, a fantasy oscillates between extremes of unease and domestication, staging both a prospective castration and a scene which protects against just such a possibility. (p. 56)

When set apart by race, the answer the Other gives is driven by fantasies of perceived jouissance. Veracity occurs when the subject gathers, through experience, knowledge that either confirms or refutes the fantasy. Racial fantasies exert a powerful psychic reality in their own right (Calvo 2008), as we see illustrated in the fundamental fantasy imposed on South African white children educated to either believe superiority over their others or face corporal punishment for transgressing against supremacist ideologies. Given such conditions, we witness the futility of mental hygiene in segregated education.

So what is perversion? In this context, it is the use of physical and psychic control over children's bodies in order to satisfy a desire for power and dominance: jouissance. It is akin to what Sheldon George (2011) explicates in *Realism's Racial Gaze and Stephen Crane's The Monster: A Lacanian Reading.* George discusses jouissance as approached without the taboo of incest limiting their drives by white slave owners. In Glen's case, older boys in his school could pursue their jouissance and perform perverse acts hidden behind veneers of patriotism and governance. Retief (2011) recalls the prefects' repeated lectures:

> "Fricking wastes of white skin," John says now, looking at all of us. I don't know yet but this is another one of his standard turns of phrase. At Youth Preparedness lessons, John will stand next to the school commandant, who'll lecture us to ready ourselves for lifelong struggle against racist terrorists like Nelson Mandela. Back in the dormitory, he'll call meetings to repeat what the commandant said, and say, "That's why you shouldn't behave like kaffirs, guys—if you're lucky enough to be born white, you shouldn't waste it." (pp. 102–3)

Any act that brought whites down to the level of blacks was transgressive. Eugenic service camouflaged fetid acts of physical and sexual abuse. Typical of a perverse psychopathology, apartheid condoned and justified all manner of taboos.

Perversion, we can say, occurs where racism takes the form of a justification of one's fetishistic tendencies as a necessity to police the other's jouissance seeking behaviors. There is no apparent risk of castration for this hedonistic pleasure when it is sanctioned by society. "Castration means that jouissance has to be refused in order to be attained on the inverse scale of the Law of Desire" (Lacan 2006, p. 827). Fundamentally, to refuse jouissance is to accept prohibition, which allows the Subject to enter into the Symbolic realm. To continually pursue jouissance, the pervert must remain within the Imaginary. The Other governs the law, forbidding or permitting acts of jouissance for the Subject. However, the recalcitrant Subject—the pervert—refuses the Symbolic order in preference for jouissance.

Examining the intricacies of sexuality and racism uncovers that though expressed through the libido, perversion is not a sexual/genital drive. Perversion is on the side of wielding power through sexual violence, a phenomenon we witness often in difference-based conflict (Papineni 2003). Retief (2011) provides an account in which sex, masturbation, and nakedness take on the signification of power and dominance against helpless children. He writes:

> Sex is John's penis sticking out like a tree orchid, the steam billowing through the downstairs bathroom. Masturbation fantasy is a padlock snapping over a penis; it is Sven, naked, punching a younger boy one day in the showers and causing him to double up. In short, sexuality is something dark and secret, imbued with shame and violence—something connected to the jack bank. (p. 146)

Sexualized oppression protects one's power through performed physical dominance over an *other's* body, thereby disavowing one's lack and powerlessness. This kind of sexuality occurring at the level of the body however, takes on the quality of unpleasurable pleasure, which would be the fulfillment of jouissance.

The complexities of racism as perversity are understood through Straker (2004), a white South African working in the country during. She confesses:

> First, the fetish was used to cover our own lack, that is, to cover our own sense of powerlessness. Second, it was used to cover the lack in ideal whiteness; and third, it was used to express the perverse wish to obliterate difference. (p. 413)

To maintain a semblance of power, (having realized that anything prior to this was simply a fantasy) the fetishistic racist must find the commodity that will symbolize power. Institutions such as slavery and apartheid stem from this fetishism in order to fulfill the desired taboo and flaunt the external symbol of power and prowess (George 2011).

With no accessibility to black commodities, Glen and his peers remained impotent unable to partake of the gratification of whiteness. Consequently, they assaulted each other. Older boys exploited their younger and more vulnerable schoolmates as fantasy objects upon which they could exercise their racism. Through sexualized acts of dominance, they practiced the pedagogy of supremacies. The jouissance deemed possible through the fetishization of younger boys was the same jouissance Straker (2004) and her colleagues sought through their community work with black clients. Perversion, that is racism, sullied all aspects of human relations within the country, even professions, like social work, that should have been noble. Straker concludes, "[R]acism is indeed a morally reprehensible perversion of justice" (p. 407).

A moral view is vital to understanding the justification of a perverse label on racism. As a social condition of humanity, perversion is traditionally grounded in measures of moral character (Roudinesco 2009). At the root of perversion, stems deviance from a moral code of behavior and "no matter how hard scholars have tried to avoid discussing perversion with reference to moral principles, they have generally failed to live up to the expectations of an 'objective' and 'neutral' science" (Nobus 2006, p. 8). Nobus's statement clarifies the interpretation of racism as perverse for regardless what angle we apply, objectively, neutrally, or scientifically, racism still, rightly so, appears immoral in its perpetration. Whether we take away theological and religious moral compasses, there is reasonably at the level of social justice, an ugliness and violence to racism by any human standards. Further, the idea of objectivity in racial affairs, which are in their very nature subjective, has been something with which social scientists contend. Epistemological violence occurs when the Subject is detached from the analysis of race.

As an example of justified perversity, in epistemology, we might examine a racist study conducted in 1979/1980 by J. J. Ray, who asked white South Africans what they thought of black people. Some of the responses to questions posed included, "The blacks are a rather ugly race"; "Blacks are not very hygiene-conscious"; "Blacks generally don't show much inclination to work"; and "drunkenness is one of the greatest problems with blacks." Critically, the questions both ethically and morally raise concerns but the researcher justified his questions by stating these attitudes toward black people reflected white people's attitudes toward black people in other parts of the world where similar questionnaires were distributed. Ultimately, his study reflected the epistemological violence of research based on notions of white supremacy. To justify such violence as legitimate scholarship reveals a perverse structure, which Ray (1979) attempts to conceal by relying on superficial distinctions between "racial discrimination" and "racism":

> One element in understanding this is the distinction made by Banton [(9)] between "racism" and "racial discrimination". With the aid of a vast array of historical evidence, Banton points out that racism is a scientific or quasi-scientific theory. It is a systematic belief in black genetic inferiority. Banton questions whether much of the racial antagonisms of modern-day Britain are motivated by such a theory. He feels that they are simply due to the inevitable conflict between different cultures. (n.p.)

Further critical examination of Ray's research exposes those who entrenched in the cycle of racist jouissance, justify their actions by projecting their perversity onto those they oppress. He concludes that white South Africans were hard on blacks because they feared them rather than despised them in spite of the obvious repugnance and contempt expressed in the responses to his survey. Ray's conclusion uncovers the underlying fantasies of the oppressors, for how could the one wielding the whip fear the other being whipped? The white person maintains a perverted stance of racism by projecting his lack onto the black body. He justifies his racism as "helping," "guiding," "educating," and "bettering" racialized people prone to self-destructive, base, and hedonistic desires.

Ray (1980) states:

> If South African racist practices cannot be explained by greater racism in attitudes, how, then, can they be explained? A very obvious explanation flows from such work as that by Sales [(25, 26)], who shows that authoritarianism in both behaviour and attitudes is increased by perceived threat. South Africans are hard on blacks not because they despise them but because they fear them. There are, no doubt, very good grounds for such fear. The accuracy of this explanation is borne out by the now well-documented finding that South Africans suffer from especially high levels of chronic anxiety [see Van Der Spuy and Shamley [(28)]. (n.p.)

The view of violent attitudes as "social conservatism" is warped even in the zeitgeist of the time. In addition, the researcher's testament to white South Africans suffering from chronic anxiety reveals a pathological structure to their social dominance.

Fundamentalist authoritarianism was part of the education of white boys often associated with religiosity (Duckitt 1992). In Glen's case, the authoritarian education took the form of deprived acts of physical and sexual violence as well as epistemic violence against [white] boys that did not meet the South African ideal of whiteness. Thus, black or white, South Africa was educating its children through perverse and oppressive pedagogy, scarring the future generations on both sides of the divide.

## THE FANTASY OF WHITENESS

It is wise to be conscious of what drives a person to perversion; forethought requires consciousness of the desire that molds the fantasies of perverts. Hence, critical psychoanalysis is quite valuable in its exposition of what underlies racism where efforts to debunk ideologies of racial superiority scientifically fail. Regardless of what modern science and education has taught, there is still a desire that drives toward racism, toward perversion. In white South Africa, as we see in Glen's memoir, the desire was driven by a fundamental fantasy of whiteness.

Lacan (1981, 1998, and 2006) used the term "fundamental fantasy" to describe the primary fantasy from which all other Imaginary fantasies take form. Therefore, from whiteness, as fundamental fantasy, come other collective fantasies of racial dominance and identity. Blackness as a racial signifier is subsequently derivative of whiteness as a [racial] master signifier. Black must be black in relation to white (Fanon 1967). White was an emotionally loaded color for the white people, and according to Jordan's (1968) account; "Whiteness, moreover, carried a special significance for Elizabethan Englishmen: it was, particularly when complemented by red, the colour of perfect human beauty" (p. 8). For many white South Africans it was an unattainable quality—rendering it fantasy.

Whiteness as *master signifier* (a signifier without a signified) in racial discourse is per Seshadri-Crooks (2000), a signifier of complete mastery, self-efficacy, and the jouissance of oneness. Evidently, no one can fully possess these qualities, individually or collectively, hence the unsignified status. While in school, racist pedagogy insisted Glen and his peers exhibit all of the qualities of whiteness. Any deviation from unattainable qualities was rewarded with physical attrition. The boys were damned to oppression by the fantasy of whiteness. Ironically, demands for whiteness—complete mastery, self-efficacy, and the jouissance of oneness—further collapsed the fantasy as the boys turned on each other in desperate displays of weakness, and looked to their abusers for direction and validation. Seshadri-Crooks also states that as a master signifier of race, whiteness is neither a physical nor an ideological property but "establishes a structure of relations, a signifying chain that through a process of inclusions and exclusions constitutes a pattern for organizing human difference" (pp. 3–4). The education of white boys in apartheid South Africa illustrates that the derived differences of the master signifier become pathological manifestations of fear and anxieties, which stem from the incapacity to tolerate lack and take the form of racism.

The fear of castration by whiteness is a fantasy in the Imaginary realm and denials of the castration are the previously mentioned privilege of the Imaginary realm. Straker (2004), as a white South African, admits the unattainability of whiteness even for those with the "right" skin color:

> Few whites reach the desired status of whiteness to which they may aspire. To be white in Western terms means to have power, and this the possession of very few. Power may still elude those whose skin color facilitates the attainment of privilege. Privilege may be possessed by many, but power by few. . . . In addition to not attaining whiteness (in terms of owning power), some whites recognise that whiteness itself is limited. Whiteness is castrated or limited because of its failure to live up to its own democratic and humanitarian ideals. (p. 409)

In describing the guilt, shame, and fear that comes from being white in South Africa's apartheid regime, Straker illustrates that whiteness is a fundamental fantasy. The desire to maintain a fantastic identity, position, and power threatened by the realization that it was never owned, becomes a disavowal of reality, which manifests as racism. We know disavowal is the primary position leading to perversion and it operates on two levels: a psychic split, in which one part knows that the fantasy is not real, and the other part that wishes it was and thus acts as if it is so.

The explanation of racism as perversion can be expounded by Verhaeghe's (2008) statement:

> Because of his or her disavowal, the perverse subject does indeed recognise lack and the regulating law—but for others, not for itself. One half makes us suspect we are dealing with an equal, even a hyper-equal who is more *au fait* with the conventions than we are. The other half confronts us with the perversion of these conventions that are useful only for being replaced by the lack-disavowing perverse law. The pervert's speech testifies to this equivocalness: yes and no are interchangeable, any word can mean what the perverse subject wants it to mean, and the only law that matters is that which imposes jouissance on the other. (p. 430)

The effect that the authority of whiteness has on the white body is potentially castrating for the white person who cannot live up to the fantasy of whiteness. Submitting to this lack would essentially racialize the white person and trigger a neurotic subjectification as discussed in the previous chapter. The racist would rather disavow his lack and maintain the fantasy of whiteness than be at par with those he has systematically racialized. Straker (2004) corroborates:

> Confronting the de-idealized whiteness created in us a wish to cast a veil over the flaws in the ideal of whiteness, at least in relation to our own whiteness. One way of doing this, which we noted in ourselves, was to use the Other . . . in the process of covering up lack, the interests of the minority group [Black people] were then patronizingly and paternalistically promoted, these interests having been predetermined for the group. (p. 415)

Straker's confession is an admission of perversion by individuals who were aware of their wrongful treatment of the people they were supposed to serve but they carried on objectifying black people in order to feel better about their lack. The pervert's fundamental fantasy always displaces his disavowed lack onto the other.

The perverse phenomenon is apparent in current racial politics where we find people who insist they are not racist and yet are complicit in the propagation of systemic racism. Teachers, politicians, and so many other professionals whom society have held up to a higher standard are most vulnerable to perversion because they are overcome with feelings of inadequacy when confronted with social justice matters. Rather than face their lack, they use the people to whom they owe equity and inclusion to maintain a semblance of mastery, efficacy, and oneness in their leadership roles. It is no wonder that society is dealing with an upsurge of racism and racial oppression because the ideals have changed and the fantasies have become disillusionments. People are afraid. White men in particular because it is their fantasy that has been challenged the most. It is white men most vulnerable to castration because it is white men who were raised and taught to be the gatekeepers of white supremacy, whether they liked it or not. White people are trained to be white by institutions, explains Suchet (2007), who believes that these institutions shelter white people and as such whiteness cannot be separated from institutional and social power, whether experientially or ideologically (p. 869). That means when these institutions are challenged by demands for social justice, white people are left without shelter and afraid. That is why we are seeing the rise of such terms as "white flight" and "white fright."

Within the institution of education, Glen and his peers learned to be white; however, their sheltering by these institutions was different from what we might witness in prevailing cases of white privilege. Demonstrably, the perversion of racism was through acts of physical and sexual violence. Whiteness was taking the position of abuser of black people; supremacy was to believe in the fundamental fantasy, and pedagogy was abuse and denigration. Retief (2011) recalls the mixed feelings of his indoctrination into apartheid ideology:

> Is this the essence of self-defeat, its sickly core: when you refuse to look at reality because it has become too embarrassing and painful? Or perhaps I am still on the wrong track here. Perhaps the key to my consent to being part of that great cycle of apartheid violence—the apparatus whereby white boys are bullied when they are so young so that later they will know how to beat blacks into continued submission—does not lie in John. (pp. 105–6)

Older boys chose indifference to the trauma inflicted on younger boys despite their own experiences of it. Confronted by their lack, which became more apparent with cognitive development, the victims became perpetrators of the violence. Desperate boys engaged in the eroticism of humiliation and sexualized oppression of those identified as contrary to ideals of whiteness.

## MELANCHOLIA AND DIFFERENCE

For melancholic white South Africans that confronted their disavowal of their lack of ideal/phallic whiteness, jouissance was gained through the commodification of racialized others. In their acts of perversion, they found comfort in knowing that while the other was castrated, they were still intact but there was also guilt for secretly celebrating that they were not the castrated one. For Straker (2000), this celebration brought back the shame, which they tried to deal with by overcompensating in their zeal to help black people whom they patronized. In realizing this overcompensation, they once more felt shame in their objectification of the oppressed and the cycle continued.

According to Freud and Abraham, one of the symptoms of melancholia is one's relation to shame, as an egocentric shame (Freud 1917). The melancholic subject becomes so egocentric that they become the center of all existence. They have no repression of shame, will humiliate themselves and justify it to invite reproach and further justify their affect and behavior. Retief extends our understanding of this melancholic position when he confesses his continued interest in his abuser:

> Part of me really doesn't want him to thrash me. I just want to curl up in the tightness of the sheets and fall asleep again; I want John to leave me alone. Yet something wild and magnetic is also drawing me toward him, something crazy, primitive, and self-destructive. Show him that you're worthy. (p. 124)

It would seem Glen delighted in his humiliation and shame, or perhaps derived from it a sense of grandiosity. There is therefore interchangeability between the shame and grandiosity. With this clinical description, Freud (1917) further identified an unconscious discourse that suggested psychic mechanisms of repression, displacement, and inversion.

Straker (2004) takes up the idea of racial melancholia, describing it as a condition of shame and guilt for benefiting in the acts of apartheid. In racial melancholia shame is a diminishment in one's own eyes of self, while guilt was experienced in the realization that they were privileged (Straker 2004, p. 410). Similarly, Suchet (2007) grapples with the melancholia she experiences when her whiteness is brought into scope and her power challenged. This indicates racism is not a linear clear-cut concept; that is, the *master-slave dialectic* does not occur as traditionally portrayed in some sociological theories of race such as critical race theory. From a social justice perspective in order to understand the experiences of children in perverse societies we must acknowledge the complex and dialogical forms that racism and race may take, positing that sometimes the apparent "master" is as much the "slave" in the dialectic. In Retief's school as he attests, younger boys grew into their roles of oppressor through their own oppression. They became perverse in deference to the perversion surrounding them.

Melancholia relates to perversion as an identified symptom of the psychopathology (Verhaeghe 2008). Straker (2004) testifies that feelings of shame and guilt (both elements of melancholia) may be disavowed and dealt with by encapsulating them in the other as a fetishistic object in the mode of perversion (p. 407). To rephrase, the disavowal of one's lack through the dehumanization of an other is perversion. The pedagogic relevance of this lies in the classroom as a space where social justice requires the acknowledgement and containment of a propensity to perversion. We cannot offer a socially just education when we disavow the emotional and mental mechanisms that bring about the injustice in the first place.

Verhaeghe (2008) explains that disavowal is a defense mechanism of the pathological structure of perversion:

> [T]he pervert adopts a double stance. He denies the phallic lack (for himself and for the mother), while at the same time recognizing its existence (for the rest of the world in general and for the father in particular). The result is a clear-cut split: the pervert lives in a divided world where lack and the regulating law are both recognised and denied at the same time. (p. 411)

Retief (2011) confesses that by the time he was ready to graduate he had become double-stanced. One of his schoolmates points this out to him saying, "*Yissis*, hey, but you have only two settings. Either you let them walk over you or you *donner* them until they can hardly walk at all" (p. 151). Glen grew into John, the senior who had indoctrinated him into perversion. Just as he had guessed at John's self-loathing, he was suffering his own and projecting his melancholia on to younger boys. Similar to Straker (2004), the double-stance permitted a disavowal of lack exposed by the ideology of white supremacy. Verhaeghe (2008) further states that the pervert will then compel others to assume the passive position of the object, while taking the active position for itself, meaning not only will the pervert become the Other's object of enjoyment but he also submits the other to a constructed system of rules propos enjoyment (p. 411). In Glen's experience of pedagogy, we see the psychopathology of perversion passed on through education.

## PERVERSION: SADISM OR MASOCHISM

Perverse pedagogy is complex and traumatic and epitomizes "wickedness" (Devaney and Spratt 2009). When education reproduces sadistic and masochistic mechanisms to perpetuate ideologies and fantasies of dominance, authority, and patriarchy, the perversity chisels away at vulnerable psyches resulting in trauma. "The mind of such a child under the influence of hormonal shifts, becomes," according to Twemlow (2000), "Uncreative, preservative, and very narrow in focus, resulting in a despairing acceptance of the victimization because creative solutions do not occur to the victim. Thus, submission becomes a way of life" (p. 752). Concurrently, Ghent (1990) states that clinical experience confirms that the victims of empathetic or abusive childhood settings are prone to develop deep sadistic or masochistic relationships in life.

The bullying in relation to Glen's sexual orientation began before boarding school. Children too young to have any actual understanding or experience of their own sexuality were already using sexual orientation as a weapon against each other. Retief writes:

> "Moffie," says Albert, in the grade ahead of me. Moffie—faggot—what does this word mean? When I ask Albert he guffaws and whispers something to another guy
>
> True, I don't seem to really notice which girls are pretty . . .
>
> True, as I get older I increasingly become aware that I find some of the older boys attractive . . .
>
> True, I find myself glancing at these Afrikaner boys more and more whenever I get the opportunity.
>
> But if all of this amounts to anything beyond the obvious—something more than Boer versus British—I am still unable to see it.
>
> "You're a total sissy," he says. "You like boys, not girls. My pa says some boys turn into these weird, sick perverts—I bet you're one of them." (p. 34)

Several times, Retief (2011) attempts to make sense of the twisted nature and unbridled violence of pedagogy that Glen and his peers must endure. At the age of twelve, Glen enters the cycle of oppression at boarding school. Older boys, assigned authoritative duties over their juniors, operate within the prefect system. John is an older boy who enjoys using sexual tension to unsettle and disempower his younger charges. Through "an uneasy marriage of cruelty and affection" (Retief 2011, p. 99), he releases the sexual tension so that his victims are forced to take a submissive position. According to Twemlow (2000):

> Fetishizing or dehumanizing the victim/child through the splitting of humanity and aliveness produces a less alive (less unique or human) fetish object, allowing the sadistic, bullying child to act out vengeful, hateful, destructive fantasies, fueled by the painful and humiliated response of the victim. (p. 758)

Retief illustrates his oft-apparent dyadic role of sadist and masochist in bullying relationships:

> Then, at some point—I will retain nothing of the prior chain of thoughts or images—I notice John's cock is hard. Its standing out in front of him at a forty-five degree angle, bright pink from the shower water, on the one hand rather grotesque and otherworldly, like crimson bromeliad, and on the other vaguely erotic. I have never seen a mature male hard-on before. This is like a revelation of my own future. My penis becomes tumescent.
>
> John puts his finger under his penis and lifts it.
>
> "Do you want this?"
>
> What is the right answer?

> "No sir," I reply. Then hesitating—perhaps I am insulting him—what exactly does he mean by want? "Well, maybe sir. I mean, I don't know."
>
> "Retief, didn't anyone teach you it is rude to stare?" John asks. I do not reply.
>
> "Especially at a guy's dick, like a moffie. That's not lekker. That's not what we do, here." (Retief 2011, pp. 99–100)

Twemlow (2000) explains that the spiraling ritual of excitement charges the extreme humiliation of the victim, which produces high levels of sexualized and perverse undertones in the bully. He further states, "The person identified as a bully-bystander is vicariously identified with the bully where the victim-bystander identifies with the victim, both typically exhibiting a similar level of fear and arousal with ego boundary permeability" (p. 769).

The eroticized violence takes place in front of other boys both older and younger, all of them drawn into the sexual scene in the shower room. No one intervenes. There is snickering, laughter, and unconcealed enjoyment of what is occurring, but there is also fear and unease. John demands Glen bend over in the shower, then whacks him loudly on the buttocks with a cricket bat. Glen faints or loses consciousness of his body. When he regains it, John privately rewards him with affection and softness.

> "No hard feelings, hey, laaitie?"
>
> I shake my head. And at age twelve, I mean it—there is no indignation or umbrage. Just confusion. Emptiness. Terror. . . . Worming around somewhere deep inside my brain, however: something new. A beam in a freshly built house, slipping an inch or two in response to four thundering tremors. Cracks appearing in mental walls; a chisel chipping into an untried foundation block. (Retief, 2011 pp. 100–101)

"Something new" is an indication of learning happening. Glen is learning to enjoy and adopt this violence as a means of making sense of the world. With the feeling of victimization, the drama begins to feel to the masochist "like an appropriate and expected ending—as in the child who comes to the end of a favourite fairy tale whose ending he knows very well—and there is a sense of familiarity, relief, and closure" (Ghent 1990, p. 54). Closure is with innocence and freedom, Glen replaces his confusion, emptiness and terror with a new understanding. Within a few years, he becomes John:

> Later, what I recall most vividly about the moment is the enormous, surprising pleasure. Violence is glorious. I crash the cricket bat forward with every ounce of my strength: Waldo's head knocks forward against the wood. He gasps; he struggles to breathe. On about the fourth blow he begins to whimper and cry softly. I do not care: in fact this satisfies

> me. He deserves this, the little prick—now he will respect me—the triumph in my muscles and sinews is sensual, physical. (p. 151)

The intimate scenes of sexual violence, profoundly affective, draw us in as witnesses to the effects of a perverse pedagogy and the resulting psychopathology. Without a socially just pedagogy, educators' participation, like Glen's peers, becomes that of bully/victim-bystanders, aroused, fearful, ashamed, and guilty. We become either sadistic or masochistic in efforts to defend against the oppression of social difference. Where the sadist feels no empathy, has low anxiety about what he witnesses, and enjoys the privilege of impunity (Twemlow 2000), the masochist suffers from lack of cohesion of self and lacks the capacity for appropriate assertion in the world. The characteristic of sadism is the fetishizing or dehumanization of the masochist whose "aggression is generally confined to inner anger or self-defeating expressions of aggression in the wrong place, at the wrong time and against the wrong people" (Ghent 1990 p. 55).

We have witnessed the outward expressions of both of these defensive positions in numerous school shootings around the world. Oppression—victimization and bullying—leads to a serious deconstruction of the Subject. Perversity in our schools leads to such extreme outcomes such as murder and/or suicide. At the center of perverse psychopathologies is social difference.

## SEXUAL DIFFERENCE, DISORIENTATION, AND COMPLEXITIES

The reproduction of perversion is sexual disorientation. Retief (2011) asserts the difficulty of holding on to or even acquiring sexual orientation when he states:

> Years later, life will provide me with words for these and later feelings of inadequacy. Stockholm syndrome. Battered victim's disease. Internalized homophobia. The ineluctable sense, as I watch John acting so masculine and nonchalant, talking to one of the other Standard Sixes about cricket scores, that there is something wrong with me for having warranted this punishment. (p. 101)

The apartheid discourse of race and sexuality negated sexual subjectivity. Ratele and Shefer (2013) state that white sexualized racism immobilizes black subjectivity and illustrate the immobility through *Fanon's Fact of Blackness*. Fanon's analysis of a black man's anxieties in white company due to his perceived terrorism of whiteness renders the black man immobile, afraid to act or speak lest he cause the white sensitivities discomfort. "Consequently, a black man cannot but question himself when he observes the look in a white woman's or white man's face" (p. 199). Similarly, internalized homophobia caused Glen to introject the melancholic perversion surrounding him and attributed it to something he caused. He saw himself as defective; when actually he was an object for the fulfilment of jouissance in a defective pedagogy.

An education system that prioritizes social fantasies of dominance and superiority at the expense of the children's safety, well-being, and mental hygiene creates disoriented learners. Glen's disorientation was not limited to his sexuality nor was it limited to his secondary socialization. It permeated all aspects of his developing mind, collapsing meanings, and challenging his self-identification.

Intersecting with this complexity of racial and religious identity was the complexity of his sexual identity. Eriksen (2007) unfolds the meaning of complexity with reference to social discourses of difference. He states that complexity encompasses three dynamic conceptualizations: a great number of relationships mutually influencing each other; an irreducible property of human worlds; and an outcome of a way of looking at the world. Although Eriksen looks at complexity from a theoretical perspective and in regards to academic or cultural research, I see this type of complexity in Glen's education as he navigates the social and cultural discourse to which he is a mere object. In his nostalgia for his school days, Retief (2011) discloses the complexity of misappropriation of language, which rendered efforts of self-representation ineffective. Retief tries to reconcile impressions of Catholicism, Englishness, and masculinity. He struggles to grasp social discourse as one both in and out of the social categories he must navigate.

> "I never want to hear you say kaffir," Mommy says to me, even though this is the standard term for black people on the elementary school playground and even with some of my teachers. "We Catholics believe all people are children of God and should be treated well." (p. 27)
>
> If the Afrikaners are racist, what does that make us English? We also have maids and gardeners. . . . We even vote much the way the Afrikaners do, as far as I know. (p. 28)

> The truth is, I feel this difference, this Englishness, right in the core of my body, in the pit of my chest, where my teacher Miss Jeanette says my heart is supposed to be . . . (p. 29)

> I'm strange even for an Englishman. What other boy in the world is so crazy about telling stories to himself about Middle Earth Wizards? (p. 31)

> But the other guys at school tease me: "You're just a bangbroek," they say, a scaredy-cat. "No guts." (p. 31)

Once more we witness the contradictions in primary and secondary socialization. The social understanding gained at home is negated by the expectations put upon Glen as a white boy in South Africa. At boarding school, the English values are superseded by the perverse values of apartheid. Words his mother told him were wrong to use were legitimized through violence and oppression. According to Bem (1967), if a person holds two cognitions that are inconsistent with one another, he will experience the pressure of an aversive motivational state called cognitive dissonance (p. 183). Expanding on the theory put forward by Festinger (1962), Bem explains that cognitive dissonance creates a pressure which the individual will seek to remove, among other ways, by altering one of the two "dissonant" cognitions. Cognitive dissonance at any age can create feelings of anxiety and insecurity in one's self-perception. For a child still developing one's identity, this makes his own subjectivity most likely the cognition to be altered or negated. The dissonance between what Glen learned at home and what he was learning at school created a pressure in which he became the victim, the collateral damage.

Bem (1967) further states that for self-perception to develop, one relies on a community that enables interactions:

> Verbal statements that are self-descriptive are among the most common responses comprising self-perception, and the techniques employed by the community to teach its members to make such statements would not seem to differ fundamentally from the methods used to teach interpersonal perception in general. The community, however, does face severe limitations in training the individual to make statements describing internal events to which only he has direct access. (p. 184)

The child requires support in a community already deficient to develop a sense of self, but the community in Glen's childhood was not only deficient but also perverse. He had little to work with that could enable him to develop a healthy self-perception about his sexuality and resorts, like many of his peers, to fetishization as a form of defense against the internal destruction with which he was faced.

Complexity is apparent in Glen's participation in erotic violence as both sadist and masochist. Retief (2011) writes:

> As the years go by, we move from being victims to perpetrators . . . all the way through high school, military basic training, and then the whites-only conscript force, where, armed with tanks and rifles, our job will be to control forty million black South Africans. (p. 127)

The boys became either sadistic or masochistic reflecting the psychopathology of the nation of South Africa. In these perverted positions, they simultaneously enjoyed and suffered social difference.

Glen's narrative is particularly significant because it touches the intersection of difference in race and sexuality. He turns our attention to the perception of sexual difference as jouissance. In schools where children learn that heterosexuality is right and normal, homosexuality is subsequently perceived as jouissance. Within these false dichotomies of moral and immoral, private or public, children are forced into either sadistic or masochistic positions of perversion, which present as bullying. "To summarize, the bully gains both social power and personal satisfaction from the combination of an exalted position within the peer by-standing group and personal sadistic, sexual pleasure at the humiliation of the victim" (Twemlow 2000, p. 755).

If an LGBTQ child is perceived to be flaunting something that should be private ("don't ask, don't tell" policies arise from this) or if they are perceived to be accessing jouissance, the response is an attempt by his peers to curb the hedonistic expression of self. The child is bullied, and those bullying that child are accessing their own jouissance through the act. This is homophobia. Glen internalized his homophobia because he began to view his very nature as hedonistic. Many young people internalize homophobia for this reason and like Glen they cannot embrace or even admit their sexuality because public spheres, such as schools, privatize or prohibit anything perceived as jouissance. Those that do embrace or admit their orientation suffer retribution for making it public. Many instances of racism, misogyny, and homophobia prove that it is perceived jouissance that cultivates violence, bullying, and oppression.

In social discourses of difference, disorientation is not limited to sexuality. To explain how gender and sexuality are constructed psychoanalytically, Verhaeghe (2008) states:

> Firstly, Lacan widens Freud's focus on the individual drive life by understanding it within the primary relationship between the subject and the Other . . . the displacement of the first Other's answer onto the second Other introduces gender differentiation and forms the basis for gender identity. . . . As a result identity will never be complete and will always depend on the Other, understood as both the first and second Others, along with larger sociocultural discourse. For centuries, this discourse has presented a binary division: man versus woman. This dichotomy has recently been abandoned and replaced by a wider one where homosexuality and bisexuality have found a place. . . . The result is that gender identity has become problematic for every subject, which is all the more true once we begin talking about psychopathology. (p. 404)

Gender, like sexuality, also becomes a perverse embodiment when those forced to represent normalcy, power, and the ideal suffer anxiety and confusion over how they must perform their social responsibilities. We know through feminist studies that girls and women may feel responsible for violence against them. Women or girls who dress a certain way are accused of attracting the "wrong attention." In an apt example, Moffett (2006) explains the complex blend of peer and societal pressures men in South Africa experience regarding the need to police feminine subversion (perceived feminine jouissance). She states that many men rape not because they are "tempted" rather society tells them they can (and in some cases, should) do so with impunity. Consequently, rape is a "safe" crime with unlikely legal repercussions and any shame attached to the act will be the victim's burden to bear. Similarly, when a child is bullied for his race or sexual orientation he will feel responsible for the violence inflicted upon him.

## CONCLUSION

A child understands his gender and sexuality through the discourse presented to him by the Other. What he becomes can either align with what the Other desires or be at odds with the Other's desire. In Glen's case, it was at odds with the Other's desire and therefore experienced as traumatic. Education as a second Other can be a place where these dichotomies do not have to be conflictual or opposing. Homosexuality does not have to be a violation of heterosexuality and heterosexuality should not prohibit homosexuality. Unfortunately, for children growing up within these dichotomies psychopathologies develop as a direct result, then difference presents as hostility and conflict in schools. Endorsing false dichotomies within education means, for children like Glen, becoming disoriented and internalizing trauma. Schools that manage difference and diversity as problematic or abnormal create a culture of perversity that oppresses and drives children into sadistic and masochistic positions of bullying.

The question then becomes how do children within perverse systems of education break the cycle. From Retief (2011), Straker (2004, 2011), Suchet (2007), and countless others we see that often times children cannot count on the adults to ensure a safe society. In fact, when we consider Young-Bruehl's (2012) statement that in differing degrees throughout history, children have been oppressed in belief systems that require them to serve the needs and fantasies formally subjected to allegedly inferior women, races, or alien groups that have through civil action obtained a more superior status, education for children appears impossible. If adults cannot deal with lack, how can children find a way to resist introjecting the lack without succumbing to disavowal as a defense mechanism and suffering the melancholia that comes from feelings of guilt and shame? Consequently, how can we cultivate social justice within perverse systems?

Our positions as witnesses underpin our ego-identifications—with victim or bully—in social justice matters; this in turn contributes to our self-representations in social narratives. Are we sadist or masochist when we encounter oppression? We introject the social dynamics occurring in the pedagogical environment. "Extractive introjection" is a term Twemlow (2000) uses to describe situations in which the [oppressor] attacker extracts self-representation from the mind of the victim, leaving a feeling of being emptied of thoughts and the capacity to think, and a loss of self.

We are all implicated in oppression. Failing to act perverts pedagogy in the continued cycle of oppression. "Boundary permeability as psycho-physiological state, especially in situations of trauma, results in ever changing, confusing melange of mental contents defying clear delineation" (Twemlow 2000, p. 769).

The confusion returns us to the discourse of impossibility in education and it returns us to an insistent call to glory, to narrative revolt. Through testimonies like Retief's (2011), we witness the possibility of revolt in perverse systems. Fortunately, as he grows into adulthood, free from the perverse boarding school pedagogy, Glen takes up the position of activist and surrounds himself with like-minded youth. The call to glory issues an opportunity to build defenses against oppressive cycles. In my final chapter, I propose a way of allowing for a space in which all learners within an education system are empowered through difference instead of oppressed by it.

## NOTES

1. See R. L. 2013.
2. White privilege, male privilege, and even academic privilege are such examples.

# FIVE

# Mark Mathabane: *Kaffir Boy*

Dad died when I was seventeen. After leaving boarding school I lived at home with my parents whilst attending public school for my A levels. It was difficult adjusting to parental care again after four years of life in boarding school. I do not recall much of the day-to-day activities at home during my A levels. I do not recall conversations or time spent with either of my parents. I know there was plenty, but somehow, it's not accessible to me. After four years in a girls' school, my new co-ed school was difficult to navigate. Co-ed schooling was a culture shock. I was confounded by the relationships between boys and girls and the competitiveness within the sexes. I felt like a voyeur, enjoying the sexual interplays of my peers, always from the periphery; never quite becoming a part of the culture or socializing going on around me. I managed to make some good friends, both girls and boys, and pleasantly found I got along well with my male peers. Everyone seemed more socially confident than I was but I was not the only one to have been thrust into this jungle from boarding school.

My grades were appalling. I failed every test and exam consistently throughout the two years of my A levels. I had no interest in the academic work and found the pedagogy at the school lacking. Teachers seemed apathetic in their work; one economics teacher often turned up drunk and unkempt. This same teacher, once, and to my horror, made inappropriate advances toward me. The other girls at the school said this was common practice, and we were over sixteen so it was not considered a crime. Romances between male teachers and advanced level girls were not uncommon in the school. I hated it.

At the beginning of the second year, my father cornered me as I was leaving my room. He asked why he had not seen my report card for the term. I told him it was probably coming in the mail. I lied to him. I had intercepted the mail the previous week and destroyed the card. I had also been avoiding both my parents since committing this act. I had never lied to either of my parents before but desperation made me explore new horizons of misbehavior. My father responded with concern: "We can't help you if we don't know what's going on. I need to know that you'll be okay." I did not understand what he was talking about, and through my guilt, I could do no more than shrug before running off to a cousin's house to spend the night. I could not face him after that lie.

That was the last time I spoke to my father. He died unexpectedly the following day. The guilt I had experienced from destroying the report card and subsequently lying to him was nothing compared to the deluge of emotion crushing me when I saw his lifeless body just before he was taken away through a haze of flashing lights and sirens.

Following the Christmas and New Year's holiday, the week after he died, I returned to school. I had three more terms to complete at this awful school as it was my last year of secondary schooling. My grades did not improve. At some point, I stopped attending classes altogether. I left home every day, turned up at school, and hung out with my equally demotivated friends. My teachers had no kind words and could not be bothered to ask what was going on with me. I did not tell anyone what had happened over the Christmas break. Only one male friend knew and he tried to be supportive. I was lost and I did not care to find my way.

Sometime during my final term of high school, my mother picked me up from school one afternoon. I normally walked home, as it was not too far. All my siblings had left home for work, further study, or boarding school. It was just me, my mother, and my grandmother who spent her days in the garden. Our mother-daughter relationship was strained, to say the least.

"Tapo this is it. Your final exams are in a few weeks and if you don't pass I don't know what I can do for you. I know it's been difficult without your father." My mother sighed as she spoke. She had obviously been worrying about me. We were sitting in my mother's car by the garage. My grandmother was a few feet away, sitting under her favorite tree, enjoying the shade with our dog, Rover. The three of us, three generations of women, in the same room was rare at that time. It was even rarer that my mother and I sat and talked.

"I know. I'll pass," I responded.

"What do you need from me?" my mother asked in return.

"I have to learn all of it, from first year. I'll get the books." I sighed too. It was time to take responsibility. I did not look at her during this exchange. She did not look at me either. We both stared ahead knowing we needed each other and needed to work together to make it happen. The silence and animosity had dissipated, replaced by a common goal.

The weeks leading up to the exam were like a ceasefire between my mother and me. She would wake me up at 3:00 a.m. with a cup of hot chocolate or milk, and I would sit at the dining room table learning all the work I had neglected for two years. I would study for hours, not even bothering to go to school anymore. I had no notes to refer to so I read the textbooks and filled up several notebooks as I studied. I enjoyed learning this way and discovered how much I had missed during my time at public school. In the quiet hours, I lost myself in learning, taking refuge from my guilt and anger in my studies. In those hours, I fell in love with learning again and nothing seemed cold, distant, or accusatory.

When the results came the following spring, I walked to the school to pick them up. I had not been on the campus in many months. I headed straight for the administration office where several teachers were passing around slips and commenting on students' results. My geography teacher was holding a slip commenting in Ndebele that wonders never cease. He was telling his colleagues that maybe it was a mistake because "*uChimbganda*" was a hopeless case throughout the two years he taught me. He did not see I was in the room. The secretary asked my name. I said, "Chimbganda." My teacher turned around. He asked how I did it. I took the slip from him and left without saying a word in response; and walked home never to set foot on those premises again. I took the results home to my mother. I had passed with B grades. My mother was so relieved and happy. I was, too.

## OPPRESSION AND POSSIBILITIES

In his memoir, *Kaffir Boy*, Mark Mathabane (1986) illustrates the adverse experience that estrangement due to racial oppression can cause a child. Estrangement at a young age can lead to a psychopathology that seeks to compensate for what is lost. Mathabane illustrates the ongoing mental struggle to find answers for a child who seems to encounter more uncertainty and contradictions the further he goes in his pursuit of knowledge. Through schooling, he could experience things beyond his family's limited world, an emotional situation that led to feelings of becoming superior to his father, especially. Like Freud (2006) who articulates the difficulties that education can cause between father and son, Mark found books meant nothing to his father. Throughout his education, his father is antagonistic toward his desire to read and to learn. An embittered man, Mark's father was subject to laws and oppression that rendered him ineffectual and unable to perform his parenting duties. In his preface, Mathabane (1986) gives us a clear indication of the difficult and impossible relationship he and the rest of the family endured with his father stating:

> They turned my father by repeatedly arresting him and denying him the right to earn a living in a way that gave him dignity into such a bitter man that, as he fiercely but in vain resisted the emasculation, he hurt those he loved the most. (p. X)

Even when his father gradually begins to see the benefits of his son's passion for books, there is an animosity, a begrudging stalemate between father and son.

This chapter uncovers the possibilities education offers a child with an obsessional psychopathology. Through pedagogy, Mark begins to find the answers he is looking for—answers that can help him navigate the treacherous life of apartheid. Not all his learning is fulfilling, but he certainly begins to find within the turmoil of difference and oppression a way to break free of racist constraints. As he breaks free, Mark takes up the mantle of freedom. He becomes a young man able to foresee a brighter future despite the bleak life the Other has enforced onto him. In his resistance of oppression, Mark becomes a contradiction to his father.

My focus on the father-son relationship in comparison to the mother-son relationship is not to privilege one over the other, but rather I seek to show that what matters most in a child in terms of institutionalized education and pedagogy is the school's honoring of the parental wish. The parental wish issues as a promise to the child who seeks something in which he can ground himself. Whether it's his father or mother who utters the wish, if the parent turns to education for the son's future, education should take the place of the law that speaks—the paternal metaphor. Although I use masculine (father, paternal) versus feminine (mother, maternal) language, ultimately what Mark's father represents (oppression) and what his mother represents (possibilities) gains meaning through his schooling. I do not generalize the meaning of these terms but highlight, in the case study, the role Mark Mathabane's father took in his education. When the law, also referred to by Lacan as *the-name-of-the-father* becomes the oppressor the child looks elsewhere for a law that can bring him into the symbolic.

An important aspect in Mathabane's (1986) account is the integrative quality of education that brings the primary and secondary socialization into perspective. With the incorporation of both, the child finds his desired place in the world. We see in *Kaffir Boy* the crucial need for educational systems that honor the family, perceived or rendered ineffectual by society, as the primary socializer of the child. Mark's teachers used corporal punishment, they were harsh and punitive, however their message was the same message his mother gave to him. He could be anything he desired and education was the key. Mark's world, although confused by oppression, was made livable through pedagogy and collaboration.

Mark's primary socialization was affected by the ongoing brutalization of his family and community by racist police. At a young age, he learns both his father and mother are subject to laws that rendered them ineffectual through the process of castration. Neither of his parents subsists at the level of the law, a situation necessary to reach an Oedipal resolution; in fact, they seem to be subject to a much greater authority than his young mind can comprehend. Furthermore, his parents can neither protect him nor prevent the psychic rupture and horror that resulted from the continual oppression.

> "What's a pass, Mama?" I knew vaguely what a pass was, but not its reality.
>
> It's an important book that we black people must have in order always, and carry with us at all times." She took out hers and showed it to me. I remembered seeing the book; in fact, I remembered seeing it many times; and yet, each time I saw it, it appeared dreadfully new. There was something about it which made me fearful, helpless. But I could not figure out what about it made me feel that way. It seemed a mere book. Yet it was, I was to later find out, the black man's passport to existence. (Mathabane 1986, p. 36)

Much like Lacan's metaphoric papers (Fink 1995), the papers Bantu people were forced to carry at all times represented a relationship with the law. The Bantu pass was used often and oppressively to police the movements and freedoms of black people in South Africa. The papers were not easy to obtain, making it extremely hard for Bantu people to abide by this edict. Any form of official document meant to signify citizenship by birth or otherwise was difficult for black people to obtain. Mathabane (1986) recalls the endurance of Mark's mother as she tried to get him a birth certificate so he could enroll for school. Her efforts were undermined by a system meant to withhold the papers the government valued more than the people.

Extensions of the arm of oppression, the papers were an instrument for the apartheid government to dehumanize Bantu people. To leave the Bantu reservations, Bantu people needed papers; to work, they needed papers; to walk down any street outside or inside of their shanty townships, they needed papers. The Bantu had become aliens in their own land, kept away not only by physical boundaries but also by the power and authority these papers represented. Eriksen (2011) states:

> The work amounting to making insecure situations secure takes many shapes. Imperialist powers may try to reshape their new lands to make them less threatening different, or they erect physical boundaries against the aliens, as the architects of apartheid did in South Africa. (p. 289)

These papers rendered them subjects not citizens of South Africa. The difference, as Rousseau (2003) points out, is that citizens share in the sovereign power, while subjects are under the laws of the State. The Sovereign, according to Rousseau, is inalienable from the State, while the subject has no guarantees by virtue of being non-members. The Sovereign in fact requires from subjects a reassurance of fidelity and submission as it threatens the subject with castration. The Bantu people were expected to comply with every demand even if unreasonable. In addition, Rousseau observes, "The strongest is never strong enough to be always the master, unless he transforms strength into right, and obedience into duty. Hence the right of the strongest, which, though to all seeming meant ironically, is really laid down as a fundamental principle" (pp. 3–4). Rousseau further argues that rights are created by force and every force that is greater than the first succeeds to its right. He states, "As soon as it is possible to disobey with impunity, disobedience is legitimate; and, the strongest being always in the right, the only thing that matters is to act so as to become the strongest" (p. 4). The law of apartheid was maintained by the physical separation of subjects from citizens through violence and oppression.

The oppression of the Bantu through the withholding and demanding of papers was in all intents and purposes, a mechanism for social stratification. Not complying with the demands was viewed as a threat to the social order white South Africa had created. Blacks were treated punitively and contained within boundaries that disabled them from working and supporting their families. Impunity is reserved for citizens, whom Rousseau (2003) points out are unable to transgress against the Sovereign as the members cannot have any interest contrary to the State (p. 11). Any violation to the law of the Sovereign is perceived to come from outsiders, which is why the Bantu were contained in shanties; and in discourses of alienation and transgression of State. Through oppression, the colonialists created rights and laws maintained by mechanisms of power and authority granted only to white citizens. By right, a citizen can transgress legitimately and therefore, come out as justified or legalized. The subject, however, exists in a position of transgression and criminalization. The Bantu were prohibited from stepping outside the boundaries and hierarchies created to protect the citizens of apartheid South Africa. At the beginning of his memoir, Mathabane (1986) illustrates the rungs of stratification that were commonplace in the cities and towns of South Africa as he describes the sections of his township Alexandra, just outside Johannesburg. Within the township, sections are divided by race, with black people living in the poorest parts, and the Indians, the cream of Alexandra's quarantined society, living in the commercial areas of Alexandra. Mathabane states that in South Africa black people were "considered and treated as the dregs of society, aliens in the land of their birth. Such labelling and treatment made them an angry and embittered lot" (p. 4).

Mark's narrative reveals a perpetual struggle to fulfill what was lost due to the abrasive qualities of social difference. The laws of apartheid forbade blackness to exist outside of its oppression. Consequently, Mark navigates his existence with a hungry psychopathology. He is constantly obsessing about the law according to his father, according to his community, and according to the nation of South Africa. He uses his mother's voice to guide him toward fulfilling his desire. He views the world through calculations of jouissance, comparing the lives of his more affluent black neighbors, and of those who seem to have a privileged relationship with the nation—white people. Mark sees something in the lives of white people that is fulfilling in a way he has not witnessed among his own people. Given the opportunity, he spends increasingly more time outside of his township seeking the signifier and estranged from the black community.

## ESTRANGEMENT IN PRIMARY SOCIALIZATION

At the age of forty-eight, Freud (2006) has a specific occurrence, a mental sensation (Federn 1953) at the Acropolis. This experience, which he calls *estrangement,* he explains to his friend, is attributed to feelings of guilt of "having come such a long way; there is something involved in it that is wrong, something that has for a long time been forbidden" (p. 76). Through Freud's explanation, we see that estrangement is a complex process of ego feelings, and as Federn (1953) explains:

> There exists estrangement, not only in regard to the external world, but also in regard to many mental processes, including: all cognitive processes such as remembering, thinking, reasoning, and judging; affective attitudes such as hoping, fearing, wishing, worrying, grieving; and thought processes which influence the imagined or real external world, such as deciding, beginning, terminating, commanding and obeying. (p. 207)

While there are external, relational phenomena of estrangement, the mental sensation, as Freud experienced it, connects to ego experiences in the developing child. It is for this reason that Freud concludes that this psychoanalytic phenomenon he experienced, was due to a realization that he was superior to his father—that being the desire he tried to resist—the desire to outdo his father. Freud's experience at the Acropolis might have been his ultimate defining moment. His "arrival" was not simply to the Acropolis, but he had arrived at that place every son desires, a place that signifies becoming the proverbial phallus. Nevertheless, he is filled with feelings of guilt because to arrive he had to outdo his father, displace him, and take the phallic position. Through this experience, Freud could understand the unconscious problem of the child's desire to become the father. His initial resistance to making the trip, which he describes quite intently upon visiting the Acropolis, is a regressive anxiety that indicates repressed desire. Anxiety is a very important element of estrangement as it relates to repressed desires to outdo the father and thereby destroy him. In Lacan's (1987) words "Anxiety is for us witness to an essential breach" (p. 84)

Federn (1953) clarifies, "In the estrangement of the inner world, which is a form of depersonalization, the patient no longer senses his affects as connected with his ego" (p. 310). Congruently, Freud confesses:

> It has to do with criticism of our father in childhood, with the undervaluation that had replaced that overvaluation of his character which had prevailed in early childhood. It seems as though the essential aspect of success lies in getting further than one's father, as though wishing to outdo one's father were forbidden. (p. 76)

In admitting that his estrangement came from guilt at having outdone his father, Freud is so bold as to use the term "the superiority of sons" (Freud p. 76). He felt guilty, not because he had worked hard and could now afford to enjoy life, but because his father could not even comprehend or value the same standards of accomplishment. The guilt came with feelings and thoughts of superiority, which in turn triggered a castration anxiety. Federn (1953) states "in every affective reaction there is also a stronger ego feeling which cathects more intensely that ego boundary with which we apprehend the object in question, on which the stimulus from the object impinges" (p. 285). The ego feeling of superiority counteracted with the terror and anxiety of castration, follows feelings of guilt at having "dethroned" the father, which is estrangement.

Mark's early estrangement from his father, and from blackness, leaves him seeking to assuage the feelings of superiority, guilt, and anxiety associated with the phenomenon. In Seminar IX, Lacan (2011) explains that paternal lack is at the root of pathology. He states that the Oedipus complex could be quite well constituted even when the father was not present. Whether a father is weak, submissive, battered, castrated by the wife, or whether he is sick, blind, bankrupt, or anything else, Lacan insists that the question of paternal lack is not easily answered (p. 7). Mark's knowledge of his father's lack was paradoxical and indeed complicated. He was a young boy searching for answers but his father could not offer anything but oppression because that is all his father could comprehend within his experience.

The function of the father in the family is one who is normative, according to Lacan (2011). Seeing strife and weakness reflected in his father should have made the oppressed way of life normative for Mark, but he actively resisted being anything like his father. The father must maintain an oedipal normalizing position within the family relative to the Subject's own oedipal position. Paternal lack, therefore, is about oedipal positioning, a very important aspect of the father-child relationship.

## PATERNAL LACK

Expressing sentiments we can identify in Mathabane's narrative, Mucina (2013) wrote a heartfelt and forgiving letter to his African father who had raised him during Zimbabwe's colonization. Mucina's letter exposes the fragmentation of father-child relationships under the scourge of white rule. Fathers, themselves infantilized in many ways by colonialism, could do little to raise their children with pride and dignity. Blackness, as a submissive position was a performance, a learned state of being that was instilled as early as possible to ensure safety and survival. For many Bantu children, growing up in colonized territories, watching their fathers constantly emasculated, resulted in traumatic and difficult relationships that were marred with fear, guilt, and the son's estrangement. If we consider the state of affairs in the past and present, highlighted by Coates (2015), historically, a black man trying to rise above his station was punished for insubordination. Fathers had to teach their sons to keep their heads down, not to tangle with the police or resist the oppression because it could be fatal. Even today, black men have no choice but to raise their sons in relation to the law that oppresses them. In so doing, they admit their inferiority to young men who are determined to be superior not because they despise their fathers but because they fear becoming what they have witnessed their fathers become. Black men repeat this cycle, from father to son, generation after generation, because a black man must be black in relation to the white man (Fanon 1967).

Paternal lack is best understood as a psychic rendering rather than a masculine condition, meaning it accosts at the level of the unconscious rather than in any physical form. Paternal lack is at the root of the disavowal of one's roots.

> It is necessary to have the name of the father, but it is also necessary to know how to use it, and it is from this, it is on that that the fate and the outcome of the whole affair may depend to a large extent. (Lacan, Seminar VIII, p. 13)

Mucina's testimonial to this phenomenon helps us understand Mark and his father's relationship. Mucina begins by outlining a deep-seated resentment he felt for his father, that kept him at a distance and later spurred him home, after many years abroad, to seek retribution. Upon arriving in Zimbabwe in 2003, he realizes that his father, despite Zimbabwe's independence, never got over his castration by the white man.

Like Mathabane (1986), Mucina (2013) recalls the instigation of his estrangement at the early age of five. He attempts to work through his complex feelings for and toward his father, writing, "You had taught me to hide whenever I saw a White person and, from your teachings, I understood that they posed a danger to our survival" (p. 326). Fear turned Mucina's father from a loving man who wanted what was best for his son to a man who could not reconcile his own feelings of hatred and fear with self-identity. Mucina recalls his father teaching him to speak Bantu languages as a matter of identity and pride. He recalls his father going hungry so he could eat; he recalls his father begging and scrounging for food. He recalls his father's ongoing castration (Moten 2003) at the hand of colonial law: "As you tried to navigate the colonial system at its lowest level, I imagine you felt inadequate as your two children died due to malnutrition and poverty" (Mucina 2013, p. 328).

Mucina (2013) also attempts to articulate the moment he realized he had outdone his father. His father was illiterate and Mucina's accomplishment of learning just three letters of the alphabet on the first day of his schooling was all it took to outdo his father (p. 332). The ensuing beating for challenging his father's authority was enough to remind him of his father's physical dominance but the psychic estrangement had already occurred. A clear pattern emerges as father and son engage in an ongoing power struggle, ultimately leading to the irreparable breakdown of their relationship. He writes:

> Why I had to always get under your skin I cannot adequately explain but I think it had something to do with my wanting power. Sadly, because of your low parenting skills all my provocation led to greater degrees of violence as you too wanted power. We were locked in the cycle of violence. (p. 366)

Colonialism and oppression negated the role of many black fathers in Africa and other parts of the world (Connor and White 2011). Unfortunately, the power struggle between father and son could never be properly or normally resolved because of the colonial strain put upon it. Colonialism left a legacy of estranged sons and castrated fathers struggling to find common ground. Similarly, as Mark's narrative proceeds, it is clear to see that the rupture that occurred on the night of his father's castration left a deep and abiding need for answers, precisely to one question: What is the law?

## THE AETIOLOGY OF OBSESSIONAL NEUROSIS

The harrowing account provided by Mathabane (1986) of the night his father's lack was exposed sheds light on the overreaching arm of oppression. Children may not be the direct targets but the actions of racist authorities ultimately destroy the very foundations of family life and subsequently affect the socialization of children. A gang of police officers came around his neighborhood, terrorizing the inhabitants of the squalid shelters of Alexandra Township. Mark's parents caught in the confusion of neighbors running and screaming in futile efforts to avoid the raid, were unable to escape the harassment of the racist police. He describes the scene that unfolded before him when the police tore through their meager shelter demanding his parents produce their passes:

> My father became speechless. He parted his parched lips and tried to say something, but no sound came. He lowered his bony head and buried it in the palms of gnarled hands; and at that moment he seemed to age a thousand years, a pitiful sight. The policeman playfully prod-

> ded my father's penis with a truncheon. I gasped with horror. . . . My father forced a fake smile. It was not a spontaneous smile—my father never smiled. It was a begging smile, a passive acceptance of the policemen's authority. After smiling my father again dropped his eyes to the floor. He seemed uncharacteristically powerless and contrite, a far cry from the tough, resolute, and absolute ruler of the house I knew him to be, the father whose words were law. I felt sorry for him. (p. 22)

In witnessing the castration of his father, Mark experiences a range of emotions—horror, pity, and superiority—feelings Freud posited in the oedipal theory were often directed toward the mother upon the realization that she does not possess the phallus. When the child experiences these emotions toward his mother, the father becomes the phallic symbol for the child to emulate. In Mark's case, both mother and father were exposed as lacking the phallus.

A physically present father who cannot bring his child into the Symbolic according to Lacan might as well be gone and absent entirely; for "What is essential is that the subject, from somewhere or other, should have acquired the dimension of the name of the father" (Lacan, Seminar VIII, p. 13). The name of the father gives the child access into the Symbolic. When his father was exposed as lacking in his capacity to stand as phallic symbol, Mark was old enough to know to pity the destruction of his father by the law. He had assumed his father was the law and within the Oedipal context, this occasion resulted in estrangement. His father became something he refused to identify with or desire to emulate. It is at this point that Mark's pathology begins to form. Mathabane (1986) elucidates on the boy's reaction to what he witnessed done to his father. Mark sees his father as an alien, strange to him and his instinct is to deny the tears that threaten to make him like his father. Instead, Mark fills with rage beyond his comprehension but branded into his being until his death (pp. 22–23). Unlike his father, Mark refuses to bow to the authority of the police officers who speak with the authority of the apartheid law. Mark's feelings of hate and anger were powerful affects for a child so young because although children feel hate from a young age it is often of an ambivalent nature as they go through their oedipal phases. The nature of Mark's hate was different. He confesses this hate and anger were beyond his comprehension. We might think of his feelings at the level of the unconscious as symptomatic of a neurotic pathology.

In keeping with Freud's (1924) theory of the Oedipus complex, we surmise that this deep-seated hatred and anger were because his father had suffered social castration, which meant Mark would never have a chance to resolve his unconscious rivalry with his father. When a child witnesses his father groveling, when initially he thought his father signified the law, there is a moment of psychic rupture. Any resolution that would bring the child from the Imaginary into the Symbolic becomes impossible. Lacan (2011) states there must be a successful resolution that brings the child into the Symbolic, therefore the psychic trauma Mark experienced was the onset of a psychopathology that would lead him to question everything and everyone including himself. He lost any recourse for the Symbolic as the paternal metaphor he had identified before that night was destroyed right in front of him. His father's lack exposed through a careless act of oppression was a stark lesson on the power of the law. Lacan's (2011) words affirm this sad state of affairs:

> You should understand the importance of the lack of the particular signifier that I have just spoken to you about, which is the name of the father in so far precisely as it grounds as such the fact that there is law, namely the articulation of the signifier in a certain order; the Oedipus complex, or the oedipal law, or the law of the prohibition of the mother, for example the signifier which signifies that within this signifier, the signifier exists. (Lacan, Seminar VIII, p. 5)

Mark was destitute without the name of the father and the law it signifies to ground him. Instinctively, he decides he would not beg or plead, as it had not helped his now ineffectual father. What hope did he have without a paternal metaphor? His hatred for the police officers who had so carelessly destroyed the fabric of his still developing psyche was a reaction to losing both the father he had thought he knew and the law his father represented. "While hysteria is associated with a surplus of unpleasure and trauma," according to Verhaeghe (2008), "the opposite is true for obsessional neurosis: the supposition is that there was an excess of pleasure that in itself was experienced as traumatic" (p. 384). The excess of pleasure in dethroning the father is also traumatic because with the father's destruction comes a punitive eviction from the Symbolic. The cost of estrangement at such a young age is the loss of the security the Symbolic provides.

Following the genesis of his estrangement, Mark developed obsessional neurosis, which Bracher (1994) outlines as a pathological condition marked with compulsions and obsessions aimed at fulfilling the master signifier's role, and the obsessional attempts to calculate jouissance or in other words, pass into the signifier. In addition, according to Bracher, all the obsessional's energy is devoted to filling everything with the phallic master signifier and avoiding the Real. Accordingly, per Arena et al. (Bracher 1994):

> What is paradoxical is that, in order to support this position of mastery, he lives condemned to carry on his back the weight of a guilt that is not his own, and to pay with forced labour a debt that is no-one's. (p. 149)

Arena et al.'s statement sheds light on the futility of a child attempting to be his own master signifier. The master signifier's role is to bring the child into the Symbolic and Mark's desire is to enter the Symbolic. As he continually seeks, he becomes a scholar of the world surrounding him.

He studies various artifacts and cultural symbols, critiques religion and other customary rituals, constantly seeking a way to the Symbolic system of neat and orderly socialization that can correct the damage done by the rupture and destruction he witnessed repeatedly at the hands of the oppressive government. In Mark's memoir, we encounter a child who experiences paternal lack and strives to compensate for it through his education. According to Verhaeghe, the obsessional says, "I must and will always succeed, either for or counter to the Other" (p. 384) and "what the obsessional experiences as success is always a surplus, causing anxiety and guilt (p. 387).

## THE OBSESSIONAL'S SYMPTOM

The obsessional's symptom presents as a question: What is the law? He insists on not only identifying the law but also inhabiting it as a defense. In his exploration of the township, the world beyond it and education, Mark persistently asks, what is the law? He learns early to watch, to analyze, to be critical of everything pertaining to his race, his family, and the law; quickly or at least subversively resisting anything that hinders a privileged relationship with the law. Mathabane (1986) writes about the effect his father's repeated arrests had on Mark and the rest of the family. Mark gained insight into the experience of Bantu men. The boy realized that the world he inhabited was designed to disadvantage him; it was designed to keep him unstable and insecure. Mathabane writes: "Knowing that, my heart sank, and I began to wonder whether life—black life—was really worth living. But what other life was there to live?" (1986, p. 100).

His father had his own wisdom, which he tried to confer to Mark, but the irreparable damage of his castration made anything he attempted to teach his son seem ineffectual. Mathabane (1986) confesses that his father's beliefs about his free will and destiny made little sense to him. He was skeptical of some group of ancestors somewhere controlling his life (p. 102). Mark could see only lack in his father's teachings. He could not see how these beliefs, values, and rituals could save him from the black man's fate he had witnessed. His father's teachings instinctively stirred resistance within him. Driven to rectify and atone for what had happened to his father, Mark simultaneously resisted and fought any element of lack that might entrap him. Verhaeghe (2004) explains that for an obsessional the Other's authority is ridiculed as unable to provide the necessary strict system of rules that can take care of desire in a neat and orderly fashion.

A child is supposed to learn about his values and beliefs from his family, primary socialization. However, as a child, Mark's critique of his father's pedagogy was guided by the obsessional question. Mark questioned his father's relationship with the law; if what his father constituted could not save him from utter humiliation, how could it be the law? Tribal beliefs and values clearly had no authority over what happened to his father and therefore they would not save him or any of his family. There had to be something else. Mark searched through interactions with other people in the township and somehow it made no sense to him. The modern non-traditional families seemed to be faring better than Mark's family and his father's ancestors. He participated recalcitrantly, afraid his father would beat him if he opposed him. Eventually, Mark begins to understand that there is more to life than his father's severe and embittered pedagogy. Mark begins to recognize a similar searching for the law outside of their family and home in his mother.

After her husband was arrested, Mark's mother had to provide for her children in a manner that was both deeming and dangerous. She would take her children to garbage dumps to forage through the refuse in search of food and items they could peddle. Her husband was always in the precarious position of subject (Rousseau 2003), with no rights in South Africa, and she made up for his absence, physical and paternal, by leading her children to search for the law outside of their home. She risked her husband's wrath and recrimination if it could give her children the law. Mark's mother played the significant role of providing hope, where her husband represented oppression. Mark's mother would have long conversations with her husband, trying to persuade him to let go of the ancestors and embrace Christianity. The discord between his parents convinced Mark he was right to keep questioning his father's pedagogy.

Always in search of the law, Mark considered what he observed of Christianity. In particular, he analyzed the whiteness in Christianity and juxtaposed it to the blackness he had experienced in the township. For both Mark and his mother, Christianity was not about faith or a belief in the spiritual. They were interested in the law it signified. Mathabane's (1986) analysis of two portraits, one depicting heaven and God, the other, hell and the Devil. In one portrait God is shown as a blue-eyed white man flanked by white saints and white angels in a serene environment. The latter portrait featured a naked black man distorted to resemble the Devil, complete with a tail, horns, writhing vipers, wild red eyes, and a wide mouth spewing flames and smoke. In the scene, the devil is stabbing pathetic black people with a fork and a menacing fire appears to be their outcome (p. 61).

In the previous chapter, I discussed whiteness as master signifier; now through his searching, I demonstrate that Mark could identify the law that whiteness signified. His understanding of it filled him with apprehension as he began to understand in his obsessional way the law of apartheid. Like Bev in chapter 3, Mark developed a deep-seated fear of white people. Like Bev, much of his understanding of difference between black people and white people was illustrated through the movies he watched. Mark also watched westerns and, like Bev, he saw the Indian as evil and the white as perfect and pure. Mathabane (1986) writes:

> Maybe, I repeatedly told myself, white people have placed these restrictions on the movement of black people in the white world because they did not want them to unwittingly wander into an Indian village or into a gladiator arena or into a cowboy shootout, and end up getting killed. (p. 54)

The question of the law, when answered, constitutes a possibility. For the obsessional, the possibility represents a way into the Symbolic. Mark thought the apartheid law was saving him. Unfortunately, the apartheid law was keeping him in the Imaginary where his obsessional questioning fed on fantasies and facts that could not answer his question. He was stuck, subject to a law based on whiteness, an empty but oppressive signifier. As long as the law was constituted in this oppressive master signifier, blackness, and by extension, Mark was "essentially flimsy or ephemeral . . . more heard than seen" (Retief 2011 p. 24); an object for those who were privileged by the apartheid law. Mark needed a more fulfilling encounter with the law that signified freedom, rather than oppression. Again, offering hope, his mother directs him toward education. She desires for him access to a master signifier that empowers rather than oppresses. Ultimately, education offers a way into the Symbolic. His mother tells him educational attainment will allow him to be anything he desires.

## EDUCATION AS THE PATERNAL METAPHOR (FOR THE OBSESSIONAL NEUROTIC)

> "Why do you want me to go to school, Mama?" I asked, hoping that she might, somehow, clear up some of the confusion that was building in my mind.
>
> "I want you to have a future, child," my mother said. "And, contrary to what your father says, school is the only means to a future. I don't want you growing up to be like your father." (Mathabane 1986, p. 133)

Mark's mother's word had a profound effect on him. Mathabane (1986) describes it as shattering all his defenses. His mother was shepherding him toward a resolution and instinctively he let go of the defense that might have prevented him from gaining an education.

Just as we witness Mark's obsessional drive, his mother saw the same hunger in her son. Juxtaposed to her husband's bitter and violent existence, Mark's mother sets out to rescue her son from the Imaginary hell that blackness occupies. Already estranged from his father, Mark will do anything to safeguard his position of resistance, and education gives the son the ability to outdo his father.

Standing between Mark and his father is the discourse of the Subject and the law of the Other. Mark's entire narrative in *Kaffir Boy* is about getting the papers; not the ones that the apartheid government demands and his father spent a lifetime struggling to obtain. Rather, the papers education confers, papers that even the white man cannot withhold, are psychic. Mark's mother tells him how different things might be if he goes to school, not only for him but for the entire family. Unlike her father's beliefs, his mother's beliefs make more sense. Mathabane (1986) shares:

> I believe that an education is the key you need to open up a new world and a new life for yourself, a world and life different from that of either your father's or mine. It is the only key that can do that, and only those who seek it earnestly and perseveringly will get anywhere in the white man's world. Education will open doors where none seem to exist. It'll make people talk to you, listen to you, and help you; people who otherwise wouldn't bother. It will make you soar, like a bird lifting up into the endless blue sky, and leave poverty, hunger and suffering behind. It'll teach you to learn to embrace what's good and shun what's bad and evil. Above all, it'll make you a somebody in this world. It'll make you grow up to be a good and proud person. That's why I want you to go to school, child so that education can do all that, and more, for you. (p. 134)

Mathabane testifies to the enormity of his mother's trust in education for Mark. The night Mark made the decision to pursue an education, he decided to stand opposed to his father. Though his mother was equally as illiterate as his father, she was determined to guide her son toward the knowledge he had been seeking obsessively. Unlike Mark's father, his mother did not care that her son would out do her, she did not care that he would know and experience things beyond her understanding. She had never been a symbol of power or law in her son's eyes. That gave her an advantage that her husband as a man could not possess. Her lack was her privilege. Mark's father's lack was his blindfold.

Education became the signifier for freedom for Mark. As he continued in school, often withstanding the worst of poverty, he became one of the brightest students in the Bantu school in Alexandra Township. He also, through education, identified other ways to excel. He developed an interest in tennis that took him into new spheres of interactions with white people. He began to access a world where papers were more easily handed to him, often with a level of respect he could never have understood without his education. However, more importantly, education gave him a different understanding of his blackness.

From his narrative, it is easy to conclude that the position education had taken in the Mathabane family was likely taking place in many other Bantu households across South Africa. It was the young people and youth in schools who were protesting the castration of blackness. Their fathers and elders had already been rendered ineffectual through systematic racism and oppressive violence but they were seeing things differently, even in their poor schools, separated from white society, young people in schools were envisioning freedom through pedagogy.

Mathabane (1986) writes about a period of conflict and unrest as riots break out and Alexandra is aflame with cries for freedom. He joins the hundreds of youth rallying against the government seeking to force the Bantu schools to teach everything in Afrikaans. According to Ndimande (2013), the language issue became a very critical concern for black students who perceived Afrikaans to be the language of the oppressor. He explains that, "Protest against this language was inevitable; it started in sporadic forms in the early 1970s, and culminated into the notable June 16, 1976, when black students burned down schools and demanded the abolition of Afrikaans as a mandatory language of instruction" (p. 24). When it finally happens, "all the hate, bitterness, frustration and anger that had crystallized into a powder keg in the minds of black students waiting for a single igniting spark, found that spark" (Mathabane 1986, p. 259).

As a youth, Mark becomes an activist against the apartheid law with other young people from his school. During a discussion with a staff member at his school Mark declares:

> "Even if I were to become the richest man in Alexandra, sir," I said with feeling, "I could never be happy without my freedom. The books I've read have taught me different ways of life, about places where I can be free to think and feel the way I want, instead of the way apartheid wants. . . . My mind is changing, sir, I can feel it changing every day. The books I'm reading are changing the way I see the world, life, reality. I'm beginning to feel like a stranger in my own country." (Mathabane, 1986, p. 254)

Empty signifiers render a child a stranger to his own country. His time at school had begun to provide an answer to his question. He had discovered the source of meaning and the way into the Symbolic. The government's decision to teach everything in Afrikaans was a threat to take away what he had finally identified as his paternal metaphor. After searching for so long, at the cost of his relationship with his father, watching his mother beaten for encouraging him, and suffering a few beatings himself, he channeled his hatred and anger into preserving the paternal metaphor. His experience as a child, witnessing his father's humiliation, made him fight for the paternal metaphor. Freedom for him was never having to face the same castration he had witnessed destroy his father. Freedom was the papers he needed and the papers education had promised. To successfully resolve one's Oedipus complex is to come away with the papers:

> When the time comes, if things go well, if the little pigs do not eat him up, at the moment of puberty, he has his penis all ready with his certifi-

> cates: 'Daddy is the one who has conferred it on me at the right time.' (Lacan 2011, Seminar IX, p. 11)

Children in oppressive territories do not have the privilege of receiving their papers from their fathers. They find themselves at conflict with their fathers who act out of fear and bitterness for having been denied the capacity to confer the papers to their sons. They are fortunate if they can access education and an opportunity to find images and facts that reflect possibilities of freedom from oppression. More importantly, if the pedagogy available to them can make them into citizens rather than subjects of their countries.

## CONCLUSION

To the South African government, Mark was a Bantu child destined to live the life of a black person in a segregated and oppressive society. Mark grew up learning the signification of his blackness from an oft-castrated father who was bitter, violent, and without hope. His mother's provision of an alternative paternal metaphor was a way out of this cycle. Mark could imagine a different blackness and resist the one ascribed to him by his oppressors. Blackness came to mean new things, new power, and new identity. For Mark and thousands of young people reimagining their identity through education, blackness was something worth fighting for (Patterson 2010). Education was an intervention their fathers had been denied and viewed as intrusion. Even for fathers like Mucina's (2013), who wanted their children to be educated, there was an underlying fear that they would lose their sons, and worse still, their sons would become part of the system constantly castrating them.

Freedom is education's promise for many, especially immigrant and racialized children whose parents direct them toward education to cover the lack created by colonialism and oppression. Mark held on to the hope that his mother had presented to him. Even as an uneducated woman, she had a sense that if her son could get an education, he would have a better life. Mark therefore, immersed himself into the promise of education. This is a common rhetoric in many racialized family scripts. For impoverished and marginalized families, education promises more to their children than the children of historically privileged families do. Apart from the economic and social advances created through education, there is an underlying freedom from the threat of castration; a promise to someday hold the papers that curtail the vicious cycle of subjugation and oppression.

For Bantu people in South Africa, in Moten`s (2003) words:

> Black castration is not just to be seen as prospective figure and symbolic inability, since for the Black tradition, castration is not just phantas-

> matic possibility or introjection based on fleeting glance at that which is read as sexual difference, but it is also the proper name of an oft-repeated literal, historical, material event. (p. 177)

As previously indicated, neurotic racialization comes through this continued act of castration, which means for racialized children education carries a different signification. Education is freedom from this repetitive event and on-going trauma. In Mark's experience, the demands of apartheid did not abate or change, but he changed. Through his schooling and search for knowledge, he found a new understanding in the same system. Learning, not only to read and write but also to think of himself in his own terms, allowed him to forge a new direction for himself and his family. Even his father benefited from the change in his son. It was perhaps the first time anyone in that family had experienced any type of freedom.

Education today promises social freedom to many socially marginalized people, particularly those whose signifiers has been stifled through historically traumatic discourses of race, class, sexuality, citizenship, and gender, among others. Schugurensky (2007), in a paper prepared for the Diversity in Education Parents' Forum, makes some poignant observations on the plight of immigrant children and their families in the Ontario education system. He points out that many immigrants who come to Canada do so with great sacrifice and suffer poverty, marginalization, and discrimination hoping their children will have a better life by succeeding through the educational system. The statistics Schugurensky offers, however, paint a dire picture and highlight the magnitude of the problem of education in Toronto for these families. He states within the Toronto District School Board (TDSB) students living in low-income neighborhoods are less likely to complete school, and they are largely from ethnocultural groups like Portuguese students who have a dropout rate of 42.5 percent; Spanish 39.1 percent; Somali 36.7 percent; and Black Caribbean students 40 percent. Schugurensky questions the educational system on these dropout rates and makes another key observation that it is not just language barriers as many of these people speak English as a first language. He states that while some factors are beyond the scope of the school system itself, there are institutional factors ranging from educational policies and programs to the curriculum, to fundraising practices and teacher-student interactions, and these are things the educational system can modify. Also apparent in this problematic is the fact that wealthier students have more cultural capital and schools tend to discriminate against those students who do not.

Of utmost relevance to this discussion is what Schugurensky (2007) refers to as a double dynamic currently happening in Toronto pointing out that the increased pace of gentrification is generating ghettos of the poor and ghettos of the rich, which are compounded by the increased reliance of school programs and activities on fundraising. He believes this dynamic creates a type of privatization clashing against the equalization of education. Mathabane's testimony gives us cause for hope even when presented with such dire statistics and child poverty. The paternal metaphor that is education confers a different phallic signification. It allows for a different type of identification especially for those caught in social systems that render them inferior. Growing up in apartheid South Africa as a black child meant growing up continually encountering images and impressions of inferiority and baseness. From a young age, Mark witnessed these events and saw these images. From a young age, he resisted the castration that the apartheid system repeatedly meted out to every black person he encountered. Through education, the law that signified his desire, and the desire of many black youth, brought him into the Symbolic. Through pedagogy, Mark understood that freedom was the ability to think and feel the way he desired, as a citizen, not as subject, forced to seek the backdoor by the apartheid government.

# SIX

# Privileged Space

## *A Psychoanalytic Paradigm for Pedagogy*

Mr. Hlatshwayo died some time ago. He committed suicide. Somehow, it was a fitting death. There was something always sad and tortured about him. It might have been his reason for drinking, too. Maybe the Ndebele and Shona tribal conflicts affected him in some way or another. I can only speculate but he was the most influential teacher I had growing up. I have realized that now.

My friend reminds me Mr. Hlatshwayo was brutal with corporal punishment. I do not remember that. I do remember my knuckles swollen with little beads of blood that looked like rubies after being hit with the sharp end of a plastic ruler, I just do not remember which teacher did that. I think that is how I developed a low pain threshold. I find my anticipation of any pain quite overwhelming; I avoid it at any cost. This came from the long moments waiting for the ruler to finally make contact. When it did, it was always jarring as if unexpected. Now I have no tolerance when waiting for anything that might be painful or produce little beads of blood, including medical needles. I think if I did not have to wait, I would have a better threshold. Our teachers hit us hard and mercilessly in primary school. It was something inherited from the British school system. When I first enrolled at my primary school, our headmaster was a white man, Mr. Southey. He was much loved and respected—or was it feared? Mr. Southey had a well-known collection of canes for students but by the time he stepped in several teachers would have given their share of discipline. Mr. Southey was replaced by Miss Phiri, who in the way of misogyny was labeled all manner of things because people could not understand how this young Ndebele woman had succeeded in gaining such a lucrative position. My school was one of the "A" schools in the city and had a great reputation. She was deemed unqualified and must have "earned" the position through sexual favors.

"A" schools were a guarantee into any secondary school (if parents could afford the fees), were often well represented in regional and national academic and sporting competitions, and produced high rates of first class passes in examinations. Expectations were high from parents enrolling their children in "A" schools and jobs were given to well-trained teachers with experience and university degrees, especially after independence. Most of them were in historically white suburbs, far removed from the high-density housing of lower economic status. Speculators felt Miss Phiri had not earned the position on merit, especially because her name indicated Malawian ancestry and because she was an unmarried Ndebele woman. She also had no prior experience or university training and was quite young. Further investigations revealed connections within the Ministry, which angered many parents who felt their children's education had been compromised unethically. Many parents (white, Shona, Indian, and colored) removed their children from the school when Mr. Southey retired and Miss Phiri took over. Within two years, we had more children from poorer backgrounds walking long distances to attend school. By the time I left, a vast majority were Ndebele, from neighborhoods out of the school's catchment area, and there were no white, Indian, or colored children at the school. My father did not remove us from the school. By the time my youngest brother entered the school system, it was a quite different institution from that which my older brother had attended eight years earlier. As a middle child, I experienced the transition.

I was fortunate to have Mr. Hlatshwayo. It was his teaching that helped me develop a critical mind about social justice. *Animal Farm* was only part of it, though the most crucial piece. Mr. Hlatshwayo taught history beyond the textbooks. Recently, I was telling my sister one of the history lessons I learned in his class. She laughed at me, telling me I had imagined the details. I had told her that a historical figure in the first Chimurenga (liberation struggle), (also a spirit medium) had an incestuous affair with her half-brother who was a Shona king. Mr. Hlatshwayo had taught us this but it was not in any of our textbooks. He taught us this because Zimbabwean history privileged Shona people and Ndebele history revealed that one of their kings had sold his kingdom to white settlers for a bag of sugar. Both stories are true but only one was taught in the national curricula. I believe the injustices against the Ndebele affected Mr. Hlatshwayo deeply. Unlike my other teachers, he never treated Shona children worse than he treated Ndebele children. Instead, he talked to us about *Animal Farm* without explicitly drawing parallels. I did not make these connections at the time but now as I reflect on his pedagogy I see what he was doing.

It would be ideal for racial and/or sexual segregation to desist as a functional part of social structures, especially with current notions of post racialism, gender, and social equality. Yet we are beginning to see the resurgence of segregated schooling as a solution to the trauma "different" children face within the purview of education. For example, there are plans to establish a school for LGBTQ students in Manchester in the United Kingdom. Toronto already has The Triangle Program and there are countless Muslim, Christian, and ethnocentric schools all over the Western Hemisphere. Like Lane (1998), I question the choice to ignore or disregard the contemporary reenactment of what we wish to think has already passed. Lane alludes to shocking and surprising phenomena in our contemporary society and puts forward the question:

> Every citizen of Europe and North America is haunted by the spectre of racism. Despite our concern to restrict this spectre to traumatic chapters of history, it revisits contemporary society in shocking and surprising forms. Is it enough to criticize increasingly conservative strains in our political climate to understand this phenomenon, or to reclaim the past in an effort not to repeat it? (p. 1)

The regression we witness in our educational systems might be shocking, but it clearly indicates there is something unsafe in today's classrooms. There is clearly something wrong in a world where, perhaps more than any other time in history, diversity is celebrated and yet difference remains uncontained and problematized. These schools are cropping up because there is no safe space in current systems for those that are different. For these different children, much is possible to alleviate the trauma of *being* educated. By the time children reach higher education, they will have developed a standpoint that needs privileging; therefore, this chapter is an argument for privileged space rather than safe space. Privileged space is possible through a containment of difference in the present, where history resorted to segregation.

## PSYCHOPATHOLOGIES IN THE CLASSROOM

In my analysis of memoirs of childhood, my experiences have given relevance to the history of the subjects I have encountered. My working through has brought me to an explanation of how we might experience social difference as psychopathology. Based on the memoirs, treated like case studies, it is evident that transformation of traumatic experiences requires a therapeutic milieu, one in which working through might be facilitated. Within this environment, pedagogy is intervention and education is social justice.

I return once more to the question: What is the quality of education to which every child is entitled? In attempting to answer this question, I conceptualize an alternative to safe space: privileged space. Within this space the nature, presentation, and expression of psychopathology through free association is encouraged. Learners are encouraged to allow the unconscious to speak. Ultimately, I advocate for a space in which the subjective experience may find relevance, even where it might present as disruptions, eruptions, omissions, and worries over the personal, just as my own working through has manifested throughout this book.

Let us imagine that the three children Bev Sellars, Glen Retief, and Mark Mathabane by some wild fate end up in the same classroom. Regardless of what they might be learning, they approach the knowledge from their subjective positions. How might these three individuals, following such difficult childhoods, participate in a classroom without social justice?

Bev, with her neurotic identifications with the mythical "Indian," presents as a learner who cannot speak and is too afraid to try. Years of oppressive and debilitating pedagogy have instilled in Bev a fear of trying, not of failing, as failing is assumed inevitable. Bev has held on to "facts" and signifiers she has not produced herself at any point in her education. She always seeks the backdoor. Then there is Glen, perhaps no longer in denial about his homosexuality but still unable to express his desires without resorting to bullying or being bullied as an act of perversion. To come out on top, he instinctively seeks out weaker students like Bev. Glen cannot function within an equality framework. He would be lost within it as he thrives on discourses of dominance and authority. He believes there should be a hierarchy at all times. That is what makes sense to him. If he cannot be on top, then he will take the bottom willingly. He manipulates situations so that he can hurt or be hurt. Power is important to him and any environment that suggests otherwise causes him anxiety. Finally, obsessional Mark constantly tries to resist boundaries and is always challenging authority. He is insecure about his abilities and needs continual reassurance that he is the best. He works hard, too hard; and when he does not do well is extremely hard on himself. He over-compensates through compulsions to succeed. What started out as model student behavior quickly turns to a nuisance. Mark wants to prove he belongs. He wants to make everyone proud. However, in his efforts to be perfect, to fulfill his mother's dream for him, he works himself into despair. Mark and Glen have a very uneasy relationship because Mark constantly compares himself to Glen, noting what advantages Glen has over him. Glen senses Mark's desire for success and sees it as a quest for power. He feels Mark wants to dominate him. He is not sure if he should let him or assert himself over Mark.

What class can contain these three individuals and still claim safety? What class can contain ten or twenty more of these people, all seeking through education to resolve the burdens placed upon them by society? All these individuals must work through what prior pedagogy has done to them. In this classroom, they either encounter hope or oppression. I believe there can be no indifference.

In this chapter, I apply a psychoanalytic understanding of privilege and offer a way of reframing privilege in education to make privilege a positive experience, rather than one that divides and discriminates between "the haves and have-nots." I propose that we extend privilege to its extremities and subsequently afford more people the benefits of the positive and favorable aspects of privilege. If education must equalize, if we are to ensure diversity, equity, and inclusion within our schools, maybe what we need is more privilege rather than less of it. This begins with a reformulation of privilege in pedagogy and requires a reconstruction of its nuances. I propose we use privilege to create a space where we view classrooms as spaces for social justice intervention. By revisiting some of the challenges for social justice praxis in classrooms raised in chapter 2, such as the teacher's futile attempts to be "professional," I pull apart the elements of psychoanalytic paradigms that make such pitfalls for the psychoanalyst opportunities rather than barriers to teaching and learning. I revisit the matter of ethics from a psychoanalytic perspective and advocate for a facilitating environment, ultimately for love and hope.

## DEFINITIONS OF "PRIVILEGE"

In educational settings, privilege is often viewed as a negative vicissitude of social and occupational oppression. Critical theory highlights situations and positions of privilege as something to be condemned and eradicated in order to make education equitable. Critical frameworks such as Feminist Epistemology, Critical Race Theory, and Queer Theory view privileged constructions of knowledge as hegemonic. Through the deconstruction of the power imbalances ingrained through hundreds of years of racism, sexism, prejudice, and discrimination, they challenge society's reliance on oppressive pedagogies to review the very structures they seek to dismantle. Clearly, privilege as a critical concept in pedagogy is a domain fraught with tension, conflict, and ambivalence. Barnett (2010) defines privilege as the receiving of an act, service, or material good based upon perceived differences among possible recipients. His definition implies that privilege is a biased human thought process even if it occurs below the level of consciousness and thus becomes habitual, learned, perfunctory, calloused, routine, involuntary, and/or automatic. He argues, too, that it is accompanied by a positive, or favored, result for its recipients (p. 4).

As an alternative to Barnett, and as an asset to pedagogy, *epistemic privilege* as a brand of knowledge is generated by experience from a position of disadvantage and marginalization (Harding 1993). We draw this perspective from Black Feminist Theory (Harding 1993; Hill Collins 2009;

Janack 1997), which advocates for the recognition and legitimacy of the experiences of black females in society. Through epistemic privilege, we differentiate between, 1) those that are privileged because they were born into social, economic, and political power and, 2) those that are disadvantaged due to their race, class, or gender but have come to possess a different kind of power through struggle and experience. In her explanation of *Afrocentric Feminist Epistemology,* Hill Collins states that there is, for some people, a concrete experience that extends beyond knowledge into wisdom (p. 208). Black feminist theorists such as Hill Collins advocate seeing those who come from "the wrong side of the tracks," the bad neighborhoods, and/or "the disadvantaged areas" as potentially wise and knowledgeable because of what they have experienced and therefore learned through their struggles with economic hardships, oppression, discrimination, and social division. Epistemic privilege, if cultivated and nurtured, brings with it better critical thinkers, more adaptable learners, and more resilient students who see the world from a unique perspective.

The gaps and deficits of the initial structure of multicultural education gave rise to intercultural/crosscultural paradigms (James 2001, p. 181), which were also found lacking and led to anti-racist, critical race theory based practice and focused on race relations in the 1980s–1990s (James 2001, p. 184). Critical Race Theory (CRT) highlights (a) legal conceptualizations of white privilege and its associated advantages, (b) majoritarian narratives as hegemonic discourses of legitimacy that assert and help preserve the rights of privilege and whiteness, and (c) the role of interest convergence as a historically necessary and politically effective condition for the implementation of successful equity-focused change (Pollack and Zirkel 2013, p. 297). This connection is profoundly important in understanding how schooling has developed over time and the magnitude of the influence the past has on the present condition of our education systems. With present day ideas of post-raciality and multiculturalism implying racial and ethnic equality and inclusivity, it is easy for matters of racism and discrimination to be cataloged under "history" when the evidence and statistics insist otherwise.

Using Butler's concept of performativity, Chadderton (2013) working from a critical race theory perspective states:

> Drawing on aspects of both theoretical approaches allows us to work toward developing a theory of social interaction with explicitly political social justice aims based on the experiences of marginalised groups without being essentialist, which values diversity and complexity. In order to work towards developing a framework to deepen our understanding of the way racism in education shapes the experiences and subjectivities of minority ethnic students, I suggest drawing on aspects of CRT and Butler (1990, 1993, 1997, 2004b), whose work on subjectivities and performativity potentially provides a theory for exploring the

> production of identities at the same time as explicitly challenging identity categories. (p. 42)

Alternatively, Materialist CRT (Cole 2012) is a focus on the material factors surrounding educational discourse and it views racism as a "means by which society allocates privilege, status and wealth" (p. 170). It allows us to question how market forces such as profits and the labor market impact the policies and practices within the education system and how these in turn impact students and their families. Congruently, *Critical Realism* posits an emergent, transformative relation between structure and agency. It reminds us that standpoints are always delimited by the sociohistorical period of which they are a part (Edwards 2014, p. 180). If we are to foster an educational system, which serves a social justice imperative, a critical look at the positionality of all stakeholders is necessary. As previously stated, one of the biggest criticisms of the ongoing structure of the educational system is the divisive push for tolerance, which regretfully, through a notion of neutrality, maintains privilege and power for some while sidelining, silencing, and segregating the marginalized in the system. Educators especially must be objective but not neutral. Neutral means maintaining the status quo as it means ignoring power imbalances and marginalization. Objectivity however, is the examination of all situations and the rendering of social justice with the aim of ensuring diversity, equity, and inclusivity. To be objective is not to negate the subjective. Rather, it is to work from one's subjectivity towards empowering another's. Edwards advocates for this kind of objectivity by beginning with standpoint, that is,

> In the interests of strong objectivity, then, the experiences of a subjugated group within a particular social structure is a necessary starting point for interrogating reality in as much as this group is likely to pose questions that cannot arise in those groups whose lives are structured from a position of material advantage. This is not to say that the perspectives of working-class pupils are necessarily valid or objective accounts; rather, it is to say only that a critical engagement with reality must take the perspectives and differential power relations within different structural locations into account on the journey towards stronger objectivity in knowing. (Edwards 2014, p. 174)

Like other critical education theoretical frameworks, *discourse analysis* enables the discussion of education reform to widen the understanding of social justice to include those who might otherwise disappear in political and socioeconomic discourses.

Also relevant is the politics of inside/out explored through Queer Theory, which explores the borders of sexual identities, communities, and politics. Extimacy, (discussed briefly in chapter 4) coupled with queer theory, challenges false dichotomies and brings us to a place where intimacy cannot be negated. Queer theory recognizes the impossibility of moving outside current conceptions of sexuality and the privilege of those deemed normal by virtue of fitting neatly into a specific a category. A critical sexual politics, in other words, struggles to move beyond the confines of an inside/outside model. By disrupting and challenging the notion of "normal," we begin to encounter difference as privileged in any context. Essentially, this means we do not seek to label, appropriate, or misappropriate. Rather, we seek to constantly question and by so doing push against perspectives that divide society into those who are and those who are not. As Namaste (1994) states, "We cannot assert ourselves to be entirely outside heterosexuality, nor entirely inside, because each of these terms achieves its meaning in relation to the other. What we can do, queer theory suggests, is negotiate these limits" (p 224). According to Namaste, through queer theory, we can think about the how of these boundaries exist, and also how they are created, regulated, and contested. Redefining privilege, and thinking through queer theory, offers an avenue to negotiate and renegotiate constantly within the pedagogical space.

I therefore define privilege as a learner exercising the power to speak the word and to produce signifiers that are congruent with the inner being. The opposite of privilege is oppression, which we have encountered in the memoirs. I lean on Freire (2000) in *Pedagogy of the Oppressed* to extrapolate on the injustice of an education without privilege. Beginning with the following statement: "To exist humanly is to name the world, to change it" (p. 88), we encounter the relevance of privilege in pedagogy. When a child cannot name the world because she is "Indian" or because he lives under an oppressive apartheid system, we inhabit a world of despair. However, through a pedagogy that privileges, the dehumanization resulting from an unjust order is not a cause for despair but hope, responding to the incessant pursuit of the humanity denied by injustice (pp. 92–93). When the child's psychopathology insists on resolution, privilege is the key to accessing what has been lost. According to Freire (2000),

> While to say the word—which is work, which is praise, which is praxis—is to transform the world, saying that word is not the privilege of some few persons, but the right of everyone. Consequently, no one can say a true word alone—nor can she say it for another, in a prescriptive act, which robs others of their words. (p. 88)

To speak there must be communication and dialogue, which Freire states cannot exist in the absence of profound love for the world, and for people. He believes the naming of the world, which is an act of creation and re-creation, is not possible if it is not infused with love. A privileged pedagogy inspires the hope to create and re-create humanity and it speaks through love.

Love in terms of pedagogy is, as discussed previously, something we often do not speak of as "professional." A return to Todd (2003) brings us to a crucial exercise of uncovering the meaning of love in social justice teaching and learning and in all forms of teaching and learning that occurs in schools. To speak "the word" in this context is to produce signifiers, which requires desire. What desire and what love is possible between learners and teachers? Todd states:

> To be able to love means to be able to be free, love as an act of reaching out toward another disrupts the convention of oppression and domination through which "otherness" is constituted. Thus, triangulating the link between the social construction of subjectivity and the agency needed for altering the terms of domination within this construction is the individual who feels. (p. 77)

Within a privileged pedagogy, it is possible to love because the dynamics of oppressor and oppressed do not operate. When each learner can connect with *other* co-creators from a self-represented and self-defined position, there is room for negotiation in terms of power and knowledge. Such love issues a message of surrender rather than submission. There is no domination or control in surrender. Easily confused with submission, even if it is possible to confound the two, for exploitative purposes (which brings us into the ethical dimension of pedagogy), according to Ghent (1990), surrender might be thought of as reflective of some "force" toward growth. Making room for surrender to self, others, and knowledge is privileged pedagogy, which ultimately propels toward the direction of self-discovery—identity, sense of self, wholeness, and unity. Submission, on the other hand, reverses these qualities leaving an impression of commodification, objectification, and atrophy (Ghent 1990). The word that emanates from a surrendered space offers possibilities rather than impossibilities. My goal is to offer a privileged space that takes both learners and teachers from hope to love to surrender. Surrendering is the key to atemporality in social justice, for with surrender the past, present, and future recede in secondary processes (Ghent 1990).

## THE PSYCHOANALYTIC PRIVILEGED SPACE

Psychoanalysis, rejected by the scientific community, is to the arts, humanities, and social sciences a curious adjunct, not quite embraced nor dismissed but lingering in the shadows like a strange child (Levin 2001). Like Levin (2001), I focus on psychoanalysis as a social remedy that does not quite fit the bill:

> The fact that psychoanalytic treatment or thought has from time to time achieved a kind of grudging social acceptance through medicalization or cultural chic does not really undo this basic tension . . . psychoanaly-

> sis itself will remain something of a social outcast, an object of suspicion. Its basic concepts seem eccentric and therefore threatening in the eyes of the general public and much of the scientific community. (p. 189)

Being somewhat of a social and scientific pariah makes psychoanalysis what it is today—a place where privilege can dominate and thrive to the fulfillment of both analyst and analysand. What might be viewed as negative about psychoanalysis is also what makes it resilient. Levin (2001) quite aptly describes the psychoanalytic situation, stating, "The 'space' in which an analysis takes place thus appears as a foreign territory, full of strange and abject beings, and this will always pose a disturbing challenge to the functional rationality of conventional social values" (p. 189). As negative as it may sound, this is a good thing when considering matters of privilege. A strange space is one where anyone can be anything and still work through. In this strange space, psychoanalysis itself is strange, the analyst is strange, and the analysand is strange. Essentially, one fits in by virtue of not fitting in. With this perspective, we could view strangeness as a unique type of epistemic privilege where knowledge creation arises on whatever condition necessary, even abjectly. Levin (2001) continues, saying the following:

> In a democratic society—that is, in a society that genuinely encourages and protects diversity—the eccentricity of the analytic couple can be tolerated for two reasons. The first is that the private interests of the analysand are considered important by virtue of democratic principle. (p. 198)

To define privileged space in a psychoanalytic frame is to state the democratic honoring of the private interests of the analysand. In an educational setting, we could therefore define privileged space as a democratic honoring of the learner's private interests, which means at the top of the classroom agenda, is the honoring of learners as private individuals with strange interests. Levin thinks society would collectively benefit greatly from emulating this psychoanalytic exploration and expression of strangeness within ourselves. He argues that in psychoanalysis ordinary sociability is suspended, to whatever degree possible, because the norms of social interaction tend to sponge up all the embarrassing tensions of the unsayable, the unthinkable, and the unbidden, making psychoanalytic work impossible (p. 190). In the analytic session, there are no sanctions against speaking one's mind, expressing oneself emotionally, or confronting one's oppressor with affect. Such social dictates—for example, political correctness—create gaps and chasms in education. When emotionality, the unthinkable, and the unsayable are met with silence, the silence maintains social dictates and, by extension, the status quo, thus creating barriers to learning. Privileged space does not suppress strangeness; instead, it seeks out the unconscious, nudging away repressions and coaxing strangeness into the open. Thus, it presents us with opportunities for meaningful pedagogy.

Privileged space can be viewed as a container for traumatic pedagogy (Chimbganda 2015). The trauma is necessary; it must be. Also necessary is the kind of space that Levin (2001) describes:

> Freud isolated irrationality itself for intellectual investigation by blocking the path of emotional discharge through action and creating a specialized substitute container (the psychoanalytic process). Using this container, he could deliberately foster states of insecurity, uncertainty, and radical self-criticism. The result was not healing through social integration, in which the culture acts as the container, but the disillusionment of separation through a kind of internal integration, in which a new degree of autonomy is achieved at the level of the individual organism. (pp. 192–93)

From Levin, we gather that social integration through culture comes at the cost of the development of the individual. This view highlights one of biggest failings of "safe space" as its inability to contain insecurity, uncertainty, and radical self-criticism. However, if a teacher nurtures and encourages students to learn through the trauma of giving up that safety, they might develop social identifications that make it unnecessary to teach in a "safe space."

To create a privileged space in classrooms, we might begin with the ethical standpoint suggested by Weiner (2001): "Ethics place great stress on the importance of respecting our patients' rights to confidentiality, emphasizing its link to the relationship of trust, so crucial for creating a space for unconscious exploration" (p. 432). Psychoanalytic efficacy is measured through privilege. For psychoanalysis to work, the analysand and analyst must relate in a privileged space where the analysand is assured, primarily, of confidentiality but also of other crucial principles like respect and trust in a non-judgmental atmosphere. Levin (2001) states, "The analysand's belief in the security of psychotherapeutic space is essential to its construction" (p. 197). If we were to create similar spaces within classrooms, what might we achieve? What might a privileged space mean in terms of student engagement and the attainment of knowledge?

Not to be confused with privacy or secrecy, confidentiality is, as Weiner (2001) points out, a commitment to maintain boundaries and to take no action (p. 433). According to Weiner, taking no action is not a position of passivity or ineffectuality, nor is it neglect or ignorance. It is containment. Weiner continues, saying, "For analysts, the temptation to take actions to break the boundaries of the analytic container is dependent on personal and moral principles, codes of ethics, clinical judgment and, not least, the role of the law" (p. 433). She also stresses that a failure to contain as well as a failure to maintain confidentiality erodes trust, and thus "a shadow is cast over our profession as a whole" (p. 434). By building professional standards on the principles of privileged space—confidentiality, containment, and trust—might we see an improvement in teacher-student relationships?

Also, advocating for privileged space, Levin (2001) states the following:

> Confidentiality, in this stronger sense of a privileged space, is uniquely designed to diminish the social pressure to answer to the archaic superego. The purpose of this is to protect the psychic value of the patient's communication, that is to say, to preserve its "capacity to carry the contents of unconscious thought" [Bollas and Sundelson 1995]. (p. 199)

Within the security of privileged space, speech uncensored as the analysand can speak without fear of social retribution and the reactive morality of the group (Levin 2001, p. 199). Confidentiality, according to Levin, is a very deep kind of psychological bond that is established only in very special circumstances, usually having to do with the invocation of powers transcending secular social authority such as sacred blood ties, spiritual obligations, love, and friendship, all of which have survived modernization in the quasi-transcendental form of constitutionally protected relationships implying certain residual rights (p. 196). In other words, it is a reciprocal bond between the analyst and analysand that creates the imaginary boundary required for treatment. Privilege also demarcates the boundary between the analytic couple and the rest of society: "The 'privilege' of the confidentiality principle depends very much on the quality of social respect for this distinction between the analytic couple and other social relationships; but it also, paradoxically, emerges as a consequence of their differentiation, which produces a highly idiosyncratic form of discourse irreducible to the structures of social communication" (Levin 2001, p. 197).

## PRIVILEGED SPACE VERSUS "SAFE SPACE"

The illusory state of "safe space," compared to privileged space, requires we look below the surface of what is said and done. Privileged space is a holding environment that requires "a robust professional culture steeped in the ethic of confidentiality and capable of maintaining the inter-analytic circulation of clinical experience in an atmosphere of frankness and respect" argues Levin (2001, p. 198). In addition, he believes, "When some or all of these supporting frameworks are absent in the surrounding culture, psychotherapeutic space begins to collapse into a kind of social black hole" (p. 198). Unfortunately, safe space, appraised by the same standards, is a social black hole full of judgment and social persecution, which is unable to contain the emotionality required of pedagogy.

Within the illusion of safe space, we often encounter anxiety and fear driven by sanctions and barriers set up in the name of equity and social justice. The question of socially constructed and acceptable affects that are designated, political and constitutive of worlds of relation rises from Stengel's (2010) analysis of safe space. According to Stengel, "The affect, that is, the felt response to harassment, is constructed as fear (rather than, say, annoyance or anger) through practices that control affect in order to create a particular kind of world" (p. 526). The call for "safe space," says Stengel, usually comes from someone perceiving an affect-laden experience, meaning the call for "safe space" comes from someone who thinks that a discussion in a classroom might become affect-laden and thus threatening.

Within safe spaces, discrimination, vis-à-vis affect, further alienates those already alienated through racial, gender, or other prejudices. Some feelings although justified are simply not acceptable in the classroom, and those subject to triggers of affect are prohibited from seeking catharsis through expression. As Stengel (2010) points out, when one person invokes "safe space," another person is being silenced. For those identified as requiring it, safety means the shutting up and invisibility of those perceived as threatening. "By designating fears, we construct 'safe space' for some and unsafe space for others" (Stengel 2012, p. 531). It also means that we are inevitably labeling people as either safe or unsafe, which seeps into peer relations, thereby propagating divisions and segregation. In safe spaces, silencing further cultivates anxiety and fear, both of which are symptoms of repression. The repressed affect will eventually manifest itself in other ways, as is the habit of the unconscious. On the other hand, a privileged space rejects the notion that a person should feel, talk, and act a certain way by repressing affect that does not comply with societal dictates.

Admittedly, it is difficult to balance everyone's needs and desires, especially when many remain unspoken for the sake of safety. Consequently, there is a double-bind evident in popular conceptualizations of the classroom as "safe space", which Stengel (2010) sums up in three critical problems:

> (1) The need for safe space for students who experience social exclusion and harassment is the result of a political economy that was intended to create safe space for others. (2) Students who are able to articulate a need for safe space often don't need the kind of space separation offers; students who need (if only temporarily) separation often are unable to say so. (3) "Safe space" does not always or only function to defuse fear and establish safety for students; safe space may also function to create emotional relief for adults. (p. 525)

She alerts us to the teacher's own need for safety, pointing out that in many educational settings, safety is not an antidote to fear; instead, it is a disciplinary action that suppresses affect rather than uncovering it. Often teachers are left feeling bereft and anxious when emotions explode. Through fear and anxiety, teachers choose to act, often projecting insecure affects onto students identified as needing "safe space." Stengel further argues that fear does not pre-exist and prompt the call for "safe space"; rather, the call for "safe space" establishes fear as the affect present, often hiding other feelings such as anger, annoyance, or even hatred.

The affective difficulties identified by Stengel correspond with Powell and Barber's (2006) statement that both learners and teachers struggle with a [discriminating] culture, in almost psychotic anxiety, and the future created by political, cultural, and environmental inequality. "Some teachers describe an increasing sense of powerlessness," report Powell and Barber. They refer to one mechanism we use to manage anxiety and the sense of powerlessness as "pathological denial," stating, "despite the dangerous consequences, individuals and groups cultivate ways to 'not know' and to 'not learn'" (p. 43). The emotional labor of learning from experience for teachers is a task in *thinking with feeling* (Ramvi 2010, p. 340). However, *the desire not to know* is a challenge in teaching as addressed by Alcorn (2010).

> It can become an intersubjective chess game of sorts in which the anxiety that attends thought—the anxiety that generates the desire not to know—is shifted from us to our students and then given back to us. And if we continue to play the game, we shift this anxiety back to our students, who then may reshift the anxiety back to us. . . . Classes generate emotional contexts, such as shame and ridicule, that make nuanced thought difficult. In this way classes generate, spontaneously and without conscious intent, anxious moments for thinking. (p. 356)

Alcorn paints a picture of an infernal cycle of anxiety and excess of emotion that can hold teachers and their student's hostage. He states that the cycle can be better managed when teachers take responsibility for their own role in the desire not to know. Inevitably, there are consequences of pathological denial, as Stengel (2010) points out, "Affect matters, not because it replaces logic, but because it points to logics at work that are disciplined, covered over. When affect impinges on consciousness, it reminds us to go looking for logics beyond the surface, beyond what is stated" (p. 526).

Admittedly, given the harsh realities of professional practice, privilege is easily subverted by ethical and economic predicaments, which Weiner (2001) highlights as dilemmas between maintaining the confidentiality of patients while trying to stay in line with the legal and moral obligations of a broader society. According to Weiner, there are "uncomfortable situations" in analytic space that we may wish to avoid, "to defend ourselves against our beliefs and wishes" (p. 438). Thus, continues Weiner (2001), "We are caught in a psychic area where distinctions between inside and outside, between what is subjective and what is objective, between fantasy and reality are blurred. The guardian of our everyday beliefs fails and the analytic frame is under threat so that inevitably the nature of the analytic space within it is affected" (p. 438). Such aspects in clinical practice resist acknowledging that the unconscious operates within this space, for the unconscious does not fit into discourses involving binaries such as morality/immorality, legality/illegality, and normal/abnormal. For example, voicing one's racial or gender prejudices might result in social retribution. Therefore, allowing the unconscious to speak creates dilemmas that present as "unsafe" to those who are unfamiliar with how the unconscious operates.

To address these difficulties, which we can neither ignore nor sanction by creating "safe spaces," Weiner (2001) turns to a third space, which she refers to as an *ethical space* (p. 439). Viewed as another dimension of privileged space, "secondary process thinking becomes possible and inner and outer reality may be separated yet remain interrelated" (p. 440). This ethical space within the privileged dynamic distinguishes privacy from secrecy and underpins confidentiality. Creating such a space in classrooms, along with acknowledging the unconscious, produces opportunities in which the pedagogical factors often ignored or silenced in education can be fully disclosed and worked through.

Full disclosure relies on confidentiality. In classrooms, full disclosure is undermined and/or prevented by what is deemed socially appropriate. Generally, it is not considered appropriate to express one's emotions, thoughts, and biases as they have the potential to create an unsafe atmosphere—or, at least, perceived as such. In addition, while the teacher cannot control what learners think, it is generally seen as the teacher's responsibility to control what they say. Thus, as learners cannot say what they think or feel, the status quo remains unchallenged. Everyone comes and goes without actually taking risks or learning. Paradoxically, "The classroom as a 'safe space' has emerged as a description of a classroom climate that allows students to feel secure enough to take risks, honestly express their views, and share and explore their knowledge, attitudes, and behaviours" (Holley and Steiner 2005, p. 50). Among the challenges of building and maintaining a safe space for learning emphasized by Holley and Steiner (2005) is the complete eradication of conflict or disagreement through democracy.

The solution to discrimination within safe spaces is not social democratization. According to Levin (2001), who criticizes democratization as a social principle, "Democratization can itself be transformed into an instrument of repression, to the extent that it confuses the purely formal equality required for the cultivation of individual freedom with the concrete equality of sameness and literal identity" (p. 193). He juxtaposes psychoanalytic space to other social spaces pointing out that "[a]ny 'space' within society that cultivates a challenge to identifications will be suspected of undermining social cohesion and convention; any 'space' that invites the retrieval of projections and encourages the critical examination of moral assumptions and idealizing fantasies will inevitably be treated with suspicion, because it will threaten the group identification with the archaic superego" (p. 193).

In a safe space, repression becomes the socially induced norm whereby students cannot learn and cannot experience more than superficial occurrences. As a method of challenging repression, psychoanalysis deviates from social democratization, for when psychoanalysis is brought to bear, identifications protected by safe space are challenged in order to disable repetitions that have created the need for safe space in the first place. The breaking down of these identifications into the underlying mechanisms that maintain the status quo can be traumatic, however. The key to containing the trauma is in personable elements such as the natural warmth and the authority of the analyst, derived not from her person but from her capacity to maintain the [psychoanalytic] frame in reasonably good working order (Levin 2001). Within a privileged framework relationships are negotiated; and they reflect a level of mutual assumption of responsibility (Levin 2001, p. 195).

The objective in privileged space, therefore, is not to create an environment that society dictates but to create a space in which transference can be openly sourced and resourced. In privileged space, there is transference and countertransference; and repression is not the order of the day. Both teachers and learners are "allowed" to speak from a position of power and mutual responsibility. In a safe space, on the other hand, both teachers and learners inevitably repress their fears and negate their privilege. Safe space has become synonymous with silence and seclusion, a space in which there is no confidentiality. Without confidentiality, is it ethical pedagogy?

## PEDAGOGY IN A PRIVILEGED SPACE

By applying collaborative techniques of knowledge production, education stretches beyond standardized learning outcomes toward enlightenment, something we might say has fallen in short supply. Using psychoanalytic techniques of inquiry enables teachers to reach beyond the requirements of measurable curriculum including, including hope, love, and surrender. Privileged pedagogy happens when we acknowledge what the learner brings to the classroom and make knowledge of it through the intervention we provide.

It took Freud some time to understand the importance of the imaginary constructions of his patients in achieving enlightenment. Freud's initial folly, according to Verhaeghe (2001), was assuming the role of one who knows and owns the knowledge:

> Freud assumes the role of the master, who knows in matters of desire and jouissance, and who, by way of treatment, teaches this knowledge to the patient; the patient must accept these insights; and so on. And again, the generalization of this conception can be found in his ideas on sexual enlightenment. In 1907, he writes enthusiastically on the subject: the adult may not withhold the necessary knowledge; on the contrary, he has to inform children correctly, in order that their incorrect, fantasmatic birth theories may become superfluous. For Freud, it is obvious that a general enlightenment will result in a drastic drop in the numbers of neurotic adults. (p. 2)

Freud was a master at discerning the resistances and antagonisms of his patients, preempting their learning and depriving them of enlightenment. Teachers careful of making the same mistake see how drawing conclusions for learners before they can reach the stage of self-awareness robs them of the opportunity to genuinely develop self-actualization. Verhaeghe also points out that Freud could formulate the critique of his patients much better than they ever could have done themselves, each time taking the edge off the argument (p. 2). "Such a strategy can only result in two possible reactions: either one is transformed from a patient into a pupil who says yes and absorbs everything, or one reacts as Dora did, by slamming the door and leaving" (Verhaeghe 2001, pp. 2–3). In so doing, Freud robbed Dora of her own opportunity to work through. A similar practice in seasoned teachers can serve as a barrier to student learning, alienating teacher from student and student from pedagogy. It is especially detrimental when we consider the psychopathologies learners bring to the classroom in the hope of a resolution.

Upon the discovery that "educating" his patients was yielding negative results, Freud concluded that the analysand must be the one to produce the knowledge, that is, the signifiers. The analyst must give up his position of Master and allow the analysand to learn:

> Instead of teaching, the analyst has to be taught. Instead of the analyst's signifiers, those of the patient fill the scene; the patient is the one who knows, only he doesn't know himself that he knows. Knowledge coming from an external source is merely an inhibiting factor, a point clearly expressed in Freud's technical advice from this period: ideally the patient should not read analytic works, the analyst should restrain from giving precocious information and interpretation, etc." (Verhaeghe 2001, p. 3)

Freud moved from an instructive and intrusive position of "explicative interventions" in Dora's case to a position of not-knowing in the Rat Man's case. Elucidating on Freud's change in technique, Verhaeghe (2001) states the following:

> From a Lacanian point of view, this can be described as the operational character of the transference, i.e., the transference as driving force of the treatment. The analysand expects knowledge from the analyst; actually, at the beginning of the treatment, the analyst doesn't know anything at all about this particular patient, but he can use his position in such a way that it makes the patient produce signifiers, i.e., knowledge, for the one-who-is-supposed-to-know. (p. 3)

In the same vein, teachers can take up the position of listener in order to extricate from learners their brand and extent of knowledge, which is produced through experience, creativity, innovation, and sometimes, quite simply, through questions posed to the teacher who-is-supposed-to-know. These questions will guide a teacher, as they do an analyst, through the complex maze of the learner's educational needs. Questioning is the learner's way of producing signifiers and exposing his lack, therefore what he needs. The teacher can use these questions as an indication of extent of knowledge; how much he knows and how much he is capable of learning. Without the patient's questions and without the learner's questions, neither the analyst nor the teacher can know where to begin or where to stop.

In the *Fundamentals of Psychoanalytic Technique*, Bruce Fink (2007) states, "The psychoanalyst's first task is to listen and to listen carefully" (p. 1). Might we state that it is also the teacher's first task? Additionally, Fink explains how psychoanalytic listening is different from simply listening. Our usual way of listening is centered to a great degree on ourselves, our own similar experiences, our own similar feelings, and/or our own similar perspectives. When we listen this way, we relate to the speaker, uttering phrases such as "I know what you mean!" We empathize, and we sympathize; we even feel pity, and we feel we understand (p. 2). However, what happens when we cannot understand because we cannot empathize, sympathize, or even feel pity, because we do not have similar feelings or experiences and desires? We become judgmental. We consider the speaker to be silly, obtuse, and irrational. Thus, we become baffled, incredulous, and, finally, defensive. We decide that this person needs to be taught, needs correction or direction. Fink (2007) maintains "our usual way of listening overlooks or rejects the otherness of the other" (p. 2). We begin to look for ourselves in the speaker by forcing a bit of our knowledge into them. We strive to educate (p. 2). Fink states:

> What falls outside of our expectations is neither seen nor heard, and the most well-intentioned clinician almost always automatically hears what, to her mind, it would make sense for the analysand to be saying in a particular context, as opposed to hearing what the analysand is actually saying, which may be quite out of the ordinary or even nonsensical. (p. 20)

I recall teaching an undergraduate class in which a white male student declared racism and classism were in the past and only old people seem concerned about dragging the younger generations into the discourse. He declared he would be an excellent role model for any "little black girl." Behind me, a group of black and other ethnic minority girls gasped and hissed in protest. They did not however, venture to express their outrage constructively. Caught in this situation, my inclination was to inform the young man he was speaking from a position of white privilege that disrespected and dismissed the experiences of people who did not occupy the same social status he was afforded through historical injustice. Had I spoken this way, I am sure he would have not understood a word I said both literally and figuratively. He sounded stupid in my ears, very narrow minded, and perhaps it was my psychoanalytic training that helped me resist the urge to teach him. I was also annoyed at the hissing girls who, for the duration of the term, practiced this passive-aggressive resistance to the learning and teaching take place around them. At least white privileged boy spoke up!

Where subjective knowledge takes on the guise of power and tilts the scales favorably for whoever can assume that position of knowing, defense against resistance becomes necessary to safeguard that advantage. On one side of the scales are those who see the appropriation of privilege as an act of disempowerment, especially when they are expected to "check their privilege." On the other side are those seeking to exercise their epistemic privilege but cannot do so because it is deemed objectionable (Chimbganda 2015). Within a privileged space, these opposing affects are not silenced but drawn into the open so that students can learn by working through their insecurities, uncertainties, and radical self-criticisms. So, my response was to listen, to ask questions, and provide an opportunity for both the white privileged male and his hissing counterparts a space to speak truthfully.

Even the most attentive analyst often hears only what the analysand likely meant to say, filtering out the analysand's slight slip of the tongue or slur (Fink 2007, p. 20). As Finks notes, "We are used to almost automatically cutting the ribbon up into discrete units on the basis of the language as we think we know it, as well as on the basis of what we are expecting to hear in general and what we have come to expect from a particular interlocutor" (p. 21). In other words, we are prejudiced and abuse our positions of authority when we allow difference to dictate what must and can be said.

The prejudice is not one sided. Learners may also ascribe expectations based on social difference onto the teacher. According to Williams and Evans-Winters (2005), "The inability for students to separate the message and the messenger in the area of social justice teaching has interfered with the ability for students to become change agents" (p. 205). Unfortunately, when social difference subverts pedagogical collaboration, enlightenment is at stake. Differences, social stratification, and perceptions of power create complexities of pedagogy where tensions and underlying beliefs cause resistance. "Resistance is the name given to motivational forces operating against growth or change and in the direction of maintenance of status quo" (Ghent 1990, p. 109). Where anyone within the classroom feels threatened or undermined pedagogy is futile.

In imagining a privileged space, we return to the usefulness of transference and countertransference between teachers and their students or between one student and another as normal. It is up to the teacher to manage transference within the classroom. This cannot occur when she is working from a position that does not privilege the learner. Teachers would benefit from understanding transference for what it is: a universal and spontaneous phenomenon of the human mind in relation to the other (Robbins 1990). Transference is a learner's way of relating to the teacher. It might present negatively or positively, but it always seeks a response. It is the unconscious stating its presence. To be clear, the privileged relationship is not one of intersubjectivity. Fink (2007) explains thus:

> As Lacan reminded us, the very existence of transference "constitutes an objection to intersubjectivity." The analytic situation is not a forum in which two different individuals encounter each other as subjects, because the party of the first part (so to speak) lends herself to any and every projection drummed up by the party of the second part. This means that something essential about her own subjectivity fades in the encounter, stays on the sidelines. (p. 149)

Dismissing notions of intersubjectivity does not mean that the analyst or the teacher is left bereft, at the mercy of those they seek to help. It means instead that they recognize the power dynamics within the relationship and that they seek to counteract any violence that would eviscerate their charges. Inasmuch as the teacher is a subject who also can produce signifiers, it is important for the teacher to understand that by professional standards the privileged subjectivity should be that of the learner.

However, where transference is poorly managed, communication, which creates knowledge, is curtailed. The teacher, as *other* to the students, might project a negative atmosphere that usually results in the need for and subsequent production of a safe space. "The important thing from the point of view of libertarian education," for Freire (2000), "is for the people to come to feel like masters of their thinking by discussing the thinking and views of the world explicitly or implicitly manifest in their own suggestions and those of their comrades" (p. 124).

In addition, Davis (1987) states that "important to pedagogy, is the sense in which the teacher does not convey information to students but only helps students situate themselves in a certain relation to knowledge" (p. 749). He further states the importance of pedagogy as scientific positioning,[1] arguing that it is important to understand a student's relation to a dominant discourse, a discourse the student is constituted by as well as has an effect on. The discourse itself is unconscious, and when the student imagines the teacher as someone in possession and mastery of knowledge, there is "transference" in effect—that is, the student attributes to the teacher the power and prestige of the entire semiotic system (p. 752). As such, a teacher often holds the powerful position of "possessor of knowledge." This knowledge, however, can be perceived as threatening. Knowledge is better exchanged in a privileged space where no imbalance of power is perceived. Privileged space comes about through the establishment of a relationship in which the teacher's knowledge-as-power couples with the learner's empowered knowledge.

In the pedagogical situation, class, race, and the social privileges that come with social status are replaced by a collaborative exploration of knowledge by all parties. What this means is that all parties enter into this situation with a confidence that what they say and do will be protected by the relationship they have fostered. In privileged space, there are essential elements that ensure the full and satisfactory maintenance of the relationship. Both teachers and analysts are governed by ethics of care that require they act in the best interests of the analysand/learner. Otherwise, they might encounter epistemological violence (Castro-Gómez and Martin 2002). Frosh (2010) proposes that we view psychoanalytic praxis as involving "a kind of tolerance of the other that recognises it as not fully knowable, and hence resists the temptation to appropriate the other through an act of colonisation" (p. 146). Colonization in this instance refers to the forcing of one's knowledge on to the other; and, as a demand for knowledge, it can be detrimental to both teacher and student. A psychoanalytic practice that counteracts colonization is the not-knowing position.

Teachers can emulate the psychoanalytic position of not-knowing, which allows the analysand to speak from the unconscious through the practice of free association. In the psychoanalytic situation, the analysand speaks from epistemic privilege, and the analyst takes up this knowledge for analysis, neither discrediting it nor verifying it but simply privileging it. Traditionally, however, the teacher cannot enter the classroom not-knowing. The teacher is expected to know and to act as authority over what is false or true, good, or bad knowledge, all of which deprivileges the acquiring of knowledge for enlightenment.

When the teacher is permitted an excess of authority over a learner's knowledge, submission rather than surrender occurs, which means there is no love and where there is no love, there is a deficit of hope. Surrender, according to Ghent (1990), is in an Other's presence rather to an Other, which is submission. In privileged pedagogy, we want learners to let go of their defenses that maintain the status quo. We want learners to feel they can encounter feelings of dread and destruction or/and clarity and relief, even ecstasy but regardless of what they encounter, they can within a facilitating environment "come clean" as part of an even more general longing to be known, recognized, and therefore also know and recognize others (Ghent 1990).

Within safe space, much is lost to the zeitgeist of post-raciality, humanistic education, and the economies of affect (Ahmed 2004) all of which are elements of safe space pedagogy. Of cultural invasion, Freire (2009) states it is one hand an instrument of domination, and on the other hand the result of domination. He clarifies that "cultural action of a dominating character (like other forms of antidialogical action), in addition to being deliberate and planned, is in another sense simply a product of oppressive reality" (p. 154).

We need a paradigm in which what is lost through societal pressures is recoverable and re-creatable. In fact, what gets lost in trying to facilitate pedagogy in a safe space, is incongruous to acquiring knowledge and even more so to enlightenment. Taubman (2012) reminds us that what education knows but does not want to know it knows is not dissimilar to psychoanalytic knowledge. Psychoanalytic knowledge is not the pursuit of truth, but aims to speak truthfully about the things that safe space loses. Like psychoanalysis, according to Taubman, education knows that "there are no foolproof methods, that one can teach exactly the same thing in the same way in two different classes and have totally different results" (p. 24). As Verhaeghe (2001) states, "The analytic cure is a search for lost knowledge, lost as a result of its becoming unconscious; the aim of the treatment is the re-inscription of this unconscious knowledge into consciousness. The implicit expectation is that the therapeutic effects will follow automatically" (p. 1).

At some point, within a privileged frame, the teacher does more than impart knowledge; rather she intervenes at a level of intimacy we often do not encounter in classrooms. From the psychoanalytic frame we understand, as Verhaeghe (2001, p. 8) explains, that at some point the analysand cannot stand to produce signifiers as these signifiers have exposed what is lacking in her/him. Similarly, within the classroom, the intensity of trying to create knowledge can become too much for the learner. Just as the analysand begins to hesitate upon perceiving a need for truth, not mere knowledge the learner recognizes the need for truth rather than knowledge; even epistemic privilege has its limits. The more the analysand knows, the more she/he hesitates because what is required at this junction is truth. And, it is at this junction that intervention on the part of the analyst is necessary to prevent the analysand from regressing. Levin (2001) provides an apt example:

> For example, the analysand may desperately long for the analyst's maternal caress. That this longing can be experienced and communicated with a violent insistence is a function of the holding environment. That it can be thought through to the point where the analysand discovers

> his own capacity to caress himself with maternal care is the function of the frame. Thus, if the holding environment is an invitation to the analysand to regress, then the frame is an invitation to the analysand to assume responsibility for himself in precisely that area where he believes himself unable to do so. (p. 196)

The analyst does not chastise or correct the analysand's infantile needs rather through intervention she helps the analysand develop the capacity to cradle himself. This is empowerment! Thus, progression requires a well-formulated response by the analyst within a privileged space. Likewise, a teacher might intervene in response to a learner's lack, once the frame has revealed what and where the lack exists. Lack becomes the desire to learn (Lacan and Miller 1991). Without this desire to learn, the teacher is confronted with resistance.

Pedagogy should reveal lack in order to generate desire. The teacher now intervenes through teaching, not as a source of knowledge but as a speaker of truth. In other words, her position shifts from not-knowing to one-who-knows-what-is-missing. The teacher has listened carefully, to identify the learner's lack. Thus, she can begin to fill in these gaps. If the teacher speaks as the incarnation of knowledge, a regression may follow. If, however, she speaks as one who understands the learner's desire and sees where the learner lacks, there may be progress. Learning continues and both teacher and learner maintain privilege in the pedagogical situation. Adversely, should the teacher disregard this crucial aspect of teaching the student suffers. Triana (2007) states:

> The most important and central aspect of the teaching alliance is the "education diagnosis": "It is the task of discovering what is impeding your learning." Unempathic interventions may have an adverse effect of the student's capacity to learn. They may result in untimely or too intense release of unfamiliar feelings or may be overly intellectual and remote from feelings. (p. 232)

He further states that when a student encounters an educator who cannot correctly diagnose his impediments to learning, the learner's thriving toward trust, independence, and initiative in the learning relationship maybe blocked, disrupted, or become unattainable within the teacher-student relationship. Essentially, the learner feels ignored, interrupted, criticized, and thwarted in regard to further meaningful communication (p. 232)

## NOTE

1. Rom Harré and Luk Van Langenhove (1991) clarify the difference between taking a role and taking a position. Scientific positioning considers both ontological and epistemological positions are considered thereby affecting the pedagogical approach taken by the teacher.

# Conclusion

As I contemplate the practice of education, I continually question how I formulated my understanding, my thoughts, and ideas on pedagogy, particularly social justice pedagogy. What can we teach learners—specifically young learners who still have a chance to experience good enough schooling? As I ponder my role as an educator, I consider the space my work can occupy and as we talk about postmodernism and other eras, it occurs to me that there is a space for hope as I have defined it. This space is between essentialism and difference. Hope is the ability to negotiate and renegotiate personal (even sociopolitical) outcomes within interpersonal and structural binaries. A better solution would dissolve binaries altogether.

We cannot quantify hope or reduce it to a specific methodology. Nevertheless, we can teach by making our curricula not just inclusive but dynamic and create the conditions for learners and teachers to negotiate identity. Freire (2000) in *Pedagogy of the Oppressed* states:

> The teacher talks about reality as if it were motionless, static, compartmentalized, and predictable. Or else he expounds on a topic completely alien to the existential experience of the students. His task is to "fill" the students with the contents of his narration—contents which are detached from reality, disconnected from the totality that engendered them and could give them significance. Words are emptied of their concreteness and become a hollow, alienated, and alienating verbosity. (p. 71)

His analysis speaks of a disconnection and disengagement that creates little room for communion in pedagogy. He sums up the state of affairs: "Education is suffering from narration sickness" (p. 71). When students are told who they are, what they are, and what they are capable of, there is an enactment of oppression. Having one's life narrated by another, summed up in so little words, oft-harsh unyielding words, there is little hope for possibilities. Our success is deeply rooted in who we think we are. Moreover, who we think we are must be dynamic. Unfortunately, our current systems tie us into categories and essentialisms. Psychologists administer personality tests and scales, and through them we are labeled, as if that explains all we can ever be. I was fortunate to grow up in an educational system that did not administer such tests. Even though we took exams and were graded and selected into classes depending on our grades, every new school year each student could move either up or down. I never felt stuck or eternally doomed by my results.

After coming first in third grade, I never cared to do it again. I even reached the bottom of my class a few times, and most times I was satisfied just getting by. I had proved to myself that I could do it and that was all I wanted, a school system that could allow me to be my best or worst but still feel it was up to me. Education would benefit from more curricula and systems that allow learners to be at their best or their worst but never static or reduced to one identity.

The hope I value most, I acquired from home and school. My father and mother's words and the words of teachers like Mr. Hlatshwayo helped me learn how to negotiate and renegotiate my position all the way to the top, and sometimes I reached the bottom. I have carried this attitude into my professional and personal life. Recently talking to a colleague, I was surprised when she said that rebellious blood runs through me and that is what brings about revolutions. I was curious what she had witnessed in me to make this statement.

Children can learn to exercise their own identification at school and within educational systems, to discard labels and attach new ones through relationships with family, teachers, and peers. The labels put on children within the system can circumvent any ability to self-determine outcomes. It might make work easier for administrators and statisticians but it puts limits on children who normally have no choice in which system they end up. Many children today come to school (if they come at all) with overwhelming needs (Noddings 2005, p. 151).

The use of memoirs in social justice pedagogy is intended to provide the tools that can help create an atmosphere of possibility. While theory in education is vital, it must not supersede the possibilities available in experiential learning. Memoirs provide experiences to learners beyond their boarders, both literally and figuratively. Within a privileged space exercises in reading narratives of trauma become experiences of being emotional and vulnerable in front of *others.* To be able to circumvent stereotypes and misconceptions the way in which we regard our others requires a level of intimacy that a privileged space can provide. In addition, I lean on Edwards (2013) to state:

> The nature of personal truth is always provisional. We seek to be as clear as we can in order to serve both ourselves and those with whom we work, both clinically and academically. It is often in reading about the lives of others in biography and also in fiction that we tap into our own deeper lives and thoughts. (p. 392)

Reading memoirs in classes helps those engaging in the exercise of self-discovery do so in relation to their others. Such opportunities create social circles of inclusion and equity.

In chapters 3–5, I amplified the cries of distress from the historically oppressed as I bear witness to the childhoods of the three individuals who as adults wrote the memoirs. I acknowledge the adults' calls to glory in the production of my work, perceiving it as a demand for social justice in education. I began my analysis with a paradigm shift that eradicates the distinction between human rights and social justice, and posit that this begins with the way we use accounts of historical oppression, not only of the children represented in these memoirs but also of learners, of education, and of society. Our shift should move us toward a place of acknowledgement of the psychic and emotional within the educational system and beyond that to empathy, forgiveness, and love in pedagogy. It is my hope that "this discourse might move away from an instrumentalized, moralized method for 'securing' the future and toward a compassionate inquiry into the grounds of our response to the loss of human dignity (Sliwinski 2005, p. 230).

Ultimately, I advocate for two specific elements in the emotional labor that is pedagogy. Hope and love are closely related; love acts as an agent of change and provides a sense of purpose and hope that is lacking in isolated individuality (Helm 2004, p. 555). Both hope and love manifest in transference and countertransference and through Transference[1] the teacher can learn a great deal from the lives of individuals. I acknowledge the significance of the Transference within the classroom that sets the educator in the position of one who inspires and responds to what is missing? Through hope, we can teach and through love, we can respond to the desires of learners. Learners must desire to move beyond their status quo, and this desire takes root in a facilitative environment with a "good enough" teacher. Both teacher and learner must desire to grasp those difficult and troubling aspects of their humanity that make them vulnerable and/or dangerous. On the subject of hope in psychoanalysis, Buechler (1995) does not believe that it is specifically the analyst's hope that engenders hope in the patient:

> but the analyst's whole relationship to life. The patient observes the analyst's struggle to make sense of things, keep going in the face of seemingly insurmountable obstacles, retain humor and courage in situations that seem to inspire neither. The analyst stumbles, reacts without self-hate, works to recover. The analyst is willing to work hard. She is honest without being crippled by shame. She wants to live even the most difficult moments. She doesn't shrink from what is ugly in herself or the other. She is more interested in growth than in being right, more curious than self-protective. She can be wounded but refuses to be made dead. While in part this attitude may provide a model, and it may be contagious, I think that what mainly creates hope is the patient's experience of finding a way to relate to such a person. For many, this task requires substantive changes, alterations in all components of

> the emotion system. The deepened curiosity and joy, the lightened envy and hate that results engenders hope. (p.72)

If a teacher could be so open, so frank, so human, learners might be less afraid to confront difficult knowledge. Beuchler states that it is in learning how to relate with such a vulnerable person that an analysand experiences hope. This project has been an exercise in working through the vulnerabilities of the authors in the memoirs, the children in the narratives as well as my own in order to find hope in the current education system.

I have drawn significant parallels between the teacher and analyst. In this I have attempted to offer a shift from the view of educators as ones tasked through theoretical frameworks and paradigm boundaries to provide mental hygiene to the learner. These parallels make it possible to understand the emotional life of the teacher as other to the student. The teacher's task can seem insurmountable just as sometimes the analyst is faced with the anxiety of the mission. In Beuchler's (1995) words:

> For some analysts, treatment must address specific unmet developmental needs. Others, believing that if the patient can profit from all that life can teach, healing will occur, focus more on the patient's capacity for new experience. If only the patient could fully experience what is now "inattended," the patient would progress. A strong belief in either of these paradigms, or in any other conception of growth, will give analysts a sense of what their mission is. But will it make us the long-distance runners we all need to be? Will it carry us through the bleak, lifeless periods where no movement seems possible, let alone evident? (p. 68)

In this bleakness, I do not forget the parent. Before the anxiety is passed on to the teacher, it is carried by the parent, who never really lets it go. The parent worries about the child's future—what can she be, what can he achieve, and where do they belong in the complex discourses of society.

For the parent education is their hope. They hope that schooling will help their child develop into a balanced, healthy, and productive member of society. They hope unnecessary suffering will be circumvented by the necessary suffering meted out in our education systems. Like Bev Sellars's grandmother, sometimes in spite of their own horrific childhoods in schools, they still send off their most precious and loved ones to be educated. Alternatively, like Mark Mathabane's father, they curse the institution of education and hate everything that represents it. Either way, especially in the Western Hemisphere, their children are required to go to school one way or another, or there will be consequences.

In my exploration of the paradoxes created by disconnections between primary and secondary socialization, I have tried to illustrate the need for a unified approach to education that connects family life with the institutional structures of education. Within a privileged space this is made possible by acknowledging the place from which learners emerge—family. Family is the first teacher that gives the learner material with which they can approach everything they learn at school. Like Glen Retief, learners come to understand their lived experiences within the schooling system beginning with terms of references given at home. Race, gender, ethnicity, and other factors take root within the family context and then expand in the school and larger society.

Families are complex evolving entities that are vulnerable to the discourses of society. Difference is an all-encompassing word to sum up this complexity. The one thing we see illustrated in the three memoirs within the family home is love. However, once the children leave the safety of their families' love to enter the school system, love seems to be the least thing afforded to them. Love is eradicated in the business of educating. My work has focused on paradigm shifts that reconstitute love as necessary in education. Without love, pedagogy is impossible. In the clinic, the love necessary to engender hope emanates from the position the analyst takes. Once more, Beuchler's (1995) words are apt:

> The aspect of active hope that affirms a commitment to life is probably not generally communicated in the content of what is said but, rather, in the fervor of the tone, in the strength of conviction that may be signaled by directness and forcefulness of speech. In analysis, this is probably conveyed to the patient more fully by personal and professional attitudes the analyst reveals unwittingly. Love of the work, a passion for promoting life and growth, an empathic stance toward herself and others, a willingness to struggle, joy in the humor and challenge of life are some of the intangibles that make themselves known in the subtle timing and gestures of the music, rather than in the words. What the analyst focuses on, responds to, is willing to break the frame for, lets pass in silence, meets with passion, expresses in the first person, tires about, is willing to fight, says a great deal. (pp. 72–73)

What the analyst conveys, and what Beuchler speaks of, is the kind of love I centralize in privileged space. Within privileged space, love guides the focus, responses, willingness, passion, and expressions of the teacher. Within privileged space, learners with their inhibiting psychopathologies encounter love that engenders hope.

The child learns to love at home. The child learns to hate at home. The child learns to negotiate between the two at home. That is the simplistic overview of object theory and Freud's Oedipus Complex theory. In understanding the significance of the home to schooling, I turned to what psychoanalysis can teach us, and once more, I advocate for a privileged space on this merit. According to Hopper (2006):

> Group analysts are particularly sensitive to the sociality of each person's internal world, and believe that this internal sociality is recreated

> and made manifest in simultaneous Transferences and transferences, and countertransferences. These processes reflect how psychic reality originates and develops, that is, within social situations. Through their regressions, the members of groups tend to recreate their past patterns of functioning in their families of origin as well as their families of procreation, at various phases of their development, in addition to past patterns of functioning in groups of all kinds, perhaps starting with play groups and classrooms. (p. 552)

Similarly, at school learners re-create patterns and exercise the same emotions, stretching boundaries a little wider or narrowing them down a little more. Unless education can contain these exercises in affect, the learner suffers. Such unnecessary suffering is not conducive to learning the academic content we have privileged above all else in our schools.

Learning is the acquiring of difficult knowledge (Britzman 1998; 2000) and psychoanalysis has taught us that education is trauma. This work focuses not on what is taught, rather, on who is taught, and how teaching and learning takes place for the oppressed child. I demonstrate the use of power and authority over helpless minds to socialize children into oppressed positions. Maintenance of the status quo at the expenses of the victims' childhoods happen through these oppressive practices. On the other hand, where oppression was rife but education contained, the child was able to resist the status quo and find liberation through the desire for knowledge. Through my analysis of the memoirs, I highlight micro-level, meso-level, and macro-level mechanisms of social difference.

Through privileged space, we can cultivate the capacity to speak for those who have been silenced, we can redefine power for those who have been abused, and we can provide mechanisms for discovery to those who seek answers. The best part being, in privileged space, they are actively engaged at their own pace and in their words. Pedagogy that is socially just can accommodate the psychopathologies society has triggered, and it is imperative that education remediates the damage it caused in the past. Education is culpable and pedagogy complicit in dehumanizing by taking away the learners capacity to produce signifiers. Building the capacity begins with instilling hope. Hope produces love and love leads to surrender, an act which is not voluntary like submission but must come from a deeper place where surrender seems the only way forward.

Difference is trauma. I have highlighted that throughout my work. I have also highlighted that not all trauma is bad, and not all trauma is lasting. Educators might find themselves in paradoxical situations where efforts to address social transgressions often lead to transgressive pedagogy. Education, through a socially just pedagogy that privileges each learner's subjectivity and maintains the privilege of the teacher, can counteract the damaging effects of society's divisive nature. Facing our humanity means recognizing there is no such thing as a safe space in education, just as there is no such thing as color blindness or gender neutrality in wider society. The use of such language creates structures that camouflage the terrible consequences of oppressive fantasies, which negate the experiences and development of individuals who are racialized and sexually variant. My work exposes the trauma of difference and the psychic ramifications of social and educational practices built on these discourses (Hickson and Kriegler 1991; 1996). Through my examination of childhood shaped by social experiences, and through a psychoanalytically informed discussion of difference within the educational system, I have arrived to the conclusion that difference, although problematized, is human and being human is being emotional.

In considering racial and sexual difference, what children learn about difference and discrimination must be careful not to paint a picture of eternal oppression. It is true that systems have been oppressive and still are. It is true that some children are predestined by such systems to failure. However, it is also true that nothing stays the same forever. Systems are dynamic and the people within them can be, too. To teach children how to negotiate with and within their systems means to teach society how to be open and ever changing. We teach hope by allowing children to try and then fail but also to try and then succeed. We also teach them hope by allowing them to choose their actions and face the consequences.

Both knowledge and action are critical in providing a privileged space. The teacher who can harness the desire of students in order to help them learn, then act, and acquire experience through knowledge has achieved the ultimate measure of education. This is what some might call "making a difference." Crucial to social justice in education is the cycle of knowledge production and action that shifts glaciers more rapidly. As a society, we have come to know much since the days of segregation but failure to act has caused regression, which is manifest in the new crop of segregated schooling. I sincerely believe this is the result of inaction.

Through my own experiences, I have concluded that social justice in pedagogy is the acknowledgment of the erased and the marginalized. It is the practice of negotiating facts and it is equity, inclusion, and diversity in and through teaching and learning. Social justice in pedagogy is apparent in the practice of making society accountable to all learners and all learners becoming social citizens with a stake in the future. In conceptualizing a privileged space, I hypothesize a paradigm shift that acknowledges the invisible work, the labor of emotionality, and the unconscious of both teachers and learners. Acknowledging the unconscious within pedagogical spaces brings into the classroom an unconscious force that pushes society to be accountable for the traumatization of the psychic child.

Desire is an inherent quality in humanity and as such, education is the instrument society has formulated to allow for the fulfillment of desire. Through the words we speak, we create the knowledge that informs our others who and what they mean to us. Within each learner is a desire to express these feelings. Although we may not think of today's schools as especially affective or enlightening, as we focus more on sociocultural factors of citizenship, it is crucial that education does not lose, repress, or stifle the desires that make us human, especially to each other.

I believe it is time we made emotional learning and teaching a focus especially in these days when social difference has become a fatal condition. Noddings (2005) highlights the child's need to develop emotionally within education. She states that "Often, basic needs and needs associated with self-actualization coexist, and some deeply troubled children relieve their anxieties by immersing themselves in schoolwork. But more often, needy children simply cannot concentrate well enough to learn" (p. 151). She further states:

> All kinds of real, pressing needs overwhelm the academic ones we so easily infer for schoolchildren. Homelessness, poverty, toothaches, faulty vision, violence, fear of rebuke or mockery, sick or missing parents, and feelings of worthlessness all get in the way of the learning deemed important by school people. (p. 151)

Within privileged space the child does not need to cover over her needs or desires. The child can openly express them so that education can happen and the child can succeed. Even when we examine the plight of students in higher education, we have expectations that they have overcome whatever needs they might have possessed as a child to be in university. By the time we are supervising doctoral students we hardly consider their suffering as central to their education. We might not consider that the men and women earning doctorates might be in need of love and hope in order for them to successfully complete the six or more grueling years of doctoral studies. They are adults who have already "succeeded" by some standards. Except, as Bev Sellars, Glen Retief, and Mark Mathabane reveal, the suffering and pains of childhood carry on into adulthood, still insisting, still seeking satisfaction. All three authors allude to working through their trauma through their encounters with education in university. Their studies in higher education gave them the language they needed to express their trauma and provide us testimony to the complicity of education in oppressing children.

Finally, I return to the question of teacher education: How can teachers acquire the necessary skills and competencies necessary to manage transference and countertransference? Leaning on psychoanalysis theoretically is a much simpler task than figuring out how teachers can be trained to possess the same skills and competencies that analysts possess. This has been the difficulty I have encountered in any discussions and presentations conducted on the applicability of psychoanalytic paradigms for pedagogy. At a recent workshop in Australia, a university professor in obvious despair stated she is not equipped to deal with "the emotional stuff." I empathized and had no adequate response to her statement. She also talked about her own position as a white privileged female trying to teach about inequities and oppression in education. She seemed to have identified her own perceived social identity as the biggest barrier to practicing anti-oppressive pedagogy. There was a sense of helplessness and hopelessness in the group of university faculty; an overwhelming sense of impossibility.

Freud's outlook on this impossibility is clarified by Triana (2007) who states that "Because of the difficulty in acquiring the 'ideal qualifications' needed for obtaining satisfying results in the 'impossible profession,' Freud recommended that an aspirant for the 'impossble profession' undertake an 'analysis of himself'" (p. 233). Psychoanalysis, like Freud suggested, helps the teacher reach a level of maturity that is necessary to accomplish generativity—an interest in establishing and guiding the next generation as a kind of responsibility. As Triana suggests:

> The level of maturity achieved in generativity allows for an accurate opinion of oneself, the ability to keep one's talents and accomplishments in perspective, to have a sense of self-acceptance, an understanding of one's imperfections, and to be free from arrogance and low self-esteem. (p. 232)

Ultimately, social justice in education can be achieved, regardless of one's race, gender, sexuality, or other difference through an attitude of open-mindedness, a willingness to admit mistakes and seek advice and always being open to learning even from one's students. If psychoanalysis can help teachers reach this level of generativity then every classroom can be a privileged space where those learning can connect and communicate with a central figure that is making them feel empowered and able to learn even the more troubling and difficult aspects of humanity. A way forward, then, might be to make the privileged space framework available through experiential learning for teacher training candidates.

## NOTE

1. The justification for the use of the upper case and the lower case is to indicate who the official analyst is (Hopper 2006, p. 551).

# Bibliography

Ahmed, S. (2004). Affective economies. *Social Text*, *22* (2), 117–39.
Ainsworth, M. D. S., Blehar, M. C., Waters, E., and Wall, S. N. (2015). *Patterns of attachment: A psychological study of the strange situation*. Psychology Press.
Akhtar, S., and Parens, H. (2004). *Real and imaginary fathers: Development, transference, and healing*. Lanham, Md.: Jason Aronson.
Alcorn, Marshall W., Jr. (2010). "The desire not to know" as a challenge to teaching. *Psychoanalysis, Culture & Society, 15*(4), 346–60. doi:http://dx.doi.org/10.1057/pcs.2010.9.
Armbruster-Sandoval, R. (2008). Teaching smoke signals: fatherhood, forgiveness, and "freedom." *Wicazo Sa Review, 23*(1), 123+. Retrieved from https://muse.jhu.edu/journals/wicazo_sa_review/v023/23.1armbruster-sandoval.html#REF8.
Armstrong, N. (2012). What can we learn from service user memoirs? information and service user experience. *The Psychiatrist, 36*(9), 341–44. doi:http://dx.doi.org/10.1192/pb.bp.111.037523.
Assembly, U. G. (1989). Convention on the Rights of the Child. *United Nations, Treaty Series, 1577*(3).
Barnett, D. (2010). *Privileged thinking in today's schools: The implications for social justice*. Lanham, MD: Rowman & Littlefield Education.
Bartell, T. G., and Carpenter, T. P. (2008). The three rs of social justice: A review of reading and writing the world with mathematics: Toward a pedagogy for social justice. *Journal for Research in Mathematics Education, 39*(1), 95–99. Retrieved from http://search.proquest.com.ezproxy.library.yorku.ca/docview/622060595?accountid=15182.
Bell, C. R., and Lacan, J. (2014). The Lacanian Subject: Subject of Desire or the Subject of Drive? *Language and Psychoanalysis, 3*(1), 39–65.
Bem, D. J. (1967). Self-perception: An alternative interpretation of cognitive dissonance phenomena. *Psychological review, 74*(3), 183.
Bettelheim, B. (1987). *A good enough parent: A book on child-rearing*. Alfred A. Knopf.
Bhabha, H. K., and Ebrary - York University. (1994). *The location of culture*. London, New York: Routledge.
Bracher, M. (1994). *Lacanian theory of discourse: Subject, structure, and society*. New York: New York University Press
Britzman, D. P. (1998) *Lost Subjects, Contested Objects: Toward a Psychoanalytic Inquiry of Learning*. Albany: State University of New York Press.
Britzman, D. P. (2000). If the Story Cannot End: Deferred Action, Ambivalence, and Difficult Knowledge. In R. I. Simon , S. Rosenberg , C. Eppert and R. Baum (Eds.), *Between Hope and Despair: Pedagogy and the Remembrance of Historical Trauma* (pp. 27–57 ). Lanham, MD: Rowman & Littlefield Publishers.
Britzman, D. P. (2003). *After-education: Anna Freud, Melanie Klein, and psychoanalytic histories of learning*. Albany: State University of New York Press.
Britzman, D. P. (2006). *Novel education: Psychoanalytic studies of learning and not learning*. New York: Peter Lang.
Britzman, D. P. (2009). *The very thought of education: Psychoanalysis and the impossible professions*. Albany: State University of New York Press.
Britzman, D. P. (2011). *Freud and education*. New York: Routledge.

Buechler, S. (1995). Hope as inspiration in psychoanalysis. *Psychoanalytic Dialogues, 5*(1), 63–74. Retrieved from http://ezproxy.library.yorku.ca/login?url=http://search.proquest.com/docview/618638711?accountid=15182.
Buetow, H. A. (1971). The underprivileged and roman catholic education. *Journal of Negro Education, 40*(4), 373–89. Retrieved from http://search.proquest.com.ezproxy.library.yorku.ca/docview/615825896?accountid=15182.
Butler, J. (1990). Gender trouble, feminist theory, and psychoanalytic discourse. *Feminism/postmodernism, 327*.
Calvo, L. (2008). Racial fantasies and the primal scene of miscegenation. *International Journal of Psychoanalysis, 89*(1), 55–70. Retrieved from http://search.proquest.com.ezproxy.library.yorku.ca/docview/203971268?accountid=15182.
Carlin, N. (2011). Confession and forgiveness: A pastoral reading of A father's son by lionel dahmer. *Pastoral Psychology, 60*(3), 377–97. doi:http://dx.doi.org/10.1007/s11089-011-0348-5.
Carr-Stewart, S. (2001). A treaty right to education. *Canadian Journal of Education, 26*(3), 0. Retrieved from http://search.proquest.com.ezproxy.library.yorku.ca/docview/215375495?accountid=15182
Chadderton, C. (2013). Towards a research framework for race in education: Critical race theory and judith butler. *International Journal of Qualitative Studies in Education, 26*(1), 39–55. doi:http://dx.doi.org/10.1080/09518398.2011.650001.
Chikovore, J., Makusha, T., and Richter, L. (2013). Father involvement in young children's care and education in southern africa. *Father involvement in young children's lives: A global analysis* (pp. 261–78). Springer Science + Business Media, New York, NY. doi:http://dx.doi.org/10.1007/978-94-007-5155-2_15.
Chimbganda, T. (2015). Traumatic Pedagogy: when epistemic privilege and white privilege collide. In K. Fasching-Varner, K. Albert, R. Mitchell, and C. Allen (Eds.), *Racial Battle Fatigue in Higher Education: Exposing the Myth of Post-Racial America*. (pp. 29–36). Lanham, MD: Rowman & Littlefield Publishers, Inc.
Christie, P. (1998). Schools as (dis)organisations: The "breakdown of the culture of learning and teaching" in south african schools. *Cambridge Journal of Education, 28*(3), 283–300. Retrieved from http://search.proquest.com.ezproxy.library.yorku.ca/docview/619368467?accountid=15182
Coates, T. N. (2015). *Between the world and me*. Text Publishing.
Coen, S. J. (1994). *Between author and reader: A psychoanalytic approach to writing and reading*. Columbia University Press.
Cole, M. (2012). Critical race theory in education, marxism and abstract racial domination. *British Journal of Sociology of Education, 33* (2), 167–83. doi:http://dx.doi.org/10.1080/01425692.2011.649830.
Connor, M. E., and White, J. L. (2011). *Black fathers: An invisible presence in America* (2nd ed.). New York: Routledge.
Cooper, A. M. (1993). Psychotherapeutic approaches to masochism. *The Journal of psychotherapy practice and research*, 2(1), 51.
Dalal, F. (2002). *Race, colour and the process of racialization: New perspectives from group analysis, psychoanalysis, and sociology*. Hove, [England]; New York: Brunner-Routledge.
Davin, N. F., and Early Canadiana Online (CRKN) - York University. (1879). *Report on industrial schools for Indians and half-breeds*. [Ottawa?: s.n.
Davies, S., and Guppy, N. (2010). *The schooled society: An introduction to the sociology of education* (2nd ed.). Don Mills, Ont.: Oxford University Press.
Davis, R. (1987). Pedagogy, Lacan, and the Freudian Subject. *College English* (49) 749–55.
de Rementeria, A. (2011). How the use of transference and countertransference, particularly in parent-infant psychotherapy, can inform the work of an education or childcare practitioner. *Psychodynamic Practice: Individuals, Groups and Organisations,17*(1), 41–56. doi:http://dx.doi.org/10.1080/14753634.2011.539351.

Dei, George J. (Nana Sefa A. I.). (2014). The African scholar in the western academy. *Journal of Black Studies, 45*(3), 167–79. Retrieved from http://search.proquest.com.ezproxy.library.yorku.ca/docview/1564155181?accountid=15182.

Denis, V. S. (2007). Aboriginal education and anti-racist education: Building Alliances Across Cultural and Racial Identity. *Canadian Journal of Education*, 30(4), 1068–92. Retrieved from http://search.proquest.com.ezproxy.library.yorku.ca/docview/215374551?accountid=15182

Devaney, J., and Spratt, T. (2009). Child abuse as a complex and wicked problem: Reflecting on policy developments in the United Kingdom in working with children and families with multiple problems. *Children And Youth Services Review, 31*(6), 635–41. doi:10.1016/j.childyouth.2008.12.003.

Dimitriadis, Greg, and George Kamberelis. *Theory for Education*. New York: Routledge, 2006.

Dolto, F. (2013). *Psychoanalysis and Paediatrics: Key Psychoanalytic Concepts with Sixteen Clinical Observations of Children*. London, GBR: Karnac Books. Retrieved from http://www.ebrary.com.

Domenici, T., and Lesser, R. C. (1995). *Disorienting sexuality: Psychoanalytic reappraisals of sexual identities*. New York: Routledge.

Downing, L., and Nobus, D. (2006). *Perversion: Psychoanalytic Perspectives/perspectives on Psychoanalysis*. London: Karnac Books.

Duckitt, J. (1992). Education and authoritarianism among English- and Afrikaans-speaking white south africans. *Journal of Social Psychology, 132*(6), 701. Retrieved from http://search.proquest.com.ezproxy.library.yorku.ca/docview/1290710670?accountid=15182.

Dudziak, S., and Profitt, N. J. (2012). Group work and social justice: Designing pedagogy for social change. *Social Work with Groups: A Journal of Community and Clinical Practice, 35*(3), 235–52. doi:http://dx.doi.org/10.1080/01609513.2011.624370.

EchoHawk, M. (1997). Suicide: The scourge of Native American people. *Suicide and Life-Threatening Behavior, 27*(1), 60. Retrieved from http://search.proquest.com.ezproxy.library.yorku.ca/docview/1297940713?accountid=15182.

Edwards, G. (2014). Standpoint theory, realism and the search for objectivity in the sociology of education. *British Journal of Sociology of Education, 35*(2), 167–84. doi:http://dx.doi.org/10.1080/01425692.2012.747588.

Edwards, J. (2013). Ripples in mental space caused by dark matters and twisted tales: Some reflections on memory, memoirs and therapeutic work. *Psychodynamic Practice: Individuals, Groups and Organisations, 19*(4), 390–405. doi:http://dx.doi.org/10.1080/14753634.2013.854532.

Eksner, H. J. (2015). Meaning-making and motivation in urban zones of marginalization: Mapping the ecocultural context of educational goals. *British Journal of Sociology of Education, 36*(4), 595–613. doi:10.1080/01425692.2013.835712.

Eriksen, T. H. (2007). Complexity in social and cultural integration: Some analytical dimensions. *Ethnic and Racial Studies, 30*(6), 1055–69. doi:http://dx.doi.org/10.1080/01419870701599481.

Erisken, T. H. (2011). *Living in an Overheated World: Otherness as a Universal Condition*. In Sencindiver, S.Y., Beville, M. and Lauritzen , M. Editor (Eds.), Otherness: A Multilateral Perspective (239–60). New York: Peter Lang.

Evans, D., Taylor and Francis E-books (CRKN) - York University., and ebrary, I. (1996). *An introductory dictionary of Lacanian psychoanalysis*. London, New York: Routledge.

Fanon, F. (1963). *The wretched of the earth*. New York: Grove Press.

Fanon, F. (1967). *Black skin, white masks*. New York: Grove Press.

Farley, L. (2006). Repositioning identification: Reflections on a visit to historica's heritage fair. *Canadian Journal of Education, 29*(4), 1019–38. doi:http://dx.doi.org/10.2307/20054209.

Farley, L., and Mishra Tarc, A. (2014). Drawing trauma: The therapeutic potential of witnessing the child's visual testimony of war. *Journal of the American Psychoanalytic Association, 62*(5), 835–54. doi:10.1177/0003065114554419.

Federn, P. (1953). The ego as subject and object in narcissism. *Vienna psychoanalytic society* (pp. 283–322).Oxford, New York: Basic Books Basic Books. doi:http://dx.doi.org/10.1037/10571-015.

Felman, S. (1987). *Jacques Lacan and the adventure of insight*. Cambridge, MA: Harvard University Press.

Felman, S. (1982). Psychoanalysis and education: Teaching terminable and interminable. *Yale French Studies*, (63), 21–44.

Felman, S., & Laub, D. (1992). *Testimony: Crises of witnessing in literature, psychoanalysis, and history*. Taylor & Francis.

Felman, S., Laub, D., and Ebscohost E-Books - York University. (1991). *Testimony: Crises of witnessing in literature, psychoanalysis, and history*. New York: Routledge.

Festinger, L. (1962). *A theory of cognitive dissonance* (Vol. 2). Palo Alto, CA: Stanford University Press.

Fine, M. (2012). Troubling calls for evidence: A critical race, class and gender analysis of whose evidence counts. *Feminism & Psychology, 22*(1), 3–19.

Fink, B. (1995). *The Lacanian subject: Between language and jouissance*. Princeton, NJ: Princeton University Press.

Fink, B. (2007). *Fundamentals of psychoanalytic technique: A Lacanian approach for practitioners*. New York: W. W. Norton.

Francis, D. (2012). The Imaginary Indian: The image of the Indian in Canadian culture. Arsenal Pulp Press.

Frank, A. (2002). Why study people's stories? The dialogical ethics of narrative analysis. *International Journal of Qualitative Methods, 1*(1), Article 6. Retrieved date
from http://www.ualberta.ca/~ijqm/.

Freire, P. (2000). *Pedagogy of the oppressed* (30th anniversary ed.). New York: Continuum.

French, T. M., and Wheeler, D. R. (1963). Hope and repudiation of hope in psychoanalytic therapy. *The International Journal of Psychoanalysis, 44*(3), 304–16. Retrieved from http://ezproxy.library.yorku.ca/login?url=http://search.proquest.com/docview/615440159?accountid=15182.

Freud, S. (1917). Mourning and Melancholia. *The Standard Edition of the Complete Psychological Works of Sigmund Freud, Volume XIV (1914–1916): On the History of the Psycho-Analytic Movement, Papers on Metapsychology and Other Works*, ed. James Strachey, 237–58. London: The Hogarth Press, 1957.

Freud, S. (1932). Fetishism. *The Psychoanalytic Review (1913–1957), 19*, 226.

Freud, S. (1994). *Fetishism*. New York: New York University Press. Retrieved from http://search.proquest.com.ezproxy.library.yorku.ca/docview/618562153?accountid=15182.

Freud, S., and Rivere, J. (1953). *Civilization and its discontents*. London: The Hogarth Press Ltd.

Freud, S. (1909). Notes upon a case of obsessional neurosis. *Standard edition, 10*(151), 320.

Freud, S., and Strachey, J. (1962). *The ego and the id* (No. 142). New York: W. W. Norton & Company.

Freud, S., Strachey, J., and Richards, A. (1977). *On sexuality: Three essays on the theory of sexuality and other works*. Harmondsworth, Eng.: Penguin Books.

Freud, S. (2006). *The Penguin Freud Reader*. New York: W. W. Norton, 2006.

Frosh, S. (2010). *Psychoanalysis outside the clinic: Interventions in psychosocial studies*. Basingstoke, Hampshire; New York: Palgrave Macmillan.

Ghent, E. (1990). Masochism, submission, surrender: Masochism as a perversion of surrender. *Contemporary psychoanalysis, 26*(1), 108–36.

George, S. (2011). Realism's Racial Gaze and Stephen Crane's *The Monster*: A Lacanian Reading. *Experiments in/of Realism*. (Winter 2011): 69–86. Spec. issue of *Synthesis* 3

Edited by Anna Despotopoulou and Katerina Kitsi-Mitakou. Retrieved from http://synthesis.enl.uoa.gr/fileadmin/synthesis.enl.uoa.gr/uploads/Issue3/issue3_George.pdf.

George, S. (2012). Approaching the *Thing* of Slavery: A Lacanian Analysis of Toni Morrison's *Beloved*. *African American Review* 45(1), 115–30. The Johns Hopkins University Press. Retrieved August 20, 2013, from Project MUSE database.

Grant, S. (2016). *The tears of strangers*. New York: HarperCollins.

Greenberg, M. T., Kusché, C. A., and Speltz, M. (2014). 2 Psychopathology: The Role of Relationships. *Internalizing and externalizing expressions of dysfunction*, 2, 21.

Haig-Brown, C. (1991). *Resistance and renewal: Surviving the Indian residential school* (Updated ed.). Vancouver, B.C.: Arsenal Pulp Press.

Helm, F. L. (2004). Hope is curative. *Psychoanalytic Psychology, 21*(4), 554–66. doi:http://dx.doi.org/10.1037/0736-9735.21.4.554.

Halpern, J. (2001). *From detached concern to empathy: Humanizing medical practice*. Oxford, New York: Oxford University Press.

Hahn Tapper, A. J. (2013). A pedagogy of social justice education: Social identity theory, intersectionality, and empowerment. *Conflict Resolution Quarterly, 30*(4), 411–45. doi:http://dx.doi.org/10.1002/crq.21072.

Harding, S. (1993). Rethinking standpoint epistemology: What is strong objectivity? In L. Alcoff and E. Potter (Eds.) *Feminist Epistemologies*, 1st edition (p.p. 49–82). New York, NY: Routledge.

Harrison, I. B. (1979). On freud's view of the infant–mother relationship and of the oceanic feeling—some subjective influences. *Journal of the American Psychoanalytic Association*, 27(2), 399–421. Retrieved from http://search.proquest.com.ezproxy.library.yorku.ca/docview/616487546?accountid=15182.

Hartman, S. V., and Wilderson, F. B. (2003). The position of the unthought. *Qui Parle*, 183–201.

Harvey, R. (2000). *The fall of apartheid: The inside story from Smuts to Mbeki*. New York: Palgrave.

Hickey, M. (2015). Learning from the experts: A study of free-improvisation pedagogues in university settings. *Journal of Research in Music Education, 62*(4), 425–445. doi:http://dx.doi.org/10.1177/0022429414556319.

Hickson, J., and Kriegler, S. (1991). Childshock: The effects of apartheid on the mental health of South Africa's children. *International Journal for the Advancement of Counselling, 14*(2), 141–54.

Hickson, J., and Kriegler, S. (1996). *Multicultural counseling in a divided and traumatized society: The meaning of childhood and adolescence in South Africa*. Greenwood Press/Greenwood Publishing Group, Westport, CT. Retrieved from http://search.proquest.com.ezproxy.library.yorku.ca/docview/619022449?accountid=15182.

Hill Collins, P. (2009). *Black feminist thought: Knowledge, consciousness, and the politics of empowerment*. New York: Routledge.

Hollan, D. (2008). Being there: On the imaginative aspects of understanding others and being understood. *Ethos, 36*(4), 475. Retrieved from http://ezproxy.library.yorku.ca/login?url=http://search.proquest.com/docview/848011716?accountid=15182

Holley, L. C., and Steiner, S. (2005). Safe space: Student perspectives on classroom environment. *Journal of Social Work Education,41*(1), 49–64. doi:http://dx.doi.org/10.5175/JSWE.2005.200300343

Hook, D. (2013). *(Post)apartheid conditions: Psychoanalysis and social formation*. New York: Palgrave Macmillan.

Hook, D. (2011). Narrative form, 'impossibility' and the retrieval of apartheid history. *Psychoanalysis, Culture & Society, 16*(1), 71–89. doi:http://dx.doi.org/10.1057/pcs.2010.43.

Hook, D., and Long, C. (2011). The apartheid archive project, heterogeneity, and the psychoanalysis of racism. *Psychoanalysis, Culture & Society, 16*(1), 1–10. doi:http://dx.doi.org/10.1057/pcs.2010.45

Housee, S. (2010). When silences are broken: An out of class discussion with asian female students. *Educational Review, 62*(4), 421–34. doi:http://dx.doi.org/10.1080/00131911.2010.486475.

Jacques Alan Miller Extimite in Bracher, M. (1994). *Lacanian theory of discourse: Subject, structure, and society*. New York: New York University Press.

James, C. E. (2012). Students "at risk": Stereotypes and the schooling of black boys. *Urban Education, 47*(2), 464–94. doi:http://dx.doi.org/10.1177/0042085911429084.

James, C. E., and Taylor, L. (2008). "Education will get you to the station": Marginalized students' experiences and perceptions of merit in accessing university. *Canadian Journal of Education, 31*(3), 567–90. Retrieved from http://search.proquest.com.ezproxy.library.yorku.ca/docview/621570892?accountid=15182.

James, C. E. (2003). *Seeing ourselves: Exploring ethnicity, race and culture*. Toronto, ON: Thompson Educational Pub.

James, C. E. (2001). "Multiculturalism, Diversity and Education in the Canadian Context: The Search for an Inclusive Pedagogy." in *Global Constructions of Multicultural Education: Theories and Realities*, eds. C. A. Grant and J. L. Lei (Mahwah, NJ: Lawrence Erbaum Associates, 2001), 175–204.

Janack, M. (1997). Standpoint epistemology without the "standpoint"? : An examination of epistemic privilege and epistemic authority. *Hypatia, 12*(2), 125–39.

Jordan, W. D., and Institute of Early American History and Culture (Williamsburg, VA) (1968). *White over Black: American attitudes toward the Negro, 1550–1812*. Chapel Hill: Published for the Institute of Early American History and Culture at Williamsburg, Va., by the University of North Carolina Press.

Joshee, R., and Sinfield, I. (2010). The Canadian multicultural education policy web: Lessons to learn, pitfalls to avoid. *MER, 2*(1), 55–75.

Kelly, D. M., and Brandes, G. M. (2001). Shifting out of "neutral": Beginning teachers' struggles with teaching for social justice. *Canadian Journal of Education, 26*(4), 437–54. doi:http://dx.doi.org/10.2307/1602176.

Kennedy, R. M. (2011). Toward a Cosmopolitan Curriculum of Forgiveness. Curriculum Inquiry 41: 373–93.doi: 10.1111/j.1467-873X.2011.00551.x.

Kirman, W. J. (1982). Modern psychoanalysis of learning in the classroom. *Modern Psychoanalysis, 7*(1), 87–98. Retrieved from http://search.proquest.com.ezproxy.library.yorku.ca/docview/616735472?accountid=15182.

Klein, M., and Riviere, J. (1964). *Love, hate, and reparation*. New York: Norton.

Kris, E. (1948). On psychoanalysis and education. *American Journal of Orthopsychiatry, 18*(4), 622.

Kristeva, J. (2003). *Intimate revolt: The powers and the limits of psychoanalysis*. New York: Chichester: Columbia University Press.

Kumashiro, K. K. (2002). Against repetition: Addressing resistance to anti-oppressive change in the practices of learning, teaching, supervising, and researching. *Harvard Educational Review, 72*(1), 67–92. Retrieved from http://search.proquest.com.ezproxy.library.yorku.ca/docview/212287955?accountid=15182.

Lacan, J. (1987). Introduction to the Names-of-the-Father seminar, Ed. J.-A. Miller, Trans. J. Mehlman, October, 40, 81–95. (Orig. pub.) 1963.

Lacan, J. (1998). *The four fundamental concepts of psycho-analysis*. New York: W. W. Norton.

Lacan, J. (2006). *Écrits: The first complete edition in English*. Translated by Bruce Fink. New York: W. W. Norton & Co.

Lacan, J. (2010). *The mirror stage as formative of the function of the I as revealed in psychoanalytic experience (1949)*. Routledge/Taylor & Francis Group, New York, NY. Retrieved from http://search.proquest.com.ezproxy.library.yorku.ca/docview/742981254?accountid=15182

Lacan, J. (2011). The seminar of Jacques Lacan: Book V: The formations of the unconscious: 1957–58.

Lacan, J. (1981). *Speech and language in psychoanalysis: Transl. with notes and commentary by Anthony Wilden*. Johns Hopkins University Press.

Lacan, J., and Miller, J. (1991). *The seminar of Jacques Lacan* (Norton paperback ed.). New York: W. W. Norton.
Lane, C. (1998). *The psychoanalysis of race*. New York: Columbia University Press.
Laplanche, J., and Pontalis, J. B. (1974). *The language of psycho-analysis*. New York: Norton.
LeBlanc, R. J. (2013). The Limits to Reform: A Critical Discussion of the Saskatoon Public School Board's Assessment Controversy. *in education*, *17*(2).
Levin, C. (2001). The siege of psychotherapeutic space: Psychoanalysis in the age of Transparency. *Canadian Journal of Psychoanalysis*, *9*(2), 187–215. Retrieved from http:/ /search.proquest.com.ezproxy.library.yorku.ca/docview/222816388?accountid=15182.
Lewis, B. (2010). Navigating therapeutic diversity. *Philosophy, Psychiatry, & Psychology*, *17*(3), 271–74. Retrieved from http://ezproxy.library.yorku.ca/login?url=http:// search.proquest.com/docview/822368920?accountid=15182.
Lewis, G. (2013). Unsafe travel: Experiencing intersectionality and feminist displacements. *Signs*, *38* (4), 869–92. doi:http://dx.doi.org/10.1086/669609.
Lewis, G. (2014). Not by criticality alone. *Feminist Theory*, *15* (1), 31–38. doi:http:// dx.doi.org/10.1177/1464700113513084.
Lewkowich, D. (2013). Insignificant Stories: The Burden of Feeling Unhinged and Uncanny in Detours of Teaching, Learning and Reading. *in education*, *19*(1).
Longhofer, J. (2015). *A-Z of psychodynamic practice*. London: Palgrave and Macmillan.
Martino, W. (1996). Gendered learning practices: Exploring the costs of hegemonic masculinity for girls and boys in schools. *E. Ministerial Council on Education, Training and Youth Affairs (Ed.), Gender equity: A framework for action in Australia Schools, Canberra*, 124–44.
McArthur, J. (2010). Achieving social justice within and through higher education: The challenge for critical pedagogy. *Teaching in Higher Education*, *15*(5), 493–504. doi:http://dx.doi.org/10.1080/13562517.2010.491906.
Macey, D. (2012). *Frantz Fanon: A biography* (2nd ed.). London ; Brooklyn, NY: Verso.
MacKinnon, R. A., Michels, R., and Buckley, P. J. (2015). *The psychiatric interview in clinical practice*. American Psychiatric Pub.
Mathabane, M. (1986). *Kaffir Boy: A Memoir—The True Story of a Black Youth's Coming of Age in Apartheid South Africa*. New York: Free Press.
Matthews, B. (2005). *Engaging Education: Developing Emotional Literacy, Equity And Co-education: Developing emotional literacy, equity and co-education*. McGraw-Hill Education (UK).
McCaughtry, N. (2006). Working politically amongst professional knowledge landscapes to implement gender-sensitive physical education reform. *Physical Education and Sport Pedagogy*, *11*(2), 159–79. doi:http://dx.doi.org/10.1080/17408980600708379.
Meyer, E. J. (2008). Gendered harassment in secondary schools: Understanding teachers'(non)interventions. *Gender and Education*, *20*(6), 555–70.
Moffett, H. (2006). 'These women, they force us to rape them': Rape as Narrative of Social Control in Post-Apartheid South Africa. *Journal of Southern African Studies*, *32*(1), 129–44.
Moon, S. (2011). Rethinking culturally responsive teaching: Toward new (im) possibilities of curriculum studies and policy. *MER*, *3*(2), 69–102.
Moosa, F. (2011). In the apartheid archives: From perversion to paradox. Commentary on paper by gillian straker. *Psychoanalytic Dialogues*, *21*(6), 664–69. doi:http:// dx.doi.org/10.1080/10481885.2011.629562.
Moslund, S. P. (2011). Difference, Otherness and Seeds of Becoming in Transcultural and Migration Literature. In Sencindiver, S. Y., Beville, M. and Lauritzen, M. Editor (Eds.), *Otherness: A Multilateral Perspective* (183–98). New York: Peter Lang.
Moten, F. (2003). *In the break: The aesthetics of the Black radical tradition*. Minneapolis: University of Minnesota Press, 2003.
Mucina, D. D. (2013). I am your son, baba. *Child & Youth Services*, *34*(4), 323–42. doi:http://dx.doi.org/10.1080/0145935X.2013.859900.

Murray, S. (1997) "The Benefits of Journaling: 'Stories are Medicine'—'Art is Medicine'." *Parks & Recreation* (5), 68–75.*ProQuest*. Web. 24 July 2014.
Nagda, B. R. A., Gurin, P., and Lopez, G. E. (2003). Transformative pedagogy for democracy and social justice. *Race, Ethnicity and Education*, *6*(2), 165–91.
Ndimande, B. S. (2013). From bantu education to the fight for socially just education. *Equity & Excellence in Education*, *46*(1), 20–35. doi:http://dx.doi.org/10.1080/10665684.2013.750199
Noddings, N. (2005). Identifying and responding to needs in education.*Cambridge Journal of education*, *35*(2), 147–59.
Onishi, N (2015). Students in South Africa protest slow pace of change. *New York Times*. Accessed: September 10, 2015.
Papineni, P. (2003). Children of bad memories. *The Lancet*, *362*(9386), 825–26. doi:10.1016/S0140-6736(03)14277-8.
Parry, R. (2011). A critical examination of Bion's concept of containment and Winnicott's concept of holding, and their psychotherapeutic implications (Doctoral dissertation).
Patsalides, B., and Patsalides, A. (2001). 'Butterflies caught in the network of signifiers': The goals of psychoanalysis according to Jacques Lacan. *The Psychoanalytic Quarterly*,*70*(1), 201–30. doi:10.1002/j.2167-4086.2001.tb00596.x.
Patterson, M. E. (2010*). Constructions of childhood in apartheid's last decades. (Order No. AAI3382324, Dissertation Abstracts International Section A: Humanities and Social Sciences*, , 4001. Retrieved from http://search.proquest.com.ezproxy.library.yorku.ca/docview/622203910?accountid=15182. (622203910; 2010-99071-011).
Phillips, C. B. (2009). Student portfolios and the hidden curriculum on gender: mapping exclusion. *Medical education*, *43*(9), 847–53.
Pinar, W. F. (2010). Hand in hand: Multiculturalism, nationality, cosmopolitanism. *MER*, 2(1), 25–53.
Pollack, T. M., and Zirkel, S. (2013). Negotiating the contested terrain of equity-focused change efforts in schools: Critical race theory as a leadership framework for creating more equitable schools. *The Urban Review*, *45*(3), 290–310. doi:http://dx.doi.org/10.1007/s11256-012-0231-4.
Posner, T. (2008). Chapter 4: Equity in a Mathematics Classroom: An Exploration. *Journal for Research in Mathematics Education*. Monograph, 14, 127–72.
Powell, L. C., and Barber, M. E. (2006). *Savage inequalities indeed: Irrationality and urban school reform*. In Boldt, Gail M., Salvio, Paula M., Love's return: Psychoanalytic essays on childhood, teaching, and learning 33–60. New York: Routledge/Taylor & Francis Group.
Prager, J. (2009). Melancholic Identities: Post-traumatic Loss, Memory and Identity Formation. *Identity in Question*, 139.
R. L. (2013) Wanderings of the Slave: Black Life and Social Death. http://www.metamute.org/editorial/articles/wanderings-slave-Black-life-and-social-death.
Ramvi, E. (2010). Out of control: A teacher's account. *Psychoanalysis, Culture & Society*, *15* (4), 328–45. doi:http://dx.doi.org/10.1057/pcs.2009.7.
Ratele, K., & Shefer, T. (2013). Desire, fear and entitlement: Sexualising race and racialising sexuality in (re) membering apartheid. In *Race, Memory and the Apartheid Archive* (pp. 188–207). Palgrave Macmillan UK.
Ray, J. J. (1980). Racism and authoritarianism among white South Africans.*The Journal of Social Psychology*, *110*(1), 29–37.
Ray, J. J. (1979). White south africans' views of blacks. *Patterns of Prejudice*, *13*(6), 15–17. Retrieved from http://search.proquest.com.ezproxy.library.yorku.ca/docview/617289194?accountid=15182.
Retief, G. (2011). The Jack Bank. New York: St. Martin's Press.
Robbins, A. D. (1990). Transference in the classroom. *Journal of College Student Psychotherapy*, *5*(1), 35–56. Retrieved from http://search.proquest.com.ezproxy.library.yorku.ca/docview/617942091?accountid=15182.

Ross, A., Dion, J., Cantinotti, M., Collin-Vézina, D., and Paquette, L. (2015). Impact of residential schooling and of child abuse on substance use problem in Indigenous Peoples. *Addictive behaviors, 51*, 184–92.

Roudinesco, E. (2009). Our dark side: A history of perversion. Cambridge, UK; Malden, MA: Polity. New Burnswick, NJ: Rutgers University Press.

Rosseau, J. (2003). The social contract. New York: Dover Publications.

Samuels, R. (2003). Teaching about the holocaust and the subject of objectivity: Psychoanalysis, trauma, and counter-transference in an advanced writing course. *Journal for the Psychoanalysis of Culture & Society, 8*(1), 133–43. doi:http://dx.doi.org/10.1353/psy.2003.0023.

Schugurensky, D. (2007). Does education equalize opportunities? The implications of the TDSB cohort analysis for democracy and meritocracy. Paper prepared for the opening panel of the "Diversity in Education Parents' Forum" organized by the Ethnocultural Community Network of the Toronto District School Board (ECN-TDSB), Toronto.

Sellars, B. (2013). *They called me number one*. Singapore Books.

Sencindiver, S. Y., Beville, M., and Lauritzen, M. (2011). *Otherness: A multilateral perspective*. Frankfurtam Main, New York: Peter Lang.

Seshadri-Crooks, K., Taylor and Francis E-books (CRKN) - York University., and ebrary, I. (2000). *Desiring whiteness: A Lacanian analysis of race*. London, New York: Routledge.

Shimahara, N., Holowinsky, I. Z., and Tomlinson-Clarke, S. (2001). *Ethnicity, race, and nationality in education: A global pespective*. Mahwah, NJ: L. Erlbaum Associates.

Simon, R. I. (1992). *Teaching against the grain: Texts for a pedagogy of possibility*. New York: Bergin & Garvey.

Smith, W. A. (2004). Black faculty coping with racial battle fatigue: The campus racial climate in a post-civil rights era. *A long way to go: Conversations about race by African American faculty and graduate students, 14*, 171–90.

Smith, W. A., Allen, W. R., & Danley, L. L. (2007). "Assume the position... you fit the description": Psychosocial experiences and racial battle fatigue among African American male college students. *American Behavioral Scientist, 51*(4), 551–78.

Smith, W. A. (2010). Toward an understanding of Black misandric microaggressions and racial battle fatigue in historically White institutions. *The state of the African American male in Michigan: A courageous conversation*, 265–77.

Smith, W. A., Hung, M., & Franklin, J. D. (2011). Racial battle fatigue and the miseducation of Black men: Racial microaggressions, societal problems, and environmental stress. *The Journal of Negro Education*, 63–82.

Sonn, C. C., Stevens, G., & Duncan, N. (2013). Decolonisation, critical methodologies and why stories matter. In *Race, Memory and the Apartheid Archive* (pp. 295–314). Palgrave Macmillan UK.

Soudien, C. (2001). Culture, race, and ethnicity in education in south africa. *Rutgers invitational symposium on education* (pp. 101–28) Lawrence Erlbaum Associates Publishers, Mahwah, NJ. Retrieved from http://search.proquest.com.ezproxy.library.yorku.ca/docview/619690090?accountid=15182.

Spillers, H. J. (2003). *Black, white, and in color: Essays on American literature and culture*. Chicago: University of Chicago Press.

Spivak, G. (1993) "Can the Subaltern Speak?" In Patrick Williams and Laura Chrisman, eds., Colonial Discourse and Post-Colonial Theory: A Reader, pp. 66–111. Hemel Hempstead and New York: Harvester Wheatsheaf.

Stengel, B. S. (2010). The complex case of fear and safe space. *Studies in Philosophy and Education, 29*(6), 523–40. doi:http://dx.doi.org/10.1007/s11217-010-9198-3.

Stone, M. (1998). Journaling with clients. *The Journal of Individual Psychology, 54*(4), 535–45. Retrieved from http://search.proquest.com.ezproxy.library.yorku.ca/docview/619404135?accountid=15182.

Storey, K., Shute, T., & Thompson, A. (2008). Building a culture of recovery: A comprehensive recovery education strategy.*Journal of Ethics in Mental Health, 3*(1), 1–

4. Retrieved from http://search.proquest.com.ezproxy.library.yorku.ca/docview/622077015?accountid=182.

Straker, G. (2011). Unsettling whiteness. *Psychoanalysis, Culture & Society*, *16*(1), 11–26.

Straker, G. (2004). Race for cover: Castrated whiteness, perverse consequences. *Psychoanalytic Dialogues, 14* (4), 405–22. Retrieved from http://search.proquest.com.ezproxy.library.yorku.ca/docview/233296983?accountid=15182.

Suchet, M. (2007). Unraveling whiteness. *Psychoanalytic Dialogues, 17*(6), 867–86. doi:http://dx.doi.org/10.1080/10481880701703730.

Swartz, S. (2005). Can the clinical subject speak?: Some thoughts on subaltern psychology. *Theory & Psychology, 15*(4), 505–25. doi:http://dx.doi.org/10.1177/0959354305054749.

Swartz, S. (2012). The broken mirror: Difference and shame in south african psychotherapy. *International Journal of Psychoanalytic Self Psychology, 7*(2), 196–212. doi:http://dx.doi.org/10.1080/15551024.2012.656351.

Swartz, S. (2007). The power to name: South African intersubjective psychoanalytic psychotherapy and the negotiation of racialized histories. *European Journal of Psychotherapy and Counselling, 9*(2), 177–90. doi:http://dx.doi.org/10.1080/13642530701368485.

Tarc, A. M. (2005). Education as humanism of the other. *Educational Philosophy and Theory, 37*(6), 833–49.

Tarc, A. R. M. (2013). Wild reading: This madness to our method. *International Journal of Qualitative Studies in Education, 26*(5), 537–52. doi:http://dx.doi.org/10.1080/09518398.2013.786842.

Taubman, P. M. (2012). *Disavowed knowledge: Psychoanalysis, education, and teaching*. Routledge.

Taylor, S. K. (2009). Right pedagogy/wrong language and caring in times of fear? Issues in the schooling of ethnic Kurdish children in Denmark. *International Journal of BilingualEducation and Bilingualism, 12*(3), 291–307. doi:http://dx.doi.org/10.1080/13670050802153301.

Teo, T. (2008). From Speculation to Epistemological Violence in Psychology A Critical-Hermeneutic Reconstruction. *Theory & Psychology*, *18*(1), 47–67.

Teo, T. (2009). Psychology without Caucasians. *Canadian Psychology/Psychologie canadienne*, *50*(2), 91.

Teo, T. (2010). What is epistemological violence in the empirical social sciences? *Social and Personality Psychology Compass, 4*(5), 295–303. doi:http://dx.doi.org/10.1111/j.1751-9004.2010.00265.x.

Teo, T. (2011a). Empirical race psychology and the hermeneutics of epistemological violence. *Human Studies*, *34*(3), 237–55.

Teo, T. (2011b). Theory and empirical research: Can scientific ideas be violent. *Theoretical psychology: Global transformations and challenges*, 239–46.

Truth and Reconciliation Commission. (2015). Canada's Residential Schools: The Inuit and Northern Experience. The Final Report of the Truth and Reconciliation Commission of Canada.

Todd, S. (2003). Learning from the Other: Levinas. *Psychoanalysis, and Ethical Possibilities in Education*. New York: State University of New York Press.

Todd, S. (2008). Facing Humanity: The difficult task of cosmopolitan education. *Submitted to PESGB*.

Todd, S. (2009). Facing humanity: The difficult task of cosmopolitan education. http://www.philosophy-of-education.org/conferences/pdfs/Sharon_Todd.pdf.

Triana, R. (2007). Teaching as vocation. *Psychiatry, 70*(3), 229–37. Retrieved from http://ezproxy.library.yorku.ca/login?url=http://search.proquest.com/docview/220671238?accountid=15182.

Truscott, R. (2013). Obsessional whiteness and the unpaid debt of apartheid. *Social and Personality Psychology Compass, 7*(8), 537–46. doi:http://dx.doi.org/10.1111/spc3.12050.

Twemlow, S. W. (2000). The roots of violence: Converging psychoanalytic explanatory models for power struggles and violence in schools.*Psychoanalytic Quarterly, 69*(4), 741–85.

Vanheule, S., and Verhaeghe, (2004). Powerlessness and impossibility in special education: A qualitative study on professional burnout from a lacanian perspective. *Human Relations, 57*(4), 497–519. doi:http://dx.doi.org/10.1177/0018726704043897.

Verhaeghe, P. (2001). Teaching and psychoanalysis: A necessary impossibility. *Journal for the Psychoanalysis of Culture & Society, 6*(2), 271–78. Retrieved from http://search.proquest.com.ezproxy.library.yorku.ca/docview/619909927?accountid=15182.

Verhaeghe, P. (2008). *On Being Normal and Other Disorders: A Manual for Clinical Psychodiagnostics*. London: Karnac Books. Retrieved from http://www.ebrary.com

Weatherill, R. (1994). In the name-of-the-father: Absent presence. *British Journal of Psychotherapy, 11*(1), 83–91. Retrieved from http://search.proquest.com.ezproxy.library.yorku.ca/docview/618637002?accountid=15182.

Weiner, J. (2001). Confidentiality and paradox: The location of ethical space. *The Journal of Analytical Psychology, 46*(3), 431–42. doi:http://dx.doi.org/10.1111/1465-5922.00255.

Weiss, S. (2002). How teachers' autobiographies influence their responses to children's behaviors: The psychodynamic concept of transference in classroom life. part 1. *Emotional & Behavioural Difficulties, 7*(1), 9–18. doi:http://dx.doi.org/10.1177/136327520200700l002.

Williams, D. G., and Evans-Winters, V. (2005). The burden of teaching teachers: Memoirs of race discourse in teacher education.*The Urban Review, 37*(3), 201–19. doi:http://dx.doi.org/10.1007/s11256-005-0009-z.

Winnicott, D. W. (1992). *The child, the family, and the outside world*. Boston: Da Capo Press.

Winnicott, D. W. (1965). *The maturational processes and the facilitating environment: Studies in the theory of emotional development* (pp. 37–55). M. M. R. Khan (Ed.). London: Hogarth Press.

Winnicott, D. (1960). The theory of the parent-child relationship, *International Journal of Psychoanalysis*, 41: 585–95

Woodson, C. G. (1933). *The mis-education of the Negro* (1st Africa World Press ed.). Trenton, NJ: Africa World Press.

Young-Bruehl, E. (1996). *The anatomy of prejudices*. Cambridge, Mass.: Harvard University Press.

Young-Bruehl, E. (2012). *Childism: Confronting prejudice against children*. New Haven: Yale University Press.

Zembylas, M. (2002), "Structures in feeling" in curriculum and teaching: theorizing the emotional rules. Educational Theory, 52: 187–208. doi: 10.1111/j.1741-5446.2002.00187.x

Zembylas, M. (2012). Pedagogies of strategic empathy: Navigating through the emotional complexities of anti-racism in higher education. *Teaching in Higher Education, 17*(2), 113–25. doi:http://dx.doi.org/10.1080/13562517.2011.611869.

Zembylas, M. (2013). The emotional complexities of "our" and "their" loss: The vicissitudes of teaching about/for empathy in a conflicting society. *Anthropology & Education Quarterly, 44*(1), 19–37. doi:http://dx.doi.org/10.1111/j.1548-1492.2012.01175.x.

Zhao, G. (2012), Levinas and the Mission of Education. *Educational Theory*, 62: 659–75. doi: 10.1111/edth.12003.

Zornig, S., and Levy, L. (2011). Trauma and deprivation: The relationship between early object relations and the constitution of a sense of self. *International Forum of Psychoanalysis, 20*(1), 26–30. doi:http://dx.doi.org/10.1080/0803706X.2010.501814.

Zuesse, E. M. (1983). The absurdity of ritual. *Psychiatry: Journal for the Study of Interpersonal Processes, 46*(1), 40–50. Retrieved from http://search.proquest.com.ezproxy.library.yorku.ca/docview/616787570?accountid=15182.

# Index

# About the Author

**Tapo Chimbganda** was born and raised in Zimbabwe before her family emigrated to Ireland. In Canada, she obtained her doctorate at York University and currently works in community mental health and higher education. As a practicing psychoanalyst and educator who focuses on social justice and mental health, she is committed to establishing critical and socially relevant theory and practice that is progressive in social vision and radical in action. Through experience gained in England, Ireland, and Canada, and through clinical practice and instructional work in universities, schools, community organizations, juvenile detention programs, and mental health institutions, Tapo has developed a social consciousness that has greatly added to her drive as an advocate for social justice.

www.ingramcontent.com/pod-product-compliance
Ingram Content Group UK Ltd.
Pitfield, Milton Keynes, MK11 3LW, UK
UKHW041123071026
15587UKWH00009B/155

9 781498 511957